Praise for
The Quest for Viable Peace

"*The Quest for Viable Peace* develops a simple and essential idea—that security is necessary for peace to become viable and that peace must pay for it to endure. The authors have much to share on how to plan intervention operations effectively; indeed, this volume will serve as a manual for establishing priorities in such operations. It should be read not only by planners and practitioners but also by U.S. policymakers who remain unconvinced that the effort is worthwhile and/or unaware of the steps to take in devising such operations."

—MARK BASKIN
Senior Associate, Center for International Development, SUNY

"*The Quest for Viable Peace* is a first-rate contribution to the literature on this vitally important topic. Thoroughly researched, it deserves to be widely read, discussed, and, indeed, acted upon."

—MATS BERDAL
Professor of Security and Development,
Department of War Studies, King's College London

"Taking international operations in Kosovo as its starting point, *The Quest for Viable Peace* broadens our understanding of the nationbuilding process as a whole and provides valuable guidelines for the conduct of future such missions. Campaign analyses of this sort, which look equally at the military and civil elements of an operation through its entire length, are essential building blocks in the development of a much-needed national and international doctrine for the conduct of such missions. Jock Covey, Mike Dziedzic, Len Hawley, and their coauthors move us closer to that goal, illuminating both the recent past and the near future as they do so."

—JAMES DOBBINS
Director of the International Security and
Defense Policy Center, RAND Corporation

"Success in any stability operation depends on weaving the various civilian and military lines of effort together like strands of a rope. The campaign plan needs to ensure that all dimensions are brought into play: not only security but also the political, economic, and humanitarian aspects. Peace support operations are a test of patience, understanding, and endurance; perhaps the most difficult task is to establish the rule of law where none previously existed. *The Quest for Viable Peace* captures all of this vividly and comprehensively, not least in its use of the hard-won lessons acquired by the British Army in Northern Ireland. I commend it to all those, civilians and soldiers alike, who have an interest in peace support operations."

—GENERAL SIR MICHAEL JACKSON
Chief of the General Staff, British Army

"Presenting an excellent set of essential strategies for building durable peace by means of intervention, this volume is a prodigious, extremely high-quality, valuable work. It should occupy a prominent position in the literature of peace operations."

—ROBERT B. OAKLEY
U.S. Ambassador (Ret.)

The Quest for Viable Peace

The Quest for Viable Peace

International Intervention and Strategies for Conflict Transformation

EDITED BY JOCK COVEY,
MICHAEL J. DZIEDZIC, AND
LEONARD R HAWLEY

UNITED STATES INSTITUTE OF PEACE PRESS
Washington, D.C.

ASSOCIATION OF THE UNITED STATES ARMY
Arlington, Virginia

United States Institute of Peace
1200 17th Street NW, Suite 200
Washington, DC 20036-3011

First Published 2005. Second Printing 2006.

Printed in the United States of America

The paper used in this publication meets the minimum requirements of American National Standards for Information Science—Permanence of Paper for Printed Library Materials, ANSI Z39.48-1984.

Library of Congress Cataloging-in-Publication Data

The quest for viable peace : international intervention and strategies for conflict transformation / edited by Jock Covey, Michael J. Dziedzic, and Leonard R. Hawley,
    p. cm.
    Includes bibliographical references and index.
    ISBN 1-929223-67-6 (paper : alk. paper)
    1. Peace-building. 2. Peace-building—Serbia and Montenegro—Kosovo (Serbia)
3. Peacekeeping forces—Serbia and Montenegro—Kosovo (Serbia) I. Covey, Jock, 1944-
II. Dziedzic, Michael J. III. Hawley, Leonard R., 1947-

JZ5538.Q47 2005
327.1'72—dc22   2005043011

To those who toil and sacrifice for the cause of peace,
and to the spouses of those who write books about it.

Contents

Preface

T he inspiration for this book sprang from the final conversation between Jock Covey and Michael Dziedzic as the latter completed his duties as strategic planner for the UN Mission in Kosovo in October 2000. There clearly was much to learn from that experience. Uppermost in Jock Covey's mind was the need to capture the essence of the British military's approach to peace enforcement. This led to a conversation with Tom Leney, director of the Role of American Military Power (RAMP) project at the Association of the United States Army (AUSA). The result was the concept for a book sponsored by RAMP that would seek to depict both the civilian and the military roles in transforming internal conflict.

This book, therefore, is a product of the Role of American Military Power project. The editors are deeply indebted to the original director of that project, Tom Leney, for his vision, guidance, and financial support. RAMP provided funding for honoraria, expenses for the conduct of authors' workshops, staff support, and assistance with research. Most of the actual work on the book took place while Scott Feil ran the RAMP project. A consummate professional and accomplished scholar, Scott brought discipline to the process and rigor to the analysis. His able staff provided vital assistance. The research effort was skillfully spearheaded by Sasha Kishinchand, and planning for events was adroitly managed by Alex Daskalakis. Johanna Mendelson-Foreman, while organizing a parallel project on postconflict reconstruction, was always generous with her time, insights, and support.

Although AUSA provided the venue for most book-related events, two other organizations deserve special recognition. The International Institute for Strategic Studies (IISS) in London hosted both the initial authors' workshop, at which the framework for the strategy chapters was developed, and the final international conference, at which the draft chapters were presented for feedback from prominent scholars and practitioners from the United States and Europe. Mats Berdal, director of Studies at IISS, was gracious in his hospitality and generous in his support for both of these sessions. Professor Richard Millett, Oppenheimer Chair of Modern Warfighting Strategy at the Marine Corps University, and Major General Donald R. Gardner, USMC (ret.), president of the Marine Corps University Foundation, were also lavish in their assistance, providing facilities and sponsorship for a workshop at Quantico on Ben Lovelock's chapter on the military strategy for defeating political violence. This forum was the occasion for an invaluable exchange of ideas among various doctrinal communities.

Michael Dziedzic began this project under the aegis of Dr. James Schear, director of Research at the Institute for National Strategic Studies, continued it while working under Dan Serwer, director of the Balkans Initiative at the United States Institute of Peace, and completed it under Paul Stares, director of Research and Studies at the United States Institute of Peace. Their backing, support, and encouragement were essential to sustaining the project and bringing it successfully to conclusion. Nigel Quinney provided an enormous infusion of critical thinking as Institute editor, nudging the volume editors to sharpen, clarify, and condense the manuscript. Nick Howenstein was indefatigable in responding to research requirements that arose during the copyediting process.

Contributors

Jock Covey served as principal deputy special representative of the secretary-general at the United Nations Interim Administration Mission in Kosovo (UNMIK) from 1999 to 2001 and as senior deputy high representative in Sarajevo from the creation of the Office of the High Representative in 1995 to 1997.

A career Foreign Service officer, he also served twice as special assistant to the president at the National Security Council: first in 1985–86 for Near Eastern and South Asian affairs and again in 1997–98 for implementation of the Dayton Peace Accords.

Earlier, he served in Berlin, Cairo, Jerusalem, and Pretoria, participated in the Beirut cease-fire negotiations after the Israeli invasion of Lebanon, and negotiated military portions of the Israel-Egypt-U.S. Treaty implementing the Camp David Accords. He graduated from St. Lawrence University, was a distinguished visiting fellow of the Institute for National Strategic Studies at the U.S. National Defense University, and is currently a member of the Council on Foreign Relations and the Pacific Council on International Policy.

Michael J. Dziedzic was the strategic planner for UNMIK in 2000 and the principal drafter of UNMIK's "Standards for Kosovo," published in December 2003. During a thirty-year career in the U.S. Air Force, he served as a senior military fellow at the National Defense University's Institute for National Strategic Studies (1995–99), where he was director of the Peace Operations Team. In 1994 and 1995, he was a faculty member at the National War College's Department of National Security. He also served as air attaché in El Salvador from 1992 to 1994 and as a political-military planner on the Air Staff at the Pentagon in 1992. Prior to that he was a tenure professor in the Department of Political Science at the U.S. Air Force Academy and a visiting fellow at the International Institute for Strategic Studies in London (1987–1988). Since June 2001, he has been a program officer in the Research and Studies Program at the United States Institute of Peace. He holds a PhD in government from the University of Texas at Austin. Dziedzic is coeditor (with Robert Oakley) of *Policing the New World Disorder: Peace Operations and Public Security* and author of *Mexico: Converging Challenges*.

Leonard R. Hawley served as U.S. deputy assistant secretary of state (1999–2001) and supervised U.S. interagency planning for international support to the mission in Kosovo and to several other international missions designed to respond to regional crises. Previously, he served on the National Security Council staff as director of multilateral affairs, coordinating U.S. political-military planning for international interventions. In this capacity, he was responsible for implementation of Presidential Decision Directive 56, the Clinton administration's directive for integrated planning and coordination of multilateral contingency operations. Before this assignment, he acted as deputy assistant secretary of defense responsible for multilateral peacekeeping and humanitarian relief operations. He has also worked on the staffs of both the U.S. House of Representatives and the U.S. Senate. He has several years of experience in ground combat units with overseas assignments in Vietnam and Germany and was a research fellow at the Naval War College and the National Defense University. He has mentored executive-branch civilian and military officials regarding interagency political-military planning for international intervention. He contributes to research efforts at a number of institutions, including the United States Institute of Peace. In 2004, he served on the policy team of the National 9/11 Commission.

✦ ✦ ✦

Stephanie A. Blair served in Kosovo with the OSCE KVM as deputy director of human rights and then as OMIK's first head of field office. In 2000 she served as an UNMIK municipal administrator. Her book, *Weaving the Strands of the Rope*, is published by Dalhousie University. She is a doctoral candidate in the War Studies Department, King's College London, whose research has taken her back to Kosovo, including during the violence of March 2004.

Dana Eyre is now works in the U.S. Agency for International Development's Office of Iraq Reconstruction, having earlier served for fifteen months as senior advisor in the USAID Mission–Iraq. Prior to this, he was senior policy advisor to the deputy special representative of the secretary-general at UNMIK, working in the European Union–led Pillar IV economic redevelopment effort. He holds a

PhD in sociology from Stanford University; his research focuses on organizational learning and planning for conflict transformation missions.

Halvor A. Hartz has served for more than thirty years in the Norwegian Police Force and since 2001 has been police chief superintendent in Norway. His distinguished international police experience includes serving as chief of staff of UNCIVPOL/UNPROFOR in 1994–95, as police commissioner of UNPSG in 1998 and of UNMIK in the summer of 1999, and as police advisor/chief of CIVPOL Division at UN Headquarters in 1999–2000.

Sasha Kishinchand recently returned from Iraq, where she worked for more than a year on USAID's Monitoring and Evaluation program. Earlier, she spent three years with the Association of the United States Army as the research director for the joint CSIS-AUSA project on postconflict reconstruction. She has an MA in strategic studies and international economics from Johns Hopkins' School of Advanced International Studies. Her publications include articles on postconflict reconstruction and on child soldiers.

Colonel Ben Lovelock is a serving officer in the UK Royal Marines. He served in the OSCE Kosovo Verification Mission before and after the 1999 NATO air campaign. He later analyzed the lessons emerging from Kosovo and other operations while serving in the Peace Support Operations department of the UK Ministry of Defence's Joint Doctrine and Concepts Centre. Until recently a politico-military planner in the European Union Military Staff based in Brussels, he is currently serving in the Multi-National Security Transition Command—Iraq.

Laura Mercean was trained as a lawyer and also has an MSc in global security. She served in the UNMIK Department of Judicial Affairs from September 1999 to August 2001. In that capacity, she first dealt with issues related to the initial process of reestablishing the penal system; subsequently, she worked on reform of the judiciary and development of a strategic plan for issues related to the appointment and removal from office of judicial personnel.

Bernard Salomé is special representative of the director of the Library of Alexandria. He has a diverse professional background in a wide range of international environments, including serving as deputy director of the G-7 Support Implementation Group in Russia and as head of the Economic Policy Office in Kosovo for the United Nations. An economist by training, he is the author of eight books on development issues and seven World Bank reports.

Dennis Skocz is a U.S. career diplomat currently assigned to the Office of NATO Policy in the Pentagon. As director of the Office of Contingency Planning and Peacekeeping at the State Department (1999–2003), he participated in postconflict planning for Kosovo, Afghanistan, and East Timor. As political counselor of the U.S. Mission to the Organization of American States (1990–93), he joined in multilateral diplomacy to resolve governance crises in Haiti, Peru, and Guatemala.

James Wasserstrom founded and heads UNMIK's Office Overseeing Publicly Owned Enterprises. Before joining UNMIK in 2002, he was a vice president for international business development at American Express Corporation. Previously, he managed a variety of political and economic development programs of the UN system in Asia and Africa, with emphases on decentralization and governance. He is a graduate of Tufts University, holds an MA from its Fletcher School of Law and Diplomacy, and speaks six languages.

Clint Williamson is the director for stability operations at the National Security Council. From April to July 2003, he served as the first CPA senior advisor to the Iraqi Ministry of Justice in Baghdad. Before being posted to the NSC in January 2003, he served as the director of the Department of Justice in the UN-administered government of Kosovo. From 1994 until early 2001, he was a trial attorney at the International Criminal Tribunal for former Yugoslavia in The Hague, Netherlands.

The Quest for Viable Peace

1

Introduction

Michael J. Dziedzic and Len Hawley

HE QUEST FOR VIABLE PEACE IN WAR-TORN SOCIETIES has become one of the defining challenges of our era. Since the end of the Cold War, international security has repeatedly been disrupted by the dysfunction or disintegration of troubled states. Multilateral interventions have been mounted in response to intolerable situations ranging from ethnic cleansing by marauding military and paramilitary forces to state hijacking by global terrorists. The rise of radical Islamist movements in states such as Afghanistan has particularly ominous, long-term implications. The stakes now include the security of homelands around the globe.

It is not the risk of great power competition that threatens international peace and security today, but rather the pathological weakness of states. While the unequaled military power of the United States may make it possible to vanquish rogue regimes with astonishing speed, securing the future will be a function of what takes their place. To drain the swamps where the sources of regional disorder, transnational terror, and humanitarian calamity breed, responsible governance must reliably emerge as the ultimate outcome of international intervention.

As Thomas Friedman observed after the attacks of September 11, 2001, "if we don't visit bad neighborhoods around the world, they will surely visit us."[1] It is not evident, however, that we have yet discovered what to do once we arrive. Typically, internal conflict persists long after an international military intervention has been mounted. We clearly should not exit prematurely. Yet neither can we afford to remain interminably. To do the latter would be inordinately costly and undermine our capacity to respond to emerging threats in other disruptive neighborhoods around the world. The only sensible way out of this dilemma is to become proficient at the demanding art of building viable peace after intervening in states chronically ridden with internal strife.

3

This book presents essential strategies for building viable peace in the wake of violent internal conflict when international intervention is a compelling necessity. The focus is on events after June 1999 that had a formative impact on strategies pursued by the international mission in Kosovo to moderate political conflict, defeat militant extremism, inculcate the rule of law, and establish a political economy that reduces rather than incites continuing conflict.[2] We strive to capture the learning process that took place as these strategies were crafted, applied, and adapted. Those looking for minutiae about Kosovo's peculiarities, for a chronicle of the peace process, or for a comprehensive description of peacekeeping functions will be disappointed. We are primarily concerned here with developing an understanding of measures that are necessary to transform internal conflict expeditiously during the initial years of an intervention, *wherever* that may become necessary.

The assertions made here are not drawn from secondary sources, external assessment missions, or scholarly papers. They derive, rather, from firsthand experience. This work is authored by seasoned practitioners, and it is primarily intended for practitioners and policymakers who will follow us in responding to strife in other war-torn corners of the globe.

The editors were directly involved in formulating various aspects of the strategies that are the essence of this book:

- Jock Covey was the principal deputy special representative of the secretary-general for the United Nations Interim Administration Mission in Kosovo (UNMIK) from July 1999 to March 2001.

- Michael Dziedzic was deployed as the strategic planner for UNMIK from April through October 2000 and subsequently was the principal drafter of UNMIK's "Standards for Kosovo."[3]

- Len Hawley served as U.S. deputy assistant secretary of state from May 1999 to January 2001 and was responsible for coordinating with senior UN officials and supervising U.S. interagency planning for international support to Kosovo's peace process.

Each chapter was written by international officials who played a direct role in Kosovo's peace process. A large part of their learning was by trial and error. This process continues in an unfinished quest for viable peace. Although the crucible that has shaped our thinking has been Kosovo, the strategies described in this work are designed to be transportable to similar situations elsewhere.

KOSOVO AS A LEARNING LABORATORY

Like all war-torn societies, Kosovo has its distinctive historical legacy and cultural idiosyncrasies. As described in chapter 2, Kosovo's history has produced a legacy that is of symbolic significance to the Serb nation coupled with a population that is predominantly Albanian. In 1989 the territory lost its autonomy and came under repressive rule by President Slobodan Milosevic's Serb-dominated regime. By 1997 militant Albanian groups had had enough and launched a war of independence.

The peace operation in Kosovo came about in a distinctive manner. It was more a product of force than of diplomacy. With the withdrawal of the Kosovo Verification Mission (KVM) under duress in late March 1999, diplomacy had run its course.[4] A scorched-earth campaign by Serb security forces rapidly ensued. Over a million members of Kosovo's Albanian community were either driven to seek refuge or displaced from their homes inside Kosovo.[5]

A seventy-eight-day coercive bombing campaign by NATO was the instrument that compelled Milosevic to capitulate. When the NATO-led Kosovo Force (KFOR) eventually embarked on its UN-mandated peace mission on June 12, it found little peace to keep. As refugees spontaneously flooded home, assaults on Kosovo's Serb minority erupted daily. Nearly half of that community fled into exile. Kosovo's ultimate political status remained unresolved.

The case of Kosovo is unique, but the quest for viable peace is not. As with all interventions seeking to establish peace and stability, the Kosovo experience has special features that must be recognized. On the other hand, it also belongs to a demanding set of cases in which the internal conflict remains violent and unresolved even after an international peace mission has been mounted. In such cases, the sources of conflict must be transformed before peace can prosper.

Kosovo constitutes a significant evolution since the end of the Cold War in the nature of multilateral interventions intended to quell violent internal conflicts. Three features that were typical of traditional peacekeeping were turned on their head.

First, interstate conflict generally had to be "ripe" for a negotiated solution before an intervention could take place. This meant that the parties already recognized the declining utility of the use of force and were reconciled to the need for international involvement. There normally had to be a peace to keep before blue-helmeted UN troops could be deployed.

Waiting for Kosovo's internal conflict to become ripe before there could be an international response was unacceptable. It would have left the ethnic Albanian population intolerably vulnerable to brutality at the hands of Milosevic's security apparatus. A coercive NATO bombing campaign, not a diplomatic process of negotiation, created conditions for the introduction of a comprehensive UN-NATO peace mission.

Second, UN missions were traditionally conducted with the acquiescence of the states involved in a dispute, which meant that peacekeepers had to observe strict neutrality.

When Milosevic's security forces were compelled to withdraw as a result of NATO bombing, a wave of violence erupted across Kosovo. Ethnic Albanians sought revenge against remaining Serbs. Rival Albanian factions fought one another for exclusive power. Entrenched, lawless power structures flourished in both the Serb and the Albanian communities. These hard-bitten rivals were implacably opposed to the peace process and exploited violence, intimidation, and illicit sources of revenue to sustain their influence and control. Confronting these endemic hostilities, international security forces were obliged to protect the peace process and assertively use force to dislodge those who sought to derail it.

Third, when the international community dealt with traditional interstate conflicts, it usually kept civilian and military roles discrete and sequential. The diplomatic peacemaking phase first would be successfully concluded between the states involved in the conflict. Only then would military peacekeepers be deployed to keep the peace that the diplomats had hammered out. This meant that civilian and military efforts were largely independent of each other.

When peace implementation began in Kosovo in June 1999, the process of making peace had scarcely begun. Kosovo's "final status" remained unresolved. Diplomats, military peace enforcers, international civilian police (CIVPOL), civil administrators, and assistance providers were expected immediately to discharge unprecedented responsibilities for governance over the territory. They also had to build functioning democratic institutions and inculcate the rule of law. This required the simultaneous capacity to make peace, impose peace, and build peace.

The difficulty and complexity of the Kosovo situation confronted practitioners with challenges that could not be overcome using traditional practices. Shackles that had previously constrained thinking and practice were broken. This made the Kosovo case a fertile source of innovation. The intervention also was a harbinger of many of the central challenges associated with transforming internal conflict that would beleaguer subsequent interventions in Afghanistan, Iraq, Haiti, and various locations in Africa.

CONFLICT TRANSFORMATION VERSUS POSTCONFLICT RECONSTRUCTION

In cases like Kosovo, the forces that drive continued violent conflict are deeply entrenched. Conditions that are conducive to further fighting must be transformed before peace can take hold. Thus, the most fundamental distinction to draw in planning a peace and stability operation is between situations in which violent internal conflict actually has been extinguished and situations in which violent conflict continues or is likely to reignite. If conflict has been extinguished, the strategic challenge can be confined to "postconflict reconstruction." If it has not, the operation must aim at nothing less than "conflict transformation."

The gravest threats to international peace and stability involve situations in which conflict persists and violent competition for power has not yet ended. Staunching an unfolding humanitarian calamity, as in Kosovo; routing global terrorists, as in Afghanistan; removing a threatening rogue regime, as in Iraq; and preventing the violent demise of the state, as in Haiti, are recent cases that have provoked international intervention. All these interventions encountered local environments replete with internal conflict. Under such circumstances, simple reconstruction programs coupled with hasty exits will inevitably fail. Only by seriously addressing the need to transform persistent internal conflict in the postwar period can a viable peace evolve—and in a manageable time frame.

Postwar Kosovo witnessed daily violence and killing. In June 1999, when NATO's air campaign forced President Milosevic to capitulate and withdraw his marauding security forces, conflict was far from extinguished. Rival ethnic factions had not achieved their war aims and remained determined to continue fighting, albeit through less overt means. Compounding this source of instability, a power vacuum existed that was quickly exploited by aggressive extremist militias that sought to assert de facto control through intimidation and violence. Their efforts were often financed by illicit revenues generated from criminal enterprises.

Underlying conditions spurring Kosovo's bitter struggle for power would have to change before peace could begin to emerge. The situation would have to be transformed by dislodging forces unalterably opposed to the aims of the peace process while simultaneously nurturing institutions and domestic conditions capable of sustaining peace. War-hardened power structures would have to be supplanted, and nonviolent alternatives for the pursuit of political and economic aspirations would have to take root.

The functions associated with postconflict reconstruction—enhancing governance and participation, security capabilities, justice and reconciliation, and social and economic well being—are all essential aspects of the international response to cases like Kosovo.[6] They are not, however, a strategy for transforming conflict. Rebuilding efforts alone cannot extinguish conflicts that continue to smolder or transform extremist power structures that copiously fuel the fires. When this is the strategic challenge, building peace at the end of a war is not a straightforward matter of performing postconflict reconstruction and handing the reins of power over to local leaders. This formula is likely to be a blueprint for perpetual instability and gathering danger. A strategy to transform internal conflict, coupled with a long-term reconstruction effort, is the only realistic approach for policymakers and practitioners.

Strategies for dealing with cases like Kosovo will not succeed, therefore, if they are based on a faulty, unexamined premise that all interventions are synonymous with "postconflict" situations. If statesmen and policymakers fail to recognize the difference between a situation that is truly postconflict and one that requires transformation of continuing violent internal conflict, then they will apply inappropriate and inadequate strategies that fail to instill a peace that holds.

DETERMINING THE NEED FOR CONFLICT TRANSFORMATION

How can one determine whether a postwar situation demands conflict transformation? The questions posed below are designed to help policymakers and strategists assess the situation facing an impending intervention. A determination must be made if entrenched sources of instability and violence are likely to obstruct the road to a viable peace in the postwar period. If some or all of the sources of continuing conflict are present, then the strategies that have evolved in Kosovo for transforming internal conflict will likely be relevant.

What Kind of Peace Is This?

The most basic determination a military commander must make before committing to battle is, What kind of war is this? Likewise, policymakers should contemplate the nature of the campaign for peace that is about to be waged. In a benign postconflict environment, peace may result from the straightforward implementation of a previously negotiated settlement. In more contentious situations like Kosovo, however, "peace" is but the continuation of conflict by other violent means. When intervening in fractured societies that are struggling to emerge from violent internal conflict, the foremost question to answer is, What kind of peace is this?

- *Are there unrequited war aims over which the disputants remain willing to fight?* When the intervention has taken place to prevent the unfolding of a humanitarian catastrophe, fundamental and inflammatory intergroup disputes are likely to persist after the arrival of international forces. Even if the disputants sign a peace settlement paving the way for an international mission, unresolved conflicts may persist. In Kosovo a number of rival factions accepted the international intervention to end the war, but the territory's future status remained unresolved. There was not even a process in place to address this existential issue.

- *Has the old regime disintegrated, creating a power vacuum that, if left alone, will be filled through violent means?* The disintegration or removal of a regime will likely lead to a bitter internal struggle for power. In the absence of respected institutions to manage the process of determining who should govern, and in a situation awash in weapons and militant factions, recourse to political violence is apt to be reflexive. In Kosovo an incipient civil war roiled between rival political factions *within* the ethnic Albanian community over which faction would govern.

- *What conditions must be met before elections can effectively substitute for force in determining who governs?* Unless the rights of minority populations can be reliably guaranteed, majority rule is likely to be perceived as a continuation of a life-and-death, zero-sum form of politics by at least one of the parties to the conflict. Minimum essential conditions of security, rule of law, and respect for minority rights must be met before elections are held. Premature elections called before political violence has been adequately constrained can be an invitation for political extremists to obtain office, thus legitimizing obstructionism. If elections had been held prematurely in Kosovo, a polarizing outcome would likely have spurred further hostilities. Indeed, in the weeks before the first election in 2000, there was an upsurge in assassinations and political violence.

✦ ✦ ✦

Conflict transformation is required when the assessment of the political landscape exposes the ugly reality that powerful incentives for continued conflict exist. For a viable peace to emerge, the political conditions that spawned conflict must be transformed

- from intolerant, zero-sum confrontations in which incentives and payoffs for continued violence persist,

- to a system of governance where the competition for power can be conducted through nonviolent processes.

Must Violent Extremists Be Defeated for a Safe and Secure Environment to Emerge?

Security is the essential precondition for viable peace. Only in a benign post-conflict setting does it make sense for intervening military forces to confine their efforts to *maintaining* the existing environment so that civilian entities can go about implementing the peace.[7] If violent extremists must be defeated, this outcome should be recognized from the outset; otherwise, the peace process will likely be derailed and the military will be suppressing conflict years later.

- *Is the threat conventional and military or subversive and criminal?* If intimidation, coercion, assassination, and terrorism are prevalent methods for advancing political agendas and deciding outcomes, a military strategy that employs counterinsurgency principles will be needed to secure the environment. In Kosovo informal linkages involving political extremists, paramilitary formations, intelligence operatives, and the criminal underworld remained potent forces on both sides of the ethnic divide. An assertive strategy had to be adopted in collaboration with UNMIK's civilian police to prevent sinister, informal, political-criminal networks from disrupting the peace process.

- *What indigenous security capacity must be developed to ensure that the threat of political violence is defeated?* If indigenous security forces either have disintegrated or have been responsible for the brutality and repression that led to war, international military and police will initially be required to fill the public security gap and conduct the campaign against militant extremists. In Kosovo the immediate problem was the absence of local police and the presence of the Kosovo Liberation Army (KLA) operating as a pseudo police force. Because the KLA regarded itself as a victorious army, demobilization was unacceptable to its leadership. The solution was to demilitarize, but not demobilize, the KLA. It was transformed into a civil emergency force, the Kosovo Protection Corps, which would afford its members employment and stature, at least in the near term.

✦   ✦   ✦

Conflict transformation becomes essential where paramilitary formations, warlords, militant extremists, or terrorists seek to obstruct the peace process through violence and intimidation. The security environment will need to be transformed

- from a context dominated by armed groups that are willing and able to use violence and intimidation to destroy the peace,

- to a context in which armed groups are marginalized by being subordinated to legitimate governmental authority, reintegrated into society, or defeated.

Does Lawless Rule Prevail?

The rule of law is almost universally acknowledged as a prerequisite for a lasting peace. Yet international interventions have repeatedly foundered in this regard. The most immediate requirement is to establish public order and safety. When security gaps are underestimated or overlooked, the entire peace process is likely to be placed in jeopardy. International military and police forces will have to fill this gap until local institutions can be reconstituted. However, capacity building cannot by itself produce a legal system that upholds the rule of law if the context in which nascent legal institutions operate is dominated by lawless forces rooted in the conflict that continue to act with impunity.

- *What are the threats to the rule of law?* If perpetrators of interethnic crimes, politically motivated violence, subversion, and organized criminal networks are deeply embedded in lawless power structures, the institutional context is fundamentally hostile to the rule of law. In such a context, even comprehensive vetting and training programs for local police, judges, and jailers will be insufficient, since those who seek to uphold the law will not long survive. Peace missions that have exclusively emphasized capacity building have met with unsatisfactory results for this reason. To enable the rule of law to take root, the international community must prepare the ground properly. This may require the peace mission to have at its own disposal a very broad spectrum of capabilities to dislodge criminalized power structures. In Kosovo, the primary threat to the rule of law was networks of extremists that had insinuated themselves into the structures of power in both of Kosovo's ethnic communities.

- *What is the indigenous capacity to uphold the rule of law?* If voids exist in the indigenous capacity to maintain public order, enforce the law, and operate the judicial and penal systems, the international community will have to perform these functions on an interim basis, perhaps lasting years. This can be the case when holdovers from local police forces and other components of the legal system have been an integral part of the repression and dysfunction that made the intervention necessary. In less dire situations, in which the challenge is to repair systemic weaknesses, a partnership between international and local actors will be required to retrain and reconstitute the legal system. A holistic approach is required in assessing local capacity, and the proper balance must be struck between replacing collapsed institutions with international actors and merely strengthening them through mentoring and assistance. In Kosovo there was essentially no indigenous capacity. Initially, KFOR not only had to fill the void in law enforcement, which had been anticipated, but also had to perform both judicial and penal functions. It took a year or two before sufficient international civilian resources could be mobilized to fill the many gaps in the local system of justice and law enforcement. The process of developing adequate local capacity would take even longer.

✦ ✦ ✦

Conflict transformation is essential in cases in which lawless rule prevails. Both the capacity of indigenous institutions and the context in which they operate must be changed. The institutions must be transformed

- from instruments of state repression where political and criminal elites enjoy impunity,

- to servants of the public capable of preserving order, protecting basic rights—especially for minority groups—and applying the law equitably.

Does Illicit Revenue Dominate Political Motivations and Fuel Continuing Conflict?

If those in power harbor powerful economic incentives that are served by continued conflict, peace cannot prosper. A viable peace cannot emerge when power is wielded primarily by elites who are rooted in and have continuing linkages to criminal enterprises. Those who are engaged in the illegal economy strive to preserve their power and wealth through ruthless means while depriving the formal economy of growth and the state of revenue. In a political economy that feeds conflict, criminal and illicit activities dominate the political and economic realms. Because wealth and power are inextricably linked, the strategist must be able to distinguish between a political economy that is criminalized and conducive to conflict and an open and inclusive one that is capable of sustaining peace.

- *Do economic transactions take place predominantly in the formal or informal marketplace?* If an informal, underground economy predominates, criminalized and corrupt networks will likely seek to manipulate and pervert the development of a legitimate formal economy. Informal economies consist of both gray and black markets. Gray markets involve unregistered transactions in ordinary commodities, some of which are carried out in illegal ways, such as cigarette smuggling; black markets involve activities that are patently illegal, such as trafficking in arms, drugs, women, and children. An assessment should be made of the relative significance of the formal and informal economies and the vulnerability of the formal economy to infiltration and capture by political-criminal power structures. In Kosovo, as a result of the ruinous economic policies of Josep Broz Tito and Slobodan Milosevic, the formal economy was in shambles. This predicament was compounded for the ethnic Albanian population by discriminatory policies that left it largely without options in the formal economy throughout the 1990s.

- *Is the state captured by a criminalized elite that sustains itself through illicit revenue from the informal economy?* If economic activity is largely illicit in nature, political elites with covert links to the criminal underworld are likely to capture the levers of power in state institutions. Conflict has probably served their nefarious purposes. An assessment should be made of factors such as: Who wins and who loses if peace prevails? What are the revenue streams flowing to major obstructionists that sustain their capacity for coercion, terror, paramilitary activities, and intelligence operations? Has social conflict been manipulated to provide a gloss of legitimacy for a repressive, criminalized regime? International resources will need to be concentrated on severing the nexus between illegal economic activity and political power if a viable peace is to emerge. In Kosovo murky and often criminalized political-economic linkages had sustained both the Milosevic regime and the violent struggle of the KLA against Milosevic's mafia state.

✦   ✦   ✦

Conflict transformation is required when illicit sources of revenue provide the motivation and means for obstructing the peace process. In such cases, the political economy must be transformed

- from a situation in which the gray and black markets predominate and illicit wealth determines who wields political power,

- to a functioning formal economy in which the integrity of revenues required for essential state services is protected.

An accurate assessment of the country's violence-prone power structures that promote continued conflict forms the basis for designing appropriate strategies in the quest for viable peace. The questions above are intended to serve as indicators so that policymakers or strategists responsible for future interventions can determine whether the central challenges they face are similar to those encountered in Kosovo. To the extent that an assessment determines the need for conflict transformation, the four strategies we present in this book will likely be relevant.

CORE IDEAS IN THE QUEST FOR VIABLE PEACE

In circumstances as daunting as those that beset Kosovo in mid-1999, peace implementation is never easy, fast, or cheap.[8] Fostering the transformation of internal conflict demands holistic strategies along with the resources and resolve to carry them through in a multiyear campaign. The chapters that follow trace the evolution in thinking that has taken place among practitioners in the field in recent years, with the Kosovo experience serving as the learning laboratory. Several core ideas unify this discussion: viable peace, conflict transformation, mission transition, strategies of conflict transformation, linkages, the primacy of the peace process, and the custodian of the peace process.

Viable Peace

Chester Crocker describes the process of state failure as a footrace "between legitimate governmental institutions and legal business enterprises, on the one hand, and criminal networks, often linked to warlords or political factions associated with security agencies, on the other. . . . When state failure sets in, the balance of power shifts ominously against ordinary civilians and in favor of armed entities operating outside the law."[9]

Establishing a viable peace requires the reversal of this process. In the wake of state collapse and internal war, a domestic balance of power must be restored in favor of legitimate institutions of government. Violence-prone power structures must be dislodged. To accomplish this, the motivations and means for pursuing violent conflict must diminish. Peace becomes viable when the capacity of domestic institutions to resolve conflict peacefully prevails over the power of obstructionist forces. As portrayed in figure 1.1, viable peace is the decisive turning point in the transformation of conflict from imposed stability to self-sustaining peace.

A viable peace does not end international engagement. To complete the transformation to self-sustaining peace, continued international oversight, peace-building activities, and long-term developmental assistance will be needed. Local institutions will still require reinforcement, civil society will have to mature, and the more protracted processes that lead to a self-sustaining peace (e.g., political moderation, social reconciliation, and a more egalitarian distribution of wealth) will need to be nurtured. This is the realm of postconflict reconstruction. It may take a decade, a generation, or longer before peace becomes fully self-sustaining. Viable peace, however, can emerge far more quickly if appropriate strategies are pursued and properly resourced from the outset of an intervention.

Conflict Transformation

In cases akin to Kosovo, the peace process must deal with the continuation of a violent internal struggle for power pursued by means other than open warfare. Success in achieving viable peace, therefore, hinges on transforming the way in which power is obtained, maintained, and exercised. Transformation entails diminishing the means and motivations for violent conflict while developing more attractive, peaceful alternatives for the competitive pursuit of political and economic aspirations. The strategic imperative should be to transform internal conflict in the first years of an intervention. This would permit an evolution from internationally imposed stability to a peace that is viable and, therefore, manageable at a greatly reduced cost to the international community.

Mission Transition

Transition applies to the stages of involvement of the international community. An international peace mission progresses through successive stages, from imposed stability to self-sustaining peace, evolving to a less intrusive and more affordable presence as a genuine peace settlement is effectively implemented.

The proper cause-and-effect relationship must be recognized between a transformation of internal conflict and a transition in the international presence. Simply put, conflict transformation must drive mission transition. Desired ends

Figure 1.1. Viable Peace: The Turning Point in Conflict Transformation

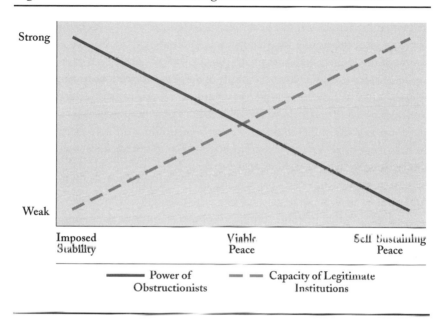

have to be achieved before transitions are considered. Peace should be viable before the mission hands off its most important responsibilities.

Measuring the success of an international mission involves determining whether sufficient transformation has been achieved in diminishing violence-prone power structures and developing institutions capable of resolving disputes peacefully. This end state must determine the pace of transition for the peace mission. Once the violent, internal struggle for power has been transformed and peace has become viable, international involvement can transition to a level that is much less intrusive, less resource intensive, and, therefore, more easily sustained over the long term. If appropriate transformation strategies are pursued and properly resourced from the outset of an intervention, a viable peace will be far more likely to emerge in a timely and affordable manner.

Strategies of Conflict Transformation

The first step is to diagnose the sources of internal conflict properly. In Kosovo conflict transformation was required to deal with four continuing sources of conflict: uncompromising political aims, capacity for militant extremism, lawless rule, and a criminalized political economy. Thus, four interdependent strategies aimed at moderating political conflict, defeating militant extremists, institutionalizing the rule of law, and building an open and inclusive political economy were necessary. These strategies for conflict transformation directly parallel the four pillars of effort identified in 2002 in the Post-Conflict Reconstruction Task Framework, a joint project of the Center for Strategic and International Studies and the Association of the United States Army.[10] This framework details lines of action that are essential for strengthening the capacity of domestic institutions to resolve conflict peacefully. When the postintervention phase is in reality the continuation of hostilities by other means, however, achieving a viable peace will also require the transformation of conflict so that these fragile institutions are able to prevail over the power of obstructionist forces. The stages of conflict transformation for each of these four strategies are summarized in table 1.1.

In cases like Kosovo, to make the transformation from imposed stability to viable peace, realistic strategies are required that address the violence-prone power structures that promote continued conflict. Capturing the essence of these four transformation strategies as they evolved in the crucible of Kosovo is the central aim of this book.

Linkages

The four strategies to transform internal conflict are interdependent. For instance, dialogue among rivals, as called for in the political strategy, cannot thrive unless it is buttressed by efforts to defeat militant violence, an objective of the security strategy, and by the provision of tangible economic benefits to demonstrate that peace pays, as sought by the political-economic strategy. Efforts to contain and diminish criminalized power structures must be supported by the development of legitimate political and economic institutions that are capable of sustaining peace. Such linkages make it imperative that these strategies for transforming conflict be effectively interwoven.

The Primacy of the Peace Process

Until peace has become viable, the requirements of the peace process will need to be given top priority by all in a mission. A passive, fragmented, or incoherent approach only undermines the process of transformation and prolongs the international presence. Thus, the primacy of the peace process should be the overarching guidance for all civilian and military peace implementation efforts. In Kosovo this guidance was expressed as a paramount mission directive: we support those who support the peace process and actively oppose those who obstruct it.

The Custodian of the Peace Process

The custodian is the central actor in achieving a viable peace. Success will largely depend on how adroitly this appointed leader mobilizes international support

Table 1.1. Stages and Strategies of Conflict Transformation

Strategies of Conflict Transformation

Stages of Conflict Transformation	Moderating Political Conflict	Defeating Militant Extremists	Institutionalizing the Rule of Law	Developing a Legitimate Political Economy
Internal Conflict	Political discourse completely breaks down.	Factional hostilities rage.	Lawlessness rules; the legal system is an instrument of repression.	The political economy is criminalized.
Imposed Stability	Peace is a continuation of conflict by other means.	Armed groups and informal power structures are predominant.	The local system is unable to administer justice; the environment is hostile to rule of law.	Obstructionists derive means and motives from the informal economy.
Viable Peace	Conflict is managed with international safeguards.	Armed groups are reintegrated or have lost popular support.	Local institutions are able to protect minority rights and confront impunity with the aid of international safeguards.	Peace pays: the state is financially viable; the formal economy offers alternatives.
Self-Sustaining Peace	Conflict is resolved peacefully by domestic political processes.	The security sector is reformed and subordinated to political authority.	Local institutions maintain order, law, and justice with domestic safeguards.	The formal economy outperforms gray and black markets.

and unifies the various components of the mission behind realistic strategies to implement the peace process.

HOW THIS BOOK IS ORGANIZED

We begin by providing an overview of contextual factors that have a profound impact on the strategies that are the essence of this work.

Chapter 2, "The Historical Context of Conflict in Kosovo," by Michael Dziedzic and Sasha Kishinchand, offers a brief account of the evolution of the conflict in Kosovo and the course of the international intervention. Those well versed in developments there can turn to chapters 3 and 4 for an examination of the big picture as it looks to political-military planners preparing for an international intervention and to the international official who leads the effort as custodian of the peace process.

In chapter 3, "Advance Political-Military Planning: Laying the Foundation for Achieving Viable Peace," Len Hawley and Dennis Skocz describe the process of advance interagency planning. High on the list of essential tasks involved in this effort is the preparation of a strategic approach to transforming entrenched, violence-prone power structures and cultivating favorable conditions in the region and the host country for an intervention. Innovation is a central feature of laying a foundation for an intervention, for each situation is unique and demands a tailored approach to the transformation of local power.

In chapter 4, "The Custodian of the Peace Process," Jock Covey examines the challenges facing the senior civilian responsible for an international intervention. He argues that the civilian and military components of the mission must be brought together promptly and effectively. The key is to infuse both with a shared sense of purpose—the primacy of the peace process—around which all efforts are to be unified. In addition to integrating the mission's internal components, the custodian must continually seek to mobilize support and resources from a wide range of self-interested international actors, none of which will have as their primary purpose the success of the peace process. In the Kosovo mission, Covey explains, it was invaluable to think and behave like a weak little country in order to maneuver around the competing agendas within the international community.

The next four chapters examine interdependent strategies essential for transforming internal conflict. These chapters follow a common format. A strategy can be described as having three components: ends, ways, and means. Using these elements as the organizing structure, each chapter begins with an assessment of the strategic challenge that confronted the mission and the objective, or *end,* that was to be accomplished. This section of each chapter begins with a review of the lessons that practitioners derived from previous experience and applied in Kosovo. The *way* an objective is pursued is the essence of strategy. Each chapter is devoted to the way a strategy was implemented, the key strategic choices that were made, and the innovations that were necessary to meet the challenges that Kosovo presented. Each strategy required a specific set of *means*, or resources and processes to carry out the strategy, and these are briefly described. In concluding their chapters, the authors take stock of the extent to which implementation has progressed toward viable peace in Kosovo.

In chapter 5, "Making a Viable Peace: Moderating Political Conflict," Jock Covey argues that the factions in Kosovo were still committed to their mutually exclusive war aims, just as if they were still engaged in armed combat. The thrust of the political strategy was to encourage rival leaders to recognize that their interests would be better served through peaceful political processes. An environment conducive to political dialogue had to be nurtured, obstructionism had to be contained, and political leaders had to be gradually persuaded to reassess their interests and to take risks associated with thinking differently about their future. The competition for power among rival factions could then be channeled into processes governed by legitimate institutions that could be sustained effectively at lower levels of oversight by the international community.

In chapter 6, "Securing a Viable Peace: Defeating Militant Extremists," Col. Ben Lovelock argues that KFOR's Multinational Brigade Center integrated tried-and-true counterinsurgency methods with core principles derived from peace operations in an effort to transform the sources of insecurity. In an evolution called fourth generation peace implementation, the essence of the strategy was to find, fix, and strike against the sources of violent obstruction to the peace process and to separate militant extremists from their popular support. Thus, the role of military commanders went well beyond simply providing security. It embraced transforming the security environment by taking violence out of the political equation. To defeat militant extremists, there was a requirement to work effectively within the overall context of the primacy of the peace process and a comprehensive framework of civilian activities.

In chapter 7, "Safeguarding a Viable Peace: Institutionalizing the Rule of Law," Halvor Hartz, Laura Mercean, and Clint Williamson explain that the strategy adopted in Kosovo evolved beyond merely establishing local capacity to embrace the removal of obstructionists opposed to the rule of law. Conditions required the peace mission to play a decisive role in completing the continuum from intelligence to incarceration. Effective safeguards also had to be embedded in local institutions to provide long-term assurances that the police, judiciary, and penal system would reliably serve the public interest, respect minority rights, dispense justice equally, and maintain their autonomy from corrupting political forces. The experience in Kosovo indicates the vital importance of establishing an environment capable of sustaining the rule of law.

In chapter 8, "Forging a Viable Peace: Developing a Legitimate Political Economy," Stephanie Blair, Dana Eyre, Bernard Salomé, and Jim Wasserstrom turn the spotlight on the challenges of transforming a political economy that is conducive to conflict. They describe the efforts made in Kosovo to separate criminally obtained wealth from the exercise of political power. A top priority must be undercutting the economic foundations of obstructionist power. Equally important, peace must pay so the coalition for peace can prevail. This is essential if elites are to take risks for peace and if all parties to the conflict are to develop a stake in sustaining the peace. Also crucial to the transformation process are establishing the fiscal autonomy of the state and expanding the formal economy at the expense of the gray and black. Alternatives to employment in the underground economy need to become sufficiently available so that there is broad interest in maintaining transparent and accountable political and economic structures.

The final two chapters widen the focus of analysis beyond individual strategies to examine, first, the interrelatedness of these four strategies and, second, the broad lessons that Kosovo has to offer about transforming internal conflict. In chapter 9, "Linkages among the Transformation Strategies," Michael Dziedzic and Len Hawley emphasize that achieving viable peace requires coherent civil-military action to exploit the linkages among the four transformation strategies. The chapter reviews interlocking linkages that influenced developments in each of the four transformation strategies in Kosovo and then discusses key integrating mechanisms that are needed to leverage the synergistic effects of these dependencies.

In chapter 10, Michael Dziedzic moves the discussion from the particular to the general. Kosovo belongs to a set of cases in which conflict transformation is required, and this concluding chapter begins by summarizing the distinguishing attributes of these cases. It then provides a general statement of the lines of action that are central to each of the strategies involved in the quest for viable peace. The chapter concludes by underlining the invaluable role played by the custodian, the importance of the notion of the primacy of the peace process, and the advantages that a strategic focus on attaining viable peace brings to peace implementation.

NOTES

The authors wish to acknowledge the generous feedback and helpful suggestions of Chris Holshek, Dayton Maxwell, and Robert Polk. While any defects that remain are solely attributable to the authors, this work has been substantially enhanced by their assistance.

1. Thomas Friedman, "Ask Not What . . . ," *New York Times,* December 9, 2001, sec. 4, 13.

2. The term "political economy" refers to the relationship between wealth and power in society. The Overseas Development Institute defines this field of study as "concerned with the interaction of political and economic processes in a society: the distribution of power and wealth between different groups and individuals, and the processes that create, sustain and transform these relationships over time." Sarah Collinson et al., *Power, Livelihoods, and Conflict,* Case Studies in Political Economy Analysis for Humanitarian Action, HPG Report 13 (London: Overseas Development Institute, 2003), 3.

3. UNMIK, "Standards for Kosovo," UNMIK/PR/1078, December 10, 2003, 3.

4. The Kosovo Verification Mission was established on October 25, 1998, to ensure compliance with the tenets of UN Security Council Resolution 1199. It operated under the aegis of the Organization for Security and Cooperation in Europe (OSCE).

5. Some 860,000 Kosovars were eventually registered as refugees in Macedonia, Albania, and elsewhere around the world. UN High Commissioner for Refugees, "The Balkans: Kosovo," www.unhcr.ch/cgi-bin/texis/vtx/balkans-country?country= kosovo (accessed October 26, 2004). By the end of May 1999, some 580,000 persons were estimated to be displaced and "rendered homeless" inside Kosovo. NATO, "NATO's Role in Relation to the Conflict in Kosovo," http://www.nato.int/kosovo/ history.htm (accessed October 26, 2004).

6. The pathbreaking work on postconflict reconstruction that provides inspiration for this book is found in Robert Orr, ed., *Winning the Peace: An American Strategy for Post-Conflict Reconstruction* (Washington, D.C.: CSIS Press, 2004).

7. In Bosnia the utter inefficacy of relying exclusively on civilian actors (whether unarmed international police or members of the local justice system) to confront entrenched underground extremist networks was demonstrated during the latter half of the 1990s.

8. Five years seems to be the minimum time requirement to achieve an enduring transformation. James Dobbins et al., *America's Role in Nation-Building: From Germany to Iraq* (Santa Monica, Calif.: RAND, 2003), 165–166. The conclusions of this report, which presents seven case studies on postwar transformation (Germany, Japan, Somalia, Haiti, Bosnia, Kosovo, and Afghanistan), are consistent with those in this book.

9. Chester A. Crocker, "Engaging Failing States," *Foreign Affairs* 82, no. 5 (September-October 2003): 36.

10. The four pillars are "governance and participation" (which make up an essential component of the strategy advanced in this book for moderating political conflict), enhanced "security capabilities" (which are a vital aspect of efforts to defeat militant extremists), "justice and reconciliation" (which are integral to the task of institutionalizing the rule of law), and "social and economic well-being" (which are central to efforts to develop a legitimate political economy). See Orr, *Winning the Peace*, 305–327.

2

The Historical Context of Conflict in Kosovo

Michael J. Dziedzic and Sasha Kishinchand

Editors' Note: This chapter is provided for those unfamiliar with the circumstances that precipitated international intervention in Kosovo. Those acquainted with these events may wish to proceed to chapter 3.

THE HISTORICAL LEGACY

Kosovo's history has produced a legacy that is of symbolic significance to the Serb nation but a population that is predominantly Albanian in ethnicity. (The most recent census, in 1991, indicated that 82 percent of Kosovo's nearly two million people were ethnic Albanian, 10 percent Serbian, and 8 percent other.)[1] As the location of major Serbian Orthodox monasteries and site of the mythic Ottoman defeat of the Serbs in the Battle of Kosovo Polje (1389), Kosovo helped to define the Serb nation. It is regarded by Serbs as the cradle of their civilization.

Albanian nationalism is also rooted in Kosovo, dating from the 1878 League of Prizren, which sought to unify Albanian-speaking peoples residing in present-day Albania, Kosovo, Macedonia, and Montenegro. Kosovo remained part of the Ottoman Empire until the First Balkan War in 1912, when Serbia and its allies asserted control of the region. After World War I, Kosovo was governed as part of the Kingdom of Serbs, Croats, and Slovenes. Albanians, the dominant ethnic group, were forced to either accept subjugation or emigrate.[2] This situation was reversed under Italian occupation during World War II, when Kosovo was annexed to Albania, producing a Serb exodus and restoration of Albanian dominance.

Kosovo

Under Josep Broz Tito's rule (1945–80), Kosovo was accorded autonomous status within the Serb Republic, one of the six republics that composed Yugoslavia. Albanians were recognized as a national minority with rights to education in their own language. Political control was reinforced through economic subsidies and ultimately the apparatus of a police state. Demonstrations in 1968 prompted the Yugoslav government to grant Albanians increased freedoms. The Constitution of 1974 significantly enhanced Kosovo's status, recognizing it as an autonomous province with its own legislative assembly, judiciary, territorial defense force, police, and central bank. Kosovo was the poorest part of Yugoslavia, and federal investment in the 1970s and 1980s had only begun to modernize its agrarian economy when Yugoslavia went into persistent economic decline. Kosovo faced the gravest consequences, its unemployment rate rising to more than 20 percent by the late 1980s.[3]

In 1981, a year after Tito's death, Kosovo Albanians agitated for recognition as one of Yugoslavia's constituent republics, provoking repressive action by federal security forces. Restiveness persisted throughout the 1980s. Kosovo's minority Serb population perceived its situation as increasingly tenuous, and its apprehension surfaced in the form of a 1986 public memorandum that called for a reversal of the decline in Serbia influence. In a visit to Kosovo the following year, Slobodan Milosevic recognized that incitement of Serb nationalism would propel him into unassailable control of government in Serbia.[4] In the estimation of historian Noel Malcolm, "With good reason, this Memorandum has been seen in retrospect as a virtual manifesto for the 'Greater Serbian' policies pursued by Belgrade in the 1990s."[5]

MILOSEVIC AND THE DISINTEGRATION OF YUGOSLAVIA

In 1989, the sixth hundredth anniversary of the Battle of Kosovo Polje, Milosevic revoked Kosovo's autonomy and reimposed direct rule from Belgrade, capital of the Federal Republic of Yugoslavia (FRY). This led to the dissolution of the Kosovo Assembly and deployment of thousands of additional troops and police to maintain order. Albanians were denied rights to education in their own language, and tens of thousands were dismissed from government positions. They responded by establishing a parallel government and education system under Ibrahim Rugova and the Democratic League of Kosovo (LDK), which espoused a nonviolent path to independence.

The fabric of Yugoslavia's multiethnic society was shredded in 1990 by Milosevic's drive to unite all Serbs under one state and form "Greater Serbia." This was a decisive turning point, according to Louis Sell, involving "a new strategy aimed at using armed force to create a separate Serb state, with the full knowledge that this would cause the disintegration of Yugoslavia and war."[6] During the war in Bosnia (1992–95), the nucleus of a violent Albanian resistance movement, the Kosovo Liberation Army (KLA), began to form. The Dayton Peace Accords that ended the war in Bosnia failed to address Kosovo's status, causing Rugova's nonviolent approach to begin losing credibility and eventually radicalizing the Albanian population.

By 1997 the KLA was openly claiming responsibility for attacks against police and other instruments of Serb authority. When neighboring Albania imploded early that year, the insurgent movement gained access to an arsenal that included crew-served weapons in addition to small arms. After the KLA shifted to systematic violence against Serbian police and officials, Milosevic responded by launching an offensive in early 1998, using Interior Ministry police (MUP) and the Yugoslav army. Their scorched-earth tactics were a replay of many previous episodes in Yugoslavia's progressive dissolution under Milosevic.

DIPLOMACY BACKED BY PRESSURE

The international community began to search in earnest for a means to avert another cycle of ethnic cleansing in the Balkans. In March 1998 the UN Security Council passed Resolution 1160, imposing an arms embargo on Yugoslavia, including Kosovo, that was to remain in effect until Belgrade entered into a "meaningful dialogue" with the leaders of Kosovo aimed at achieving a political solution to the issue of Kosovo's status.[7]

Milosevic responded by reinforcing his military posture in Kosovo. In May NATO announced that it was developing military options and was willing to act to end further violence. The deterrent effect was tempered, however, by a warning from the UN secretary-general that military intervention required a UN mandate.[8]

Any Security Council resolution seeking to authorize the use of force by NATO, however, faced a certain Russian veto and opposition from China. NATO members, moreover, were far from prepared to act in the absence of a UN mandate. Unconstrained by an effective deterrent, Serbian offensives and intermittent massacres continued into September. Between two hundred thousand and three hundred thousand Albanians were forced from their homes, and a groundswell of recruits were driven to join the KLA. With winter approaching and the cycle of violence spinning out of control, the specter of an impending humanitarian catastrophe loomed large.[9]

On September 23, 1998, the UN Security Council adopted Resolution 1199, calling for a cease-fire, withdrawal of Serbian forces of repression, monitoring by an international presence, return of refugees and displaced persons, and a dialogue to resolve the issue of Kosovo's political status. In the case that its provisions were disregarded, the resolution merely threatened "to consider further action and additional measures."[10] Russia made it clear that it would veto any future resolution that permitted the use of force.

With the passage of Resolution 1199, NATO's credibility was on the line.[11] Accordingly, on September 24, the North Atlantic Council (NAC) took the additional step of issuing an activation warning, or ACTWARN, directing NATO commanders to identify the forces they needed to carry out two options: limited air strikes and a major air campaign.[12]

In spite of continuing political divisions within NATO over the legal requirement for a UN mandate, the alliance's increased display of resolve provided leverage for U.S. envoy Richard Holbrooke to negotiate an agreement with Milosevic. It was ultimately necessary for NATO to issue an activation order, or ACTORD, on October 12, authorizing execution of an air campaign. Under this palpable pressure, the following day Milosevic accepted international monitoring to verify compliance with Resolution 1199 by NATO reconnaissance aircraft and by a 2,000-member Kosovo Verification Mission (KVM).[13] The KVM, established under the aegis of the Organization for Security and Cooperation in Europe (OSCE), began operating in Kosovo in December.

The KVM was not a cure for Kosovo's crisis. It provided time for international diplomacy to begin addressing the core issue: Kosovo's status. The KVM was hobbled by the absence of any on-the-ground enforcement mechanism. Indeed, the presence of international monitors actually deterred the use of force by NATO because KVM members could easily have been taken hostage by Serb forces. The KVM was quickly sabotaged when the KLA exploited its presence to recoup territory lost in earlier Serbian offensives and by renewed attacks on civilians by Serbian security forces. A massacre at Racak on January 15, 1999, in which more than forty ethnic Albanians were killed, left the chief of the KVM, Ambassador William Walker, with no choice but to verify the obvious. For this he was declared persona non grata by Milosevic, effectively vitiating the mission even though the KVM continued to operate with Walker at the helm.

As a result of the Racak massacre, UN secretary-general Kofi Annan met with the NAC on January 28 and declared that force could well be necessary when all other means had failed and that in Kosovo this point was nearing.[14] The Balkans Contact Group (France, Germany, Italy, Russia, the United Kingdom, and the United States) met in London on January 29 and demanded that Serbian and Kosovo Albanian leaders attend peace talks at Rambouillet, France, on February 6.[15]

The plan presented at Rambouillet called for the KLA to disarm within three months and for Serbia to withdraw all but a small contingent of security forces. Kosovo would enjoy autonomous self-governance, as it had before 1989.

The Kosovo Albanian delegation insisted on a provision that called for an international mechanism to be established after three years to resolve its final status.[16] Compliance with the agreement was to be enforced by 30,000 NATO troops.

The United States made it clear that the bombing option would not be exercised unless the Kosovo delegation signed the Rambouillet Accords. This was intended to place Milosevic in the position of having the last clear option for avoiding the use of force. On March 18 the Kosovo delegation signed, while Serbian representatives refused. With tens of thousands of Serbian forces massing on the border, the KVM was ordered to evacuate. As it withdrew on March 20, the Serbian offensive, Operation Horseshoe, was already in motion. Milosevic's strategic aim was to defeat the KLA by depriving it of a support base. As Ivo Daalder and Michael O'Hanlon argue, in the process Milosevic sought "both to alter the ethnic balance in Kosovo in the Serbs' favor and to destabilize Kosovo's neighbors, who had to cope with the large influx of refugees."[17]

FORCE BACKED BY DIPLOMACY

On March 24 NATO launched Operation Allied Force, an air campaign against targets in Serbia and Kosovo, in an attempt to achieve through force what diplomacy could not. The expectation was that a few days or at most weeks of bombing would persuade Milosevic to accept the bargain proffered at Rambouillet. In his address to the American people on the eve of the bombing, however, President Bill Clinton disavowed the use of ground troops to drive Serbian security forces out of Kosovo.[18] Serbian forces proved to be undeterred by bombs dropped from an altitude of fifteen thousand feet (a limitation NATO imposed on itself to avoid politically damaging aircraft losses).[19] A door-to-door ethnic cleansing campaign rapidly unfolded that produced the exodus of roughly half of Kosovo's two million–strong ethnic Albanian population. Most fled to refugee camps in neighboring Albania and Macedonia. Public support within NATO nations began to waver. Bombing alone appeared unlikely to prevent Milosevic from achieving his military objectives and then suing for peace. NATO's solidarity was at risk.

Force and diplomacy ultimately came together as planning for a ground offensive combined with incorporation of the Russians into the negotiating process to resolve the crisis. A diplomatic overture to Russia initiated by the German government provided an opening for a negotiated solution. President Boris Yeltsin appointed Viktor Chernomyrdin as his envoy, while President Clinton named Strobe Talbott to spearhead consultations for the United States. On May 4 Finnish president Martti Ahtisaari was added to represent the European Union. On

May 5 President Clinton was briefed on the initial results of NATO's planning for a ground invasion.[20]

A May 6, 1999, meeting of the Group of Eight (G-8), a body that includes both Russia and the United States, called for the establishment of an interim administration in Kosovo and the "deployment . . . of effective international civil and security presences, endorsed and adopted by the United Nations, capable of guaranteeing the achievement of the common objectives."[21] The G-8 proposal was one component of the diplomatic formula for ending the crisis; the other was Milosevic's acceptance of the following NATO conditions before military operations would be terminated:

1. A verifiable halt to Serbian violence and repression against the Albanians

2. Withdrawal of all Serbian police and military forces from Kosovo

3. Deployment of an international military force

4. Return of all refugees and internally displaced persons

5. Acceptance of the Rambouillet accords as the basis for a political framework to resolve Kosovo's status[22]

On May 27 Chernomyrdin communicated to Milosevic that he would have to either accept these conditions or be prepared for invasion. The clock was indeed ticking, since NATO calculated that a decision on the ground force option was needed by June 1 in order to complete the campaign by winter. Milosevic sought to impose conditions about the composition and command and control of the peace force, but Russia and the United States decided to resolve these issues themselves. Once this agreement had been reached, Ahtisaari and Chernomyrdin informed Milosevic, on June 2, that he would have to accept the basic conditions established by NATO and the G-8, which he did. This left the technical details of the Serbian withdrawal and deployment of the NATO-led Kosovo Force (KFOR) to be worked out by Supreme Allied Commander Europe, General Wesley Clark, and Yugoslav army commanders. The resulting Military Technical Agreement (also called the Kumanovo Agreement) was signed on June 9.[23]

THE BEGINNING OF THE QUEST FOR VIABLE PEACE

Kosovo presented the international community with the most demanding combination of circumstances yet confronted by an internationally mandated peace operation—it required the simultaneous capacity to make peace, enforce peace, and build peace while also performing the multitudinous functions of governance.

While the bombing was unfolding during the spring of 1999, uncertainty reigned about how the international community would deal with the outcome. The United Nations, rather than the OSCE, received the lead role in organizing the international civilian presence in Kosovo on June 10, 1999, under Security Council Resolution 1244. With little advance warning, the United Nations was required to exercise the sovereign prerogatives of a state for the first time. It was hard-pressed to cobble together a governmental bureaucracy for this purpose. One particularly demanding aspect of the mandate of the United Nations Interim Administration Mission in Kosovo (UNMIK) was the requirement to exercise "executive" law enforcement authority. More than four thousand armed international police had to be recruited to perform the gamut of public security functions required of a governing body, along with hundreds of civil administrators. A severely understaffed UN bureaucracy struggled for more than a year to mobilize the unprecedented numbers of personnel with the broad range of civilian skills required from its member states, which, with few exceptions, were totally unprepared for such a demand.

Owing to the sweeping nature of the mandate, no single international organization had the capacity to carry it out. Thus, UNMIK was the first UN mission designed with other multilateral organizations as full partners. It was built around four "pillars" under the leadership of a special representative of the secretary-general (SRSG), who managed the overall mission and controlled the activities of UN agencies and other international organizations that made up UNMIK. Each pillar had its own deputy SRSG, and each was to be responsible for one major component of the mission.[24]

Pillar I (Humanitarian Assistance) was led by the United Nations High Commissioner for Refugees (UNHCR). The pillar's responsibilities included repatriation and resettlement of refugees and internally displaced persons. After a year, these tasks were basically completed and Pillar I was disbanded. In May 2001 UNMIK Police and the Department of Judicial Affairs were combined to form a new Pillar I (Police and Justice). This brought all operations relating to the rule of law together in an effort to maximize the coordination of police investigations with prosecution within the criminal justice system. The Security Council originally authorized a police force of 3,110, including international civilian police officers, border police, and 10 Special Police Units. In October 1999 the council approved an increase to 4,718.[25]

Pillar II (Civil Administration) was the responsibility of the UN Department of Peacekeeping Operations (DPKO). This pillar oversaw administrative functions and services covering such areas as health and education, banking and finance, and post and telecommunications. Initially, 1,148 international staff members were authorized; by mid-2000, this figure was increased to 1,339.

Pillar III (Democratization and Institution Building) was run by the OSCE and had a mandate that included building human capacity in the areas of justice, police, and public administration; democratization and governance, human rights monitoring, and institutional development; organizing and monitoring elections; and strengthening the institutions of civil society, in particular, the media. With 450 international staff, it was the largest OSCE field presence.

Pillar IV (Reconstruction and Economic Development), managed by the European Union, was concerned with rebuilding Kosovo's physical and economic infrastructure, reactivating public services and utilities, and creating the foundation for a market-based economy. It had 64 international staff.

An inadequate level of police and staffing for UNMIK's civil administration was a severe constraint on its effectiveness throughout the first year. It was not until May 2000 that UNMIK Police even reached 75 percent strength.[26] Similarly, the United Nations had managed to hire only two-thirds of the 1,339 international staffers it needed when the standard one-year employment contracts were due to expire. With the mission facing crippling personnel shortfalls by mid-2000, the United Nations was compelled to permit UNMIK to hire directly from the field rather than rely on an understaffed and rules-bound UN Secretariat to do the hiring for it. After this, personnel were recruited fairly quickly. The European Union was also dilatory in mobilizing personnel. Indeed, for more than a year, most of its personnel were contractors hired by the U.S. Agency for International Development. The OSCE, in contrast, was able to draw on former members of the Kosovo Verification Mission to staff its operations efficiently.

The withdrawal of Serb forces proceeded without incident, allowing KFOR to announce on June 20 that all Yugoslav military and police units had departed. By July 26 the number of KFOR troops in Kosovo had reached thirty-five thousand, including some fifteen hundred Russian troops. Virtually the entire contingent was fielded by September.[27] KFOR would have little peace to keep, however. As refugees spontaneously returned home, assaults on Kosovo's Serb and Roma minorities erupted on a daily basis. Kosovo's ultimate political status remained unresolved. The quest for viable peace was just beginning.

◆   ◆   ◆

KEY DATES IN KOSOVO'S PEACE PROCESS, 1999–2004

June 10, 1999	The UN Security Council adopts Resolution 1244, authorizing UNMIK to control the territory and KFOR to secure it.
June 12, 1999	KFOR begins deployment into Kosovo.
June 20, 1999	Serbian military and police complete withdrawal from Kosovo.
July 25, 1999	SRSG Bernard Kouchner issues UNMIK Regulation No. 1, establishing UNMIK as the interim administration over Kosovo.
September 1999	More than 770,000 refugees have returned home to Kosovo.
September 7, 1999	Kosovo's police training academy starts its first class of 200 cadets.
September 20, 1999	The KLA completes demilitarization, and the Kosovo Protection Corps (KPC) is established by UNMIK.
November 6, 1999	UNMIK establishes the Central Fiscal Authority to manage Kosovo's annual consolidated budget.
December 15, 1999	Kosovo Albanian political parties agree to establish a Joint Interim Administrative Structure (JIAS) under UNMIK's control.
February 2, 2000	Violence in the divided city of Mitrovica erupts after a bus carrying Serb civilians suffers a rocket attack by Albanian extremists.
September 24, 2000	President Slobodan Milosevic loses national presidential elections to Vojislav Kostunica but refuses to accept the outcome.

October 5, 2000	Milosevic resigns under pressure from nonviolent popular demonstrations.
October 28, 2000	Municipal officials are elected with a 79 percent turnout.
May 15, 2001	SRSG Hans Haekkerup promulgates the Constitutional Framework for Provisional Self-Government.
November 17, 2001	The Legislative Assembly is elected, consisting of 120 representatives from all ethnic communities.
December 10, 2001	The Legislative Assembly holds its first session.
March 4, 2002	A coalition government is formed and provisional institutions of self-government begin to function.
April 2002	SRSG Michael Steiner announces the "Standards before Status" policy.
November 6, 2003	U.S. undersecretary of state for political affairs Marc Grossman announces a mid-2005 review date to determine whether progress toward meeting standards has been sufficient for final-status talks to begin.
March 17–18, 2004	Riots throughout Kosovo leave nineteen dead, hundreds injured, and hundreds of homes belonging to Serbs and other minorities damaged or destroyed.
October 23, 2004	Second Legislative Assembly elections are held.

Editors' Note: For those seeking greater detail about the peace process, a lengthy record of events since June 1999 exists in the quarterly reports of the UN secretary-general to the Security Council.[28] *These reports record both steady progress and numerous setbacks.*

NOTES

1. In 2000 the ethnic breakdown was estimated to be 88 percent Albanian, 7 percent Serb, and 5 percent other. Statistical Office of Kosovo, *Kosovo and Its Population: A Brief Description* (September 2003), 2–3, http://www.sok-kosovo.org (accessed October 27, 2004).

2. See Noel Malcolm, *Kosovo: A Short History* (New York: Harper Perennial, 1998), 264–269.

3. Susan Woodward puts the unemployment rate (defined as a percentage of the working population) at 23.1 percent in 1985 and estimates it at 22.2 percent by 1990. Susan Woodward, *Socialist Unemployment: The Political Economy of Yugoslavia, 1945–1990* (Princeton, N.J.: Princeton University Press, 1995), 205.

4. Laura Silber and Allan Little, *Yugoslavia: Death of a Nation* (New York: Penguin, 1997), 33.

5. The memorandum was first drawn up in 1985 as an "advisory document" for the government and later published fully in 1986. See Malcolm, *Kosovo*, 340–341.

6. Louis Sell, *Slobodan Milosevic and the Destruction of Yugoslavia* (Durham, N.C.: Duke University Press, 2002), 5.

7. The resolution suggested that such an agreement be based on principles of territorial integrity for the Federal Republic of Yugoslavia and "an enhanced status for Kosovo which would include a substantially greater degree of autonomy and meaningful self-administration." UN Security Council, Resolution 1160 (1998), S/RES/1160 (1998), March 31, 1998.

8. Agence France-Presse, "Annan Warns against Kosovo Action without U.N. Mandate," June 28, 1998. See also NATO, "Statement on Kosovo," NATO Press Release, May 28, 1998. For a detailed discussion of the interplay between force and diplomacy, see Ivo H. Daalder and Michael E. O'Hanlon, *Winning Ugly: NATO's War to Save Kosovo* (Washington, D.C.: Brookings Institution Press, 2000); and Wesley K. Clark, *Waging Modern War: Bosnia, Kosovo, and the Future of Combat* (New York: Public Affairs, 2001).

9. OSCE, *Kosovo/Kosova: As Seen, as Told*, 5, http://www.osce.org/kosovo/documents/reports/hr/part1/ch1.htm.

10. UN Security Council, Resolution 1199 (1998), S/RES/1199 (1998), September 23, 1998, paragraph 16.

11. NATO had already completed advanced planning for various military options if a cease-fire could not be attained. The North Atlantic Council had also authorized NATO planners to begin contacting alliance members to determine what capabilities they would be prepared to commit to prospective air operations. Daalder and O'Hanlon, *Winning Ugly*, 42.

12. NATO, "Statement by the Secretary General," NATO Press Statement, Vilamoura, Portugal, September 24, 1998.

13. The Kosovo Verification Mission was established on October 25, 1998, by Permanent Council Decision 263. Its tasks were to ensure compliance with the tenets of UN Security Council Resolution 1199. OSCE, "Overview," http://www.osce.org/kosovo/overview.

14. Daalder and O'Hanlon, *Winning Ugly*, 75.

15. The role of the Contact Group is discussed in detail in chapter 4.

16. Chapter 8, Article I, Section 3, of the Interim Agreement for Peace and Self-Government in Kosovo (commonly known as the Rambouillet accords) provides for an international meeting "to determine a mechanism for a final settlement of Kosovo, on the basis of the will of the people." According to press accounts, this vague reference to a referendum persuaded the Kosovo Albanian delegation to sign the agreement at the last minute. See Jane Perlez, "Kosovo Albanians, in Reversal, Say They Will Sign Peace Pact," *New York Times*, February 24, 1999, A1.

17. Daalder and O'Hanlon, *Winning Ugly*, 59.

18. President Clinton articulated three objectives: deter and punish Serb aggression against Kosovo's Albanian population, erode Serbia's military capabilities to wage war against Kosovo, and demonstrate NATO's commitment to oppose aggression. For a transcript of Clinton's address, see http://www.pbs.org/newshour/bb/europe/jan-jun99/address_3-24.html.

19. David Halberstam, *War in a Time of Peace: Bush, Clinton, and the Generals* (New York: Charles Scribner's Sons, 2001).

20. Daalder and O'Hanlon, *Winning Ugly*, 156.

21. A G-8 presidency letter of May 6, 1999, to the UN Security Council stated the conclusions of the meeting (circulated at G-8 request as a UNSC document, S/1999/516).

22. NATO, "NATO's Role in Relation to Kosovo," http://www.nato.int/docu/facts/2000/kosovo.htm

23. The full name of the agreement is the Military Technical Agreement between the International Security Force (KFOR) and the Governments of the Federal Republic of Yugoslavia and the Republic of Serbia.

24. UN Security Council, *Report of the Secretary-General Pursuant to Paragraph 10 of Security Council Resolution 1244 (1999)*, S/1999/672 (June 12, 1999), paragraph 5.

25. See UNMIK, "UNMIK Civilian Police: Facts & Figures," http://www.unmikonline.org/civpol/factsfigs.htm.

26. See UNMIK, "UNMIK Police Press Update," May 17, 2000, http://www.civpol.org/unmik/PressUpdateArchi/archive00.htm.

27. U.S. Department of State, "Fact Sheet: KFOR Deployment," *USIS Washington File*, July 26, 1999, http://www.un.int/usa/99kos726c.htm. See also NATO, http://www.nato.int/kosovo/history.htm.

28. The official document numbers and dates for the *Reports of the Secretary General on the United Nations Interim Administration Mission in Kosovo* are (in reverse chronological order): S/2004/348 (April 30, 2004); S/2004/71 (January 26, 2004); S/2003/996 (October 15, 2003); S/2003/675 (June 26, 2003); S/2003/421 (April 14, 2003); S/2003/113 (January 29, 2003); S/2002/1376 (December 19, 2002); S/2002/1126 (October 9, 2002); S/2002/62 (January 15, 2002); S/2001/926 (October 2, 2001); S/2001/218 Add. 1 (March 26, 2001); S/2001/218 (March 13, 2001); S/2000/1196 (December 15, 2000); S/2000/538 Add. 1 (June 29, 2000); S/2000/538 (June 6, 2000); S/2000/177 Add. 3 (May 25, 2000); S/2000/177 Add. 2 (March 28, 2000); S/2000/177 Add. 1 (March 3, 2000); S/2000/177 (March 3, 2000); S/1999/1250 (December 23, 1999); S/1999/1250 Add. 1 (December 23, 1999); S/1999/987 (September 16, 1999); S/1999/779 (July 12, 1999); and the *Report of the Secretary General Pursuant to Paragraph 10 of Security Council Resolution 1244 (1999)*, S/1999/672 (June 12, 1999).

3

Advance Political-Military Planning

Laying the Foundation for Achieving Viable Peace

Len Hawley and Dennis Skocz

A DVANCE POLITICAL-MILITARY PLANNING is essential to mounting a successful international intervention. A transformation of local war-hardened power necessitates an interagency planning effort well in advance of deployment. The aim of political-military planning is to harmonize the many diverse civilian and military efforts as a comprehensive strategy for achieving viable peace.

Three factors call for advance planning. First, significant dependencies among various agency efforts in a mission require unified policy direction and a coherent intervention strategy, one that integrates its political, security, rule-of-law, and economic lines of effort to achieve transformation. Second, contentious policy issues emerge from the outset that must be addressed to avoid policy gaps and subsequent disconnects on the ground. Finally, and often most important, a substantial number of international troops, personnel, and resources must be mobilized in a multinational and multilateral context and sustained, reasonably for at least five years,[1] to assure that the desired transformation of power takes hold. The pool of available capabilities, however, is seriously limited. There is no slack in the system. Advance planners are pressured to utilize limited national and multilateral capabilities for the greatest effect in order to achieve viable peace.

This chapter addresses major aspects of advance planning for an intervention to transform power. The intervention in Kosovo by a combined UN-NATO team—the United Nations Interim Administration Mission in Kosovo (UNMIK) and Kosovo Force (KFOR)—serves as the case study. After the chapter introduces the advance planning process, it outlines key contributions of the intelligence community. It then highlights ten building blocks that must be assembled for a successful intervention. Organizing a capable mission and mobilizing the international community to get the job done in a multiyear campaign are additional planning challenges discussed at the end of the chapter.

THE BIG PICTURE

When a crisis erupts on the international scene, the focus of attention is on urgently responding to human suffering and stopping hostilities. A response usually demands a massive international intervention calling for thousands of troops, tons of urgent relief supplies, hundreds of police officers, and a host of other "first responders." These activities must be supported by hundreds of millions of dollars, allocated quickly in the first months alone.

The intervention in Kosovo was big and complex. The NATO-led military force numbered almost fifty thousand troops after the first six months of the intervention. The UN-led civilian mission needed 4,718 police officers, 1,339 civil administrators and staff, and 450 institution-building advisers and trainers. Nongovernmental organizations (NGOs) sent thousands of relief workers and hundreds of human rights investigators. Several training programs and academies needed to be up and running in the region within a few months. Reconstruction costs totaled about $2 billion in the first year alone.

Such a massive effort cannot be sustained indefinitely. The political will of international contributors will likely fade over time, and an expensive, interminable mission will soon lose support. Indeed, once military forces are deployed and stability is imposed, considerable talk soon emerges about exit strategies—which has the deleterious effect of undermining the fragile transformation process before it begins to take root locally. Because interventions are usually promoted as temporary, short-lived intrusions to end a crisis, participating governments usually want to exit soon after the compelling need dissipates.

This reality creates considerable pressure on a mission. As leaders of the international intervention, the custodians of the peace process must "manage down" the local conflict as rapidly as possible to a less costly level that is sustainable over time.

Advance planners, therefore, anticipating this pressure on the intervention force to "go home," need to craft a strategic approach aimed at achieving viable peace within about three years. When viable peace emerges in that time frame, the entire operation can be reduced to a more affordable level in order to sustain the peace process over the longer term.

Transformation has to be achieved, but time can run out. As discussed in chapter 1, a viable peace in a war-torn society should be the near-term objective of an intervention so that the international community can sustain the intervention in the future. Hence, the compelling necessity for managing down conflict among local factions requires a transformation of power that unfolds progressively in three sequential stages:

- *Stage 1: imposed stability/an unsustainable peace process.* A massive international intervention asserts control with the active support of an international military force that imposes stability throughout the territory. The task of transformation begins immediately in all lines of effort; all these efforts together work to moderate or neutralize war-hardened power. This requires extensive activity in the political, military, economic, law enforcement, and judicial spheres, but the international community cannot sustain the peace process at this high level indefinitely. The mission's overriding aim, therefore, is to substantially transform local power so that the entire effort can get to stage 2: viable peace in about three years. As a viable peace emerges, the international community should be able to substantially reduce the scale of the intervention and continue to sustain the peace process at a more affordable level of effort.

- *Stage 2: viable peace/a sustainable peace process.* As a viable peace emerges, an essential transformation of entrenched power has taken place to the extent that a downsized and affordable international mission remains in control, but in partnership with newly trained local officials. Stability is still guaranteed by international military forces, but required troop levels are substantially lower because militant extremists and obstructionists have been noticeably marginalized. The international community can sustain this lower level of effort for an extended period, realistically for another five to seven years. The mission's overriding aim during stage 2 is to continue to strengthen legitimate institutions to channel the competition for power and prepare local officials for assuming responsibilities under stage 3: self-sustaining peace.

- *Stage 3: self-sustaining peace/a self-enforcing peace process.* The locals are now in control of the major institutions of legitimate power. Obstructionists are completely marginalized. Safeguards are fully effective. However, the fledgling government needs outside international support (especially for development) and help to channel local disputes toward nonviolent resolution mechanisms. The mission's overriding aim is to monitor safeguards, advise local officials, and leverage assistance to progressively eliminate dependencies on the international community.

This "big picture" captures the core thrust of this book: the transformation of local power must precede the international community's transition to the next stage of management. Therefore, the focus of advance planning is to set favorable conditions before the intervention is launched to jump-start this essential transformation of power in a war-torn society.

THE INTERAGENCY ADVANCE PLANNING PROCESS

On any given day in the post–Cold War era, more than thirty internal conflicts are going on around the globe. In most of these bitter struggles, war-hardened faction leaders exercise power by ruthless political tyranny, military coercion, lawless rule, and criminal economic predation. These internal wars are deadly—the strong and ruthless routinely slaughter the weak and innocent.

In dealing with these horrible conflicts, policymakers need—and earnestly demand—flexibility. They want realistic options.[2] For this reason, the advance political-military (pol-mil) planning process is fundamentally different from normal agency planning processes in which planners write detailed plans to achieve stated agency objectives.[3]

In the few years leading up to the intervention in Kosovo, pol-mil planning experts crafted what is called today the "advance planning process." It embodies a coherent sequence of policy-planning tasks that eventually produces a political-military plan[4] for an intervention. The generic phases of this advance planning process are presented in box 3.1.[5]

This process guides other interagency planning efforts. In preparing for the intervention in Kosovo, for example, advance planners made the important distinction between an "intervention" and a "coalition": an intervention usually requires several different coalitions to get the job done over the duration of the mission.

The political and structural foundations of each of these coalitions must be set in place during the advance planning process. Because contingency operations are mostly multinational and multilateral, this means that ongoing sensitive policy planning efforts must be married with diplomacy. Discrete consultations among allies, regional friends, potential contributors, and international organizations are crucial to ensuring that a political-military plan wins the active support of all participants in the various coalitions participating in the intervention.

The advance planning effort for the postwar stage in Kosovo began in earnest just as NATO launched its air campaign in late March 1999. The planning effort

Box 3.1. Generic Phases of the Advance Planning Process

Advance planners refer to three documents to set the foundation for policy planning: a regional strategy provided by the State Department, a comprehensive situation assessment provided by the intelligence community, and a crisis planning scenario provided by an interagency policy working group.

Interagency planners then receive top-down guidance that initiates the planning effort: core regional aims, policy aims in preventing or responding to the crisis, and preliminary scope of the intervention.

Phase 1: Mission Analysis
- Analyzes the preliminary purpose and scope of the intervention
- Identifies major mission areas (e.g., humanitarian relief, public diplomacy) of the operation
- Outlines intervention objectives, tasks, showstoppers, and policy questions

Phase 2: Strategic Projection and Policy Issues Paper
- Forecasts the desired ends for the intervention, looking ahead about two years
- Clarifies policy issues that will emerge over the duration of the intervention

Phase 3: Strategic Approach
- Clarifies the international community's posture regarding the crisis
- Presents a political forecast of the protagonists' actions
- Outlines broad strategies and viable options for taking action:
  - Core strategy to strengthen the intervention's posture
  - Preventive strategy to avoid hostilities
  - Crisis response strategy to achieve intervention aims
  - Escalation control strategy to limit expansion
  - Hedging strategies for geostrategic shifts and disconnects
- Recommends agency preparations

Phase 4: Pol-Mil Intervention Strategy[6]
- Confirms the intervention's policy aims and posture
- Clarifies the intervention's strategic purpose, mission, and near-term ends
- Presents a strategy to mobilize, wield, and sustain international power

(continued on next page)

Box 3.1. Generic Phases of the Advance Planning Process *(cont.)*

Phase 5: Pol-Mil Implementation Plan
- Presents a policy overview on the intervention
- Outlines the purpose, mission, and desired end state
- Defines the political-military strategy
- Establishes the mission's organization and concept of implementation
- Outlines preparatory tasks
- Specifies major mission area tasks
- Defines interagency management activities
- Outlines the follow-on mission

Phase 6: Agency Operational Planning[7]
- Mobilizes national and multilateral coalition partners
- Completes agency operational plans

Phase 7: Interagency Rehearsal
- Confirms the final countdown for the intervention
- Reviews mission area management and agency plans
- Harmonizes initial agency efforts from the outset

---

proceeded on the assumption that Belgrade would comply with NATO's demands for terminating its bombing campaign. As the effort progressed, a few key countries and the United Nations undertook confidential diplomatic activities.

Ambiguities plagued the effort from the beginning. Political-military planners could not predict which international organization—the United Nations or the Organization for Security and Cooperation in Europe (OSCE)—would lead the civilian presence. Nor could they confirm whether NATO would lead the international security presence. Planners could not lay out a detailed timetable with actual milestones for progress. These issues would be analyzed as the advance planning process unfolded throughout the spring of 1999.

Obstacles to Transforming Internal Conflict

Conflict transformation is typically far more difficult than initially envisioned. Wishful thinking often prevails, and planning fallacies flourish without prudent judgment and experienced circumspection.[8] In any crisis, it is likely that the local situation will be poorly understood, adversaries and difficult actors misjudged, ill-defined threats dismissed as unlikely, potent economic incentives overlooked,[9] operational needs underestimated, partners' commitments misread, and hopeful projections about indigenous popular support simply wrong. These miscalculations suggest that political-military planners have to be extremely risk conscious and seek to reduce these misjudgments by intense yet independent intelligence assessments of the issues.[10]

There are several obstacles to ending conflict in the postwar stage.[11] Most important, rival leaders are likely to still be pursuing their unmet war aims through violence and may seek to use the postwar peace process to do so.[12] If each faction's war aims have not been satisfied, rivals are likely to be predisposed to continue fighting to achieve them. Without transformation, it is unlikely that a viable peace will eventually emerge in the postwar period.[13]

In the spring of 1999, experienced policy planners had few illusions about the difficulties presented by the war in Kosovo. Experience with the difficulties in stopping hostilities in Bosnia had given most officials a guarded posture as they faced the conflict in Kosovo. They voiced credible doubts about the ease of ending the Serb-Albanian identity conflict, especially while Milosevic's regime remained in power to obstruct the peace process. Moreover, Kosovo's ethnic war was fueled by pervasive corruption and criminal activity that was orchestrated by organized crime syndicates in the region. Even then, Kosovo kept hidden its intense clan rivalries and deadly power struggles, and many of these remained ill defined even after deployment of KFOR and UNMIK.

A Comprehensive Situation Assessment

Coming out of Somalia, Lieutenant General Anthony Zinni spoke frequently on "twenty lessons learned," in which he emphasized the necessity to start political military planning as early as possible and include everyone in the planning process. He urged planners, if possible, to make a thorough assessment of the situation well before deployment, including local culture, the personalities of the rival faction leaders, and the issues at stake in the conflict.[14]

At the outset, a comprehensive situation assessment paints the landscape for an interagency planning effort. A thorough assessment requires an open and active discourse between the policy planning community and the intelligence community early in the process.[15] Although frank discussion is crucial, such conversations are often incomplete, and this leads to unrealistic situation assessments, inadequate political forecasts, and simplistic scenarios[16] for planning an intervention.

The collection of relevant information requires early action. The intelligence community must be energized to focus on a collapsing country well before the situation becomes urgent. Intelligence collection assets are limited, and it takes time to refocus resources on an area in crisis. Perhaps more important, a crisis involving chaotic internal conflict in a failed state causes critical sources of information to disappear or to "be disappeared" during the course of war. As an internal

conflict erupts and the troubled state is overcome by turmoil, embassy reporting, bilateral contacts, and private NGO assessments tend to erode or dry up
completely. In extreme cases, most international organizations and embassies
withdraw their staff personnel, leaving behind few to gather information on the developing emergency.

Building new institutions in a troubled state requires the most elementary
knowledge of how things work in the war-torn society. Establishing a new civilian
police force in Kosovo, for example, called for information on past civil service
salaries in Yugoslavia—after considerable searching, planners discovered this basic
information unexpectedly in the library of the U.S. Federal Reserve Bank. In
some cases, however, basic information (such as the country's licensing practices
or procedures for property transactions) may not exist to support the interagency
planning effort, and planners may need to develop estimates on the basis of parallels to roughly comparable situations elsewhere.

Hence, a nontraditional intelligence collection effort is essential. Achieving
a transformation of power in Kosovo required an expanded assessment of obscure
issues that resided outside typical political and military considerations. This included information on entrenched cultural and social practices, intrafactional
rivalries, clandestine terrorist operations, human rights abuses and police brutality,
grievances of victims' groups, diversions of economic wealth, organized crime
operations, and government corruption. Box 3.2 lists the generic elements that
usually encompass such a comprehensive assessment.

Because winning hearts and minds is a central thrust of transformation,
opinion surveys also provide significant information, particularly about the local
political landscape. Are people beginning to think differently about their future?
What are the most important concerns of daily life? Who is the public's best
hope for leadership in the postwar stage? How are specific obstructionists viewed?
What are the prevailing views about the international mission? Opinion surveys
should be taken early on to appreciate the popular support for each faction as well
as public attitudes toward the desired ends promised by the international mission.

A Mission Analysis

A mission analysis, the first phase of the advance planning process, seeks to clarify
a host of issues at the beginning of the planning effort. The most important of
these include the purpose and scope of the proposed intervention, the major mission areas of the operation, and the appropriate mission area objectives, supporting tasks, key actors, showstopper issues, and immediate policy questions. Drawing
on the guidance provided by the principals in the U.S. president's cabinet, selected
staff members of the National Security Council (NSC) should form an interagency working group to oversee this first step of the advance planning process.[17]

Box 3.2. Generic Elements of a Comprehensive
Situation Assessment

1. General situation of the crisis
2. Key actors, adversaries, and factions
   - Key actor intentions, aims, commitment, and motivations
   - Anticipated actions and reactions in the near term
3. The local internal conflict
   - Political conflict
   - Military conflict
   - Economic drivers of conflict
   - Insurgent and terrorist threats
   - Weapons-of-mass-destruction threats
4. Operating environment and physical conditions
5. The proposed peace agreement and concept for implementation
6. International mission (leadership, composition, capabilities, and the like)
7. Host nation cooperation and support
8. Neighboring state support
9. Regional and international support
10. Potential contingencies for crisis escalation
11. Potential geostrategic discontinuities
12. Potential difficulties and obstacles to transformation
13. Initial entry conditions

A systematic approach to this first step is essential.[18] Over time, several generic issues have recurred frequently in various crisis planning situations. In box 3.3, these issues are codified in a series that embodies a full mission analysis.[19]

In April 1999 the State Department led an interagency mission analysis for the postwar intervention in Kosovo. Interagency planners received top-down guidance from the Deputies Committee. They reported to the Kosovo Policy Working Group, which consisted of deputy assistant secretaries from various agencies. The intelligence community provided interagency planners with a realistic crisis-planning scenario for the postwar period in Kosovo.

Interagency teams crafted an implementation concept for their assigned mission areas based on key milestones in the continuum from the deployment into Kosovo in June 1999 to a first democratic election, which was estimated to come sometime after eighteen to twenty-four months at the earliest. International partners joined the planning process early. As the mission analysis effort unfolded in April, the mission area teams shared U.S. planning concepts with key allies and other international actors, including the United Nations Secretariat, NATO, and the OSCE.

Box 3.3. Mission Analysis Areas of Inquiry

1. Current situation and priority local needs
2. Probable desired ends of the international intervention
3. Key mission area tasks
4. Status of task planning and current operations
5. Bilateral considerations with the host government
6. Regional considerations
7. Major planning considerations for the intervention
8. Key players and potential roles
9. Probable mission area objectives
10. Probable mission area coalition partners, organization, and management
11. Preferred mission area strategy and concept of operation
12. Alternative mission area approaches
13. Preferred mission area phased implementation concept
14. Intelligence requirements
15. Personnel and resource requirements
16. Legal requirements
17. Funding requirements and potential sources of funding
18. Proposed agency responsibilities—lead and supporting agencies
19. Required early decisions and actions
20. Unresolved policy issues

A Strategic Approach to Transformation

A strategic approach to transforming power in a war-torn society is at the heart of political-military planning—it sketches the pathway to viable peace. Although there are many factors to consider in crafting this pathway, the most important factor is time—the key to a successful strategic approach to transform power hinges on determining a realistic and achievable pace of change for channeling the competition for power using new processes that rely on democratic principles under the rule of law.

A transformation from imposed stability to viable peace takes considerable time—realistically about three years (e.g., the duration of stage 1). Once viable peace emerges, transformation continues in a reduced international effort (e.g., beginning of stage 2) that may last for five to seven more years of extended assistance to help bring about a self-sustaining peace. Such a phased peace process established at the beginning is beneficial in at least three ways. First, it gives faction leaders time to realize that they are unlikely to achieve their interests without compromise and participation in the peace process. Second, it affords each rival the flexibility to pursue new alternatives in the competition for power. A third benefit, one that is often overlooked, is that it allows rivals time to reorient on future opportunities presented by the peace process rather than adhere to past grudges and rigid war aims.

Timely progress at the outset is crucial for transformation. Real prospects for a better life can erode the fixation with past struggles. Rival factions often find it easier to reach agreement and "move on" to a new life if they are less preoccupied with bitter resentments and more eager to exploit opportunities created by incipient conditions, particularly economic gain. Early improvement can also encourage faction leaders to either adapt or become irrelevant. A growing sense of future opportunity is a function of improved living conditions, especially security, justice, and economic well-being.

At the beginning, the international mission tries to set favorable conditions quickly and avoid costly delays and obstructionism. Urgent needs demand time-sensitive humanitarian relief, electrical power, and public security—these basic wants require effective action in hours and days rather than weeks and months. In the earliest days, the internationals also have to move quickly to win the skeptical support of rival faction leaders on essential actions that involve demobilizing armed groups, creating work opportunities for former foot soldiers, and participating in advisory councils to help get things running in local areas.

In addition, the sequencing of potentially explosive activities requires careful judgment. The internationals must make sensible judgments regarding the pace of highly visible—and potentially inflammatory—transformational initiatives. These include the naming of provisional local civil officials, appointing local police officers, responding to victims' grievances, investigating war crimes and human rights violations, returning refugees and internally displaced persons (IDPs) to minority areas, and conducting elections to begin installing indigenous governance. As these key efforts begin to affect entrenched power, meanwhile, the international mission must anticipate—and prudently suppress—the emergence of obstructionists to the peace process. All these activities have to be sequenced to benefit the peace process in ways that convince faction leaders that the "new order" is good for their personal interests and those of their followers.

The crisis in Kosovo was nested within several other competing priorities that were essential to bringing greater stability to the Balkans. These priorities included containment of the Milosevic regime until his removal could occur peacefully in Belgrade, continuation of peace implementation efforts in Bosnia, sustainment of the fragile alliance between Montenegro and Serbia, development of stability in Montenegro, and continuation of ethnic cooperation and greater stability in Albania and Macedonia. Kosovo's independence would likely upset these wider policy aims and ignite more war in the region. These concerns tended to slow the pace of change in Kosovo.

Given the importance of these wider factors, the approach to Kosovo's transformation was a temporizing strategy. Its political aim was to eventually constitute
Kosovo's "substantial autonomy"—which some would regard as independence in all
but its name. In getting there, the temporizing strategy would have to achieve
several objectives, not all complementary:

- Quell Albanian extremists' urges for Kosovo's immediate independence and
  Serbian fears of Albanian dominance

- Stop further ethnic violence even though community hatred raged

- Wait for moderate political forces to emerge in Serbia to oust the Milosevic regime

- Meet the urgent demands of Kosovo's war-torn society

- Allow new political entities in Kosovo to grow and take risks to support the
  peace process

- Provide realistic expectations for the eventual handover of autonomy to
  moderate Kosovar political figures

The strategic approach had to find the right balance among all these efforts in how
Kosovo's transformation would unfold. Meanwhile, the international community
had to sustain its enormous contributions to the UN-NATO intervention in the
multiyear campaign. At the same time, European contributors needed to continue
their concerted efforts on the many higher-priority issues for peace and security
in the Balkans. The implication was that the international community had to
take full control of Kosovo's transformation and defer the issue of final status
until that controversy could be addressed without violence by an increasingly
moderate Kosovar public. This would take even more time.

SHAPING LOCAL PARTICIPATION IN THE TRANSFORMATION PROCESS

A key advance planning task involves determining how to shape local participation
in the transformation process. Planners need to set conditions for the international
mission to establish structures for building a working partnership with indigenous
officials. At the top, the overall political director of the mission, normally the UN
special representative, usually establishes a political advisory council consisting of
leading local figures and influential leaders. This high-level council serves as the
central advisory body for strengthening political cooperation between the mission's
leadership and various faction leaders.

On the military side, the international force commander usually constitutes
a joint military committee consisting of the top military commander from each

faction. This committee addresses implementation of military security and related activities.

On the civil administration side, the UN mission typically establishes several joint functional committees to oversee the establishment of effective civil administration functions such as education, health care, transportation, communications services, and cultural practices, among others. All these joint committees serve to ensure participation of local officials in the decisions and actions of the international mission.

Kosovo's transformation required several working partnerships. As discussed in chapter 5, however, cooperation was never easy. Nearly every issue was contentious, and UNMIK and KFOR had to demonstrate that the peace process was going to move forward, despite efforts by some to exercise veto power over moving ahead.

TEN BUILDING BLOCKS FOR A SUCCESSFUL INTERVENTION

Advance planning also sets the basic framework of an intervention. Kosovo presented an exceptional challenge to the international community because the intervention entailed taking on the interim governance of a war-ravaged territory for an extended duration. Fortunately, in shaping an interim transitional authority, pol-mil planners learned from neighboring UN and NATO interventions in Bosnia (UNPROFOR and SFOR) and Eastern Slavonia (UNTAES). They also drew on former missions deployed to Kosovo, including the Balkans Contact Group's Kosovo Diplomatic Observer Mission (KDOM) and the OSCE led Kosovo Verification Mission (KVM), which eventually was foiled by Belgrade's obstructionism.

By April 1999 a consensus emerged that achieving success in Kosovo following a NATO victory would be well beyond anything attempted recently in the Balkans. In addition, initial conditions inside Kosovo were likely to be exceptionally variable and mostly indeterminate until after the war had ended. This perplexing uncertainty was exacerbated by a lack of basic information about Kosovo's prewar government that was needed to prepare plans for a new interim civil administration under UN control. Furthermore, recognizing that intense international alarm about Kosovo would likely dissipate in a few months following a NATO victory, advance planners were pressured to assemble building blocks for success on an expedited basis well before NATO's military campaign successfully ended in early June 1999.

Various authors have identified several conditions for success in the past, but they have done so without a specific focus on transforming war-hardened power.[20] Ten specific building blocks are central to our discussion on transforming power to achieve viable peace in war-torn societies.

Compelling Justification for Intervention

The cornerstone of any intervention is its compelling justification. Nearly all sizable international operations require an informal political consensus among interested governments and regional organizations regarding the compelling necessity for extraordinary common action.[21] Because affected nations view the difficulties and threats posed by a troubled state differently, most interventions are largely ad hoc formations in which interested states come together very quickly to deal with the crisis. Given that a transformation of power in a war-torn country is likely to entail a multiyear international intervention, the justification for such intrusive action has to hold force over several years.

In early 1999 Kosovo's crisis presented compelling motivations for common action. Most European governments had already made considerable contributions to bring peace to the Balkans since 1992, especially in Albania, Croatia, Bosnia, Montenegro, and Macedonia. The internal conflict in Kosovo threatened these ongoing regional efforts and potentially undermined the larger political evolution of the Balkans toward stability, economic development, and political integration into Europe. This broader effort held important security implications for Russia's continuing partnership with NATO, a vital national security interest of the United States.

Milosevic's tyranny in Kosovo threatened these core political and security interests. In addition, when Milosevic attempted to forcibly expel nearly the entire Albanian population during NATO's military campaign, a strong moral justification emerged calling for Kosovo's autonomy from Milosevic's ethnic terror. Moreover, European governments sought to halt the massive exodus of Kosovar refugees into Western Europe. This meant that Belgrade's repression of the Albanian population had to end permanently. All of these factors contributed to the emergence of the compelling Western justification, for the United Nations, NATO, the OSCE, the European Union, and many European governments, supporting a long-term intervention following NATO's air campaign.

Backing of Influential Regional Powers

An international intervention needs the backing of regional governments with power and influence.[22] As influential actors, regional powers are likely to pursue their national interests by exercising considerable political, military, and economic clout in potentially unforeseen ways. Because regional governments usually have close historical ties with at least one of the rival factions, they will likely seek to influence how the transformation of power unfolds within the troubled state. Without the helpful involvement of regional powers to implement a peace process, attempts at any transformation will likely be frustrated.[23]

The crises in the Balkans affected the national interests of several European powers, including Britain, France, Germany, Italy, and Russia. In 1994 the foreign ministers of these influential powers collaborated with the United States to form the Balkans Contact Group to shape a common crisis response policy for the region. For the most part, the Balkans Contact Group proved to be an effective informal crisis management mechanism because it was able to deal pragmatically with many policy issues on a consensus basis. Over the years, it influenced key actions taken by the UN Security Council, the G-8, NATO, the European Union, and the OSCE regarding international responses to this troubled region. In July 1998 the Contact Group deployed its own mission into Kosovo, the Kosovo Diplomatic Observer Mission (KDOM), to monitor and report on the dire humanitarian situation, thereby acting as a deterrent to ethnic violence in the territory.

Although the Contact Group focused on urgent matters within Kosovo, the G-8 took a broad, long-term policy perspective on the Kosovo conflict. The G-8 consisted of the Contact Group nations as well as Canada and Japan. This larger body took a keen interest in the Kosovo crisis, elevating the Contact Group's policy discourse to include G-8 heads of state and finance ministers. On May 6, 1999, the G-8 announced an agreement on principles for a political solution to the crisis. The Security Council later adopted these principles as the basis for political resolution of the crisis. After Security Council Resolution 1244 was passed in June 1999, the G-8 continued to be helpful in mobilizing European support for the massive peace implementation effort involving NATO, the European Union, and the OSCE.

Achievable Political Solution

An important building block is an acceptable and achievable political solution, or plausible end state, for the local conflict. An acceptable political result should channel the intense competition for power among rival factions into peaceful political processes built on democratic principles. An achievable political end is particularly important when a troubled state is engulfed by ethnic civil war.[24]

Conflict transformation requires the shift of power away from extremist, rogue warlords and their entrenched power structures to new, legitimate institutions. Participating governments and neighboring states are not disinterested in the eventual political outcome that will bring an end to a civil war. Such a political solution, envisioned as the desired end state articulated in a pol-mil plan, must be acceptable to these contributors and realistically achievable in the near term.

A successful transformation, however, often requires considerable ambiguity about the political solution from the outset—a prerequisite that is counterintuitive. An overly precise political solution at the front end will eventually lead to continued fighting, because losers in the desired political solution will see no alternative other than war. If the political end is well defined at the outset, the political manager will likely have to make it unclear well before mediation efforts begin.

Ambiguity does not suggest an "anything goes" approach. Some end states can be ruled out. Planners can artfully craft a desired political end that is, in the extreme, a flexible framework that the international community can embrace and that is "good enough" at the beginning to gain international backing for intervention without kindling unwelcome, and often undetected, armed resistance from local factions. This adaptable framework should allow for interpretations to assist the mediation process in opening up new opportunities for political reconciliation.

For Kosovo, toward the end of NATO's air campaign in early May, the G-8 foreign ministers met in Petersburg to adopt general principles for the political solution of substantial autonomy, including an ambiguous principle to serve as the basis for the forthcoming UN-NATO postwar intervention. This carefully worded principle called for

> a political process towards the establishment of an interim political framework agreement providing for a substantial self-government for Kosovo, taking full account of the Rambouillet accords and the principles of sovereignty and territorial integrity of the Federal Republic of Yugoslavia and the other countries in the region, and the demilitarization of the KLA.[25]

A month later, when the Security Council authorized the UN-NATO intervention, it embraced the G-8's imprecise answer about an achievable political end in Kosovo of "substantial self-government" as the aim of Kosovo's peace process.

Operational Assistance by Neighboring States

Neighboring states play a decisive role in the success of an intervention. Whether a particular neighbor assists in the transformation of power depends on how the peace process affects that government's interests. Hence, advance planners need to appreciate each neighbor's potential for support[26] or opposition to each faction within the troubled state. If close ties exist to at least one of the factions, neighboring states will not remain indifferent to the ultimate end of the political transformation process. Furthermore, pol-mil planners should understand the extent of each neighbor's political, military, and economic involvement with the war-torn country and anticipate how that state's participation will likely play out as the peace process unfolds.

Bordering on Kosovo, the states of Albania, Macedonia, Montenegro, and Serbia each had differing interests at stake. The first three, with strong Albanian connections, were satisfied with the Security Council's support of Kosovo's autonomy, while setting aside the question of independence because that would likely have had a destabilizing effect on them. Albania and Macedonia played critical supporting roles in sustaining the UN-NATO intervention logistically, containing KLA militant activity in border areas and hosting the OSCE's institution-building and training activities. Montenegro was a neutral actor for the most part, given its tenuous relationship with Belgrade. Serbia was a difficult obstructionist, as expected, owing to its forced departure from Kosovo.

Containment of Transnational Nonstate Threats

Transnational nonstate threats—extremist religious movements, ethnic-identity movements, underground economic cartels, criminal trafficking networks, and regional terrorist insurgencies—grew in power and influence during the 1990s. They have learned to exploit the new opportunities of globalization and flourish in regions where states exercise only weak control. These transnational threats have become a decisive influence, particularly in a region with a history of conflict. As the transformation threatens the operations of nonstate actors, the defiant ones will seek to obstruct the process by dominating influential faction leaders, sustaining their power over support groups, exploiting gaps in legal structure, and fueling armed violence to destabilize the countryside.[27]

The transnational threats to Kosovo were entrenched in the region well before the intervention, and they played a dominant role from the outset. A broad diaspora of ethnic Albanians had grown since 1989, flowing into Western Europe and providing funds to fuel the KLA resistance. At the same time, the wider criminal networks throughout the Balkans remained prosperous. In many cases, these and other transnational enterprises brought in huge profits.

Policy planners did not fully recognize the influence of nonstate actors on Kosovo's internal conflict. Consequently, the deleterious effects of regional criminal activities on Kosovo's transformation were not adequately addressed until the intervention was well under way. Moreover, planners did not adequately anticipate the need for Albanian and Macedonian assistance to contain illegal, cross border trafficking in arms, drugs, contraband, and women. These illegal activities greatly influenced the rapid expansion of organized criminal operations even before the war had ended, thereby challenging progress in neutralizing Kosovo's obstructionists to the peace process.

An Empowering Security Council Resolution

Although a Security Council resolution provides legitimacy to an intervention,[28] it also serves to empower the mission, a crucial aspect of a successful transformation. This entails vesting an international transitional administration or interim authority with substantial powers. Properly empowering the custodian of the peace process is essential to ensuring that the peace process is not derailed by obstructionists, hindered by internal squabbles among rival factions, or pushed off course by uncooperative neighbors.

For Kosovo, UNMIK's special representative of the secretary-general (SRSG) was designated the interim administrator and therefore served as the custodian of the mandate. The SRSG was vested with extraordinary powers to act as the sole executive, legislative, and judicial authority and was authorized to govern in the interests of the peace process without the concurrence of any local party.[29] Without these extraordinary powers, the UN interim administration could not have guided the attempt to transform entrenched power.[30] Appendix A in this chapter presents several ingredients for an empowering Security Council mandate.

Acceptable Military Role

Careful definition of the military's role in an intervention is a recurring requirement calling for serious consultations among contributing nations.[31] For example, how much policing the military will perform in the immediate postwar period will always need to be clarified. Without a safe and secure environment for a political process to take root, the transformation of war-hardened power is impossible. Necessity will likely require the military force to impose security, supervise the demobilization of armed groups, defeat militant extremists who use violence to obstruct the peace process, and defend the territory from cross-border military infiltration and attack.

At the same time, the military force must collaborate with the mission's civilian efforts, especially the international police, in a genuine partnership that will ensure coherency of action within the overall peace implementation effort. These demanding security operations call for the military not only to employ robust peace enforcement methods but also to conduct intrusive counterinsurgency operations against militant extremists, as discussed in chapter 6. Such coercive operations require unified direction from the mission's political leadership to ensure that intrusive military activities are consistent with the overall peace process guiding the transformation of power.

Getting to viable peace necessitates the deployment of a multinational military force that is cohesive and combat ready. Such a potent force cannot normally be fielded by the UN peacekeeping department, however. Blue-helmeted UN forces, the convenient remedy since the end of the Cold War, have proved to be a high-risk venture, producing poor results for achieving a transformation of entrenched power structures in postwar societies.

A properly formed "green-helmeted" multinational force (MNF) is a practical solution to this requirement for forces able to carry out coercive actions. This proposition suggests that in future international interventions involving the transformation of internal conflict, the Security Council should look primarily to authorizing a green-helmeted MNF in partnership with a credible UN civilian mission, at least initially. Once the security situation becomes suitable, the MNF can be converted to a robust blue-helmeted peace enforcement operation. Sponsorship of the MNF will likely have to come from a regional organization such as NATO, as in Kosovo, or it could be an ad hoc military coalition, such as the International Force for East Timor (INTERFET) in East Timor. Practical arrangements will be needed to allow a UN civilian mission and an MNF to work together effectively as genuine partners.

In the early months of 1999, advance planners kept in mind the hard times met in Bosnia by the international civilian mission. NATO had adopted a policy of separating its military force from the international civilian effort. This imprudent separation disadvantaged both missions. In preparing for Kosovo, military planners in Brussels were guided by a substantially revised NATO policy that called for close civil-military integration, even though it was unclear in the spring of 1999 which organization, the United Nations or the OSCE, would lead the civilian effort. U.S. civilian planners worked with the Pentagon under the supervision of the NSC to hammer out complementary mission area tasks and coordinating mechanisms to facilitate a full range of civilian and military peace implementation requirements. Informed by this parallel U.S. pol-mil planning effort, NATO's planners shaped KFOR's security role in ways that would support the broader civil-military campaign plan for the intervention.

In consultation with Brussels, the Security Council specified the role of NATO's military presence in Kosovo in Resolution 1244. Passed under Chapter VII of the UN Charter, the mandate envisioned a very intrusive NATO-led military presence to impose stability and ensure that the civilian effort could proceed safely in a secure environment. The mandate also called on NATO's military command KFOR to closely coordinate with the UN-led civilian mission UNMIK. The Security Council sought to ensure that both the military and the civilian components of the intervention worked toward the same goals in a mutually supportive manner. Subsequently, in the early weeks of the mission, the KFOR commander ensured that military operations, including coercive special operations against militant extremists, were nested within the political process as envisioned by the civilian leadership of the UN mission.

Effective Demobilization of Armed Groups

Although frequently overlooked in the planning process, the demobilization of armed groups is both a first-order political problem and a first-order security problem. In threatening postwar situations, most factions retain a persisting fear of surprise attack by their bitter rivals. This fear of vulnerability is likely to increase when armed factions are expected to disarm and demobilize their forces

—by giving up their arms, they will be unable to protect themselves from surprise attacks. It can be a most difficult security dilemma when bitter adversaries see no viable option other than offensive action to preempt a perceived armed attack imminently forthcoming from their predatory rival.[32]

Credible security guarantees are a prerequisite to effective demobilization. If the international security force cannot resolve the security dilemma in the minds of the rival factions, it will make little progress in gaining widespread political support for pursuing a course of moderation and compromise.[33]

Traditional disarmament, demobilization, and reintegration (DDR) operations have seldom done very well in meeting demobilization objectives, except in the most benign security environments. In addition, this traditional approach is very difficult to implement and requires many civilian experts and substantial financial resources, which are not readily available in the international community.

The other alternative is to disband armies once the fighting ends, as was done after the American Civil War in 1865—defeated Confederate soldiers were released to go back home to resume farming. However, in today's failed states, this approach puts several thousand unemployed young men on the streets and provides an open recruitment opportunity for criminal organizations and armed insurgent movements.

In Kosovo policy planners rejected these options as self-defeating. Instead, they adopted the approach of "defense conversion" by establishing the Kosovo Protection Corps (KPC) to demilitarize the KLA. KLA personnel joined the KPC and were trained to address humanitarian needs, disaster response, and community support. The KPC had no role in internal security or law enforcement—those roles were performed initially by the international community and later by the newly formed Kosovo Police Service. KPC members were paid for their service, which removed several thousand young men from the unemployment roles. Overall, this approach strategically fixed the KLA and allowed moderate political leaders to free themselves from militant pressures.

Rule of Law: Police, Justice, Penal System, and Applicable Law

The clearest lesson of the 1990s is the need to establish the rule of law from the outset of a peace mission. Yet many interagency planners held false assumptions regarding Kosovo's need for establishing effective rule of law. This resulted in a general lack of preparedness to take on the challenges posed by Kosovo's many years of lawless rule. Kosovo's transformation was impeded as a result.

The requirements for institutionalizing the rule of law must be fully understood by policy planners. Amid a white-hot ethnic war, taking ownership of the entire indigenous rule-of-law system—laws, police, courts, and jails—is likely to be required. This may include setting up a competent international police force as rapidly as possible with thousands of individual cops to create encouraging "facts on the ground."

But these requirements are likely to be extensive. Completely building, training, and supervising new indigenous institutions for law enforcement and the administration of justice is the foremost requirement. Gaining autonomy from destructive religious, ethnic, and criminal interests is fundamental to a successful transformation from lawless rule. Diminishing the power of criminal obstructionists by conducting anti–organized crime operations is still another requirement. Winning the public's confidence in the new rule-of-law system requires real equal protection. Establishing safeguards and monitoring compliance with standards of performance are other long-term requirements. Not until these requirements have been fulfilled can the internationals consider transferring "ownership" back to rising indigenous authorities, with the provision that some decisions may be reversed.

Planners for Kosovo did not anticipate the international community's general lack of preparedness to meet most of these requirements. Moreover, potential contributing nations were not ready to provide sufficient numbers of qualified officers to fill requirements. Start-up of the policing mission thus was slow and understaffed, and it left public security gaps in mission performance in the earliest days of the first year, when public security was needed most. The international community had not yet developed mission start-up kits for rule-of-law tasks that included trained police, judges, and jailers armed with enforceable security laws. As a result, the transformation of Kosovo's war-torn society to one based on the rule of law was troubled from the outset. None of these planning challenges were fully understood at the start, nor were they quickly addressed.

Legitimate Political Economy

Advance planning for the establishment of a legitimate political economy is an essential factor in the successful transformation of a war-torn society. Without a realistic political-economic strategy, the transformation will fall short of its achievable aims, and the political landscape will remain dominated by those who are empowered by corruption and criminal economic predation. Therefore, a legitimate political economy is a first-order peace problem, not just a secondary economic problem left to be solved by economists. This requirement was substantially misjudged for Kosovo.

At the outset, advance planners need to make a four-part assessment of the country's political economy. First, they should assess the current economic situation: how the country's economy works, how wealth is distributed among its various groups, what sectors have gained or lost during the war, and what sectors are likely to succeed or diminish in the postwar period. Related assessment issues include the economic basis for survival for the average family, job opportunities for young men and women who need employment, and patterns and methods of criminal economic activity that affect families, groups, and communities. Last, an analysis of infrastructure and medium-scale economic structures should be completed. This analysis will assist planners in determining the most appropriate methods available to bolster pro-peace behaviors through economic incentives.

Second, planners should clarify which sectors of the economy are dominated by criminal activity and identify the associated support groups of these illegal black- and gray-market activities. They should determine the connections these criminal activities have with rival factions in the country. Finally, planners should determine whether those who are in control of these criminal activities are likely to obstruct the peace process.

Third, the sources of wealth of the major influential figures and power brokers need careful examination. In particular, those leaders who are likely obstructionists need detailed study—what is the degree of their connection to corruption and criminal activity (not all obstructionist funding is criminal—some is state sponsored, externally funded, and so on)? Likewise, the sources of wealth of the pro-peace factions and their connections with criminal economic activity in the region need examination. The analysis of each rival faction involves anticipating the impact of postwar changes on criminal cash flows. Specifically: Whose ox will be gored by the peace process?

Last, planners should determine what means these obstructionists will likely use, including armed violence, to derail the peace process. This involves identifying how factions will likely respond to key decisions of the custodian and determining the means power brokers will use to obstruct peace process.

Once they have completed the comprehensive assessment, advance planners should identify key tasks that must be accomplished in the first months to "whiten" the gray and black portions of the country's political economy. Several urgent lines of action follow:

- Respond to the urgent humanitarian needs of the population depending on the specific situation.

- Restore electrical power and water within the first thirty days.

- Repair critical infrastructure and transport systems.

- Deploy anti–organized crime units and intelligence capacity.

- Engage the economic "movers and shakers" and gain consensus on priorities for economic development in the immediate time frame.

- Control cash flows for key viable economic enterprises in order to prevent capture by rapidly adaptive criminal elements—audit ongoing prevention efforts.

- Maintain a sense of momentum for the pro-peace coalition: build the state's economic viability and maintain a sense of economic promise in the first several months to leverage the arrival of significant aid and reconstruction assistance over a time horizon of one year and beyond.

- Gain international donations to maintain a cash flow for day-to-day operations of government.

- Pay salaries of key government workers in basic areas, including police, border control and customs, health care, and education.

- Initiate programs (e.g., make-work job programs) for transitioning from food (in-kind) to cash assistance.

The advance planning requirements for establishing a legitimate political economy in Kosovo were only partially understood. The macroeconomic planning effort embraced only a small but important part of the challenge. Indeed, a key lesson arising from the presence of criminalized power structures in Kosovo is clear: the establishment of a legitimate political economy must begin in the very first days of an intervention, and implementation across a broad front should not be delayed until after the security situation is stabilized. Many of these activities must begin on "day one."

Other Important Planning Issues

There are several other important advance planning issues, but they are beyond the scope of this book. They include a range of important mission areas, and all require a strategy to assure effective implementation. These additional mission areas include diplomatic engagement; regional stability; humanitarian assistance; AIDS and contagious disease prevention; infrastructure restoration; "consequence management" operations to address radiological, biological, and chemical incidents; protection of antiquities and historic sites; commercial business development; public diplomacy and education; natural resource and agriculture development; human rights abuses and war crimes prosecution; civil society and community rebuilding; and national reconciliation.

DESIGNING A CAPABLE INTERNATIONAL MISSION

An international intervention is always an ad hoc expeditionary formation. Various participants need to be brought together from afar into a formidable construct before the intervention deploys into a country that has been ravaged by war. An essential aim of the advance planning effort is to design a capable international mission to lead this diverse group of international actors.

The overarching issue at the outset is deciding on international sponsorship for the intervention—both civilian and military. Given the very difficult conditions typical of war-torn societies as well as the dangers of transformation, the preferred model would be a civilian interim authority coupled with a green-helmeted military MNF, as is described in this chapter. Appendix B in this chapter outlines the critical issues in designing a capable UN-MNF lash-up.

The design of the international mission in Kosovo, both UNMIK and KFOR, was embedded in UN Security Council Resolution 1244 and further developed in the secretary-general's report of June 12, 1999. These two documents set the stage for the peace implementation mission and were the first deliverables of the interagency advance planning effort that began in March 1999.

MOBILIZING SEVERAL COALITIONS

A major pol-mil planning requirement is to mobilize the capabilities of the international community to conduct the intervention with an expected duration of three to five years. This is a difficult challenge because many governments are unwilling (or simply unable) to make such a long, comprehensive commitment. Diplomatic engagement by the leaders of the intervention is important to winning concrete commitments to participate.

The pool of available civilian and military response capabilities to mount an intervention is seriously limited. These scarce capabilities are likely to be even more constrained in the coming years. Advance planners are faced with the reality that there is no idle capacity waiting to be deployed, so they are pressured to utilize limited national and multilateral capabilities for the greatest effect.

As mentioned earlier, an intervention requires several coalitions. Some of these are largely multinational in composition, while others are mostly multilateral. A military coalition, for example, is usually an ad hoc multinational organization. Other coalitions are considerably different. Nonetheless, the political and structural foundations of each of these different coalitions must be set in place during the political-military planning process in order for the intervention to succeed. Each coalition will have its own structure, organizational leadership, group of participants, and operating parameters.

Advance planners needed to include the following coalitions to achieve viable peace in Kosovo:

- A political coalition, the Balkans Contact Group (led by France)

- A military coalition, KFOR (led by the United Kingdom in NATO)

- A relief coalition (led by the UN High Commissioner for Refugees [UNHCR])

- A rule-of-law coalition (led by the UN Department of Peacekeeping Operations)

- A democratization and institution-building coalition (led by the OSCE)

- A reconstruction and development coalition (led by the European Union)

- A human rights coalition (led by the War Crimes Tribunal)

- A donor coalition (led by the G-8)

Advance planning efforts for Kosovo were married with diplomacy among potential multinational and multilateral partners. Consultations among allies, regional partners, potential contributors, and international organizations were crucial to ensuring that U.S. pol-mil planning activities won active support of other participants in each of the different coalitions called for by the intervention.

GARNERING FINANCIAL RESOURCES

Adequate funding to support various mission activities is also a major pol-mil planning requirement. Advance planners should determine how the intervention's requirements can be funded over a three-year time horizon. Successful operations will usually require hundreds of millions of dollars within this time frame, with more required in subsequent years depending on the nature of the postwar environment and the ambitions of the international community.

A sustainable intervention needs a multiyear financial strategy. It must clarify the myriad financial needs and associated funding mechanisms to pay for implementation, especially during the first three years. An intervention will normally be mandated to accomplish several military and civilian tasks that entail undertaking many humanitarian, political, military, police, political-economic, governance, institution-building, development, and human rights activities. Most of these activities will cost a substantial amount, especially in the first three years. Programmed funding sources include UN peacekeeping assessments, program funds from UN specialized agencies and international organizations, in-kind support provided by NGOs, and revenues generated by the host country's public administration.

But these sources never meet all funding requirements. Voluntary financial contributions from states are necessary to fill huge remaining shortfalls. Advance planners need to prepare a donor campaign strategy, consistent with the multiyear financial game plan outlined above. In collaboration with the UN Secretariat and the World Bank, the campaign plan should organize donor events and, when appropriate, spell out actions to encourage specific donors to take the lead in supporting key activities, particularly in the areas of civil administration, institution building, and reconstruction.[34]

CONCLUSION: PLANNING INNOVATIONS

Innovation is crucial to laying a solid foundation for an intervention. A creative process resides at the center of advance planning and subsequently adapting strategies because each situation calls for a unique approach to the transformation of local power. The international intervention in Kosovo, in particular, produced several innovations that became essential to the attempt to transform Kosovo's war-hardened power structures. Although not all these innovations were envisioned during the advance planning phase, nine of them are highlighted here:

1. The substitution of a Security Council resolution to be the *peace settlement* because one could not be negotiated before the intervention, as discussed earlier in this chapter on advance planning

2. The mobilization and integration of regional organizations under a UN umbrella through the *pillar structure*, as discussed in appendix B of this chapter

3. The temporary exercise of *interim state sovereignty* by a UN mission under Chapter VII of the UN Charter that involved the exercise of all executive, legislative, and judicial authority in Kosovo, as discussed in chapter 4

4. The establishment of *unified political direction* by the senior civilian authority and the codification of the "primacy of the peace process" in determining operational priorities for all international actors, both civilian and military, as discussed in chapter 5

5. The *genuine partnership* forged between UNMIK and KFOR by their leaders, as discussed in chapter 6

6. The evolution of *fourth-generation peacekeeping* by combining counterinsurgency doctrine with evolving peacekeeping doctrine, as discussed in chapter 6

7. The accomplishment of demobilization of an armed paramilitary group, the KLA, through *defense conversion* under the KPC, as discussed in chapter 6

8. The *imposition of public security* under Chapter VII using international armed police, adoption of applicable law, temporary executive detention, and a justice system to institutionalize the rule of law in a war-torn society, as discussed in chapter 7

9. The establishment of a central fiscal authority to govern economic policy and the development of a *legitimate political economy*, as discussed in chapter 8

Innovations are usually case specific. What was implemented in Kosovo may not be applicable in exactly the same way elsewhere, such as in Afghanistan or Sudan. Each internal conflict resides in a different region with a unique political landscape involving distinctive local leaders who have peculiar power relationships that draw on different means of confrontation. Understanding a troubled state's situational factors is crucial to political-military planning as well as to the efforts in adapting strategies to transform power in a specific case. Once these issues are understood, innovation becomes an important ingredient to bringing about viable peace in a time frame of about three years.

✦ ✦ ✦

Appendix A

AN EMPOWERING SECURITY COUNCIL MANDATE

There are a number of desirable ingredients for an empowering Security Council mandate. Advance planners should consider the following when seeking a resolution that empowers an international transitional authority.

1. *A single resolution.* To prevent divisions and separatism among international actors on the ground, there should be one resolution directing all international activities in the intervention rather than two or three resolutions governing each component of the mission.

2. *Statements of regional support.* To bolster the legitimacy of the mission, the resolution should embrace supporting precursor documents, such as a regional organization's statement of principles for a political solution to the peace process or an endorsement of a peace agreement for the conflict.

3. *Chapter VII executive authority.* Acting under Chapter VII of the UN Charter, the Security Council should direct the UN secretary-general to appoint a special representative to exercise sole executive power as the transitional authority or interim authority.

4. *Authority to interpret the mandate and settlement.* To avoid getting sidetracked by disputes over interpretation of key words of a mandate or a settlement (an often overlooked predicament), the resolution should empower the UN transitional authority to determine the meaning of the mandate and interpret its obligations for the parties. Furthermore, if this authority is not explicitly stated in the peace settlement, the mandate should extend this power to interpreting the text of the peace accord.

5. *Authority to impose stability.* To bolster the military coalition's authority to establish a safe and secure environment, the resolution should authorize the use of "all necessary means" by the international military and police forces to enforce implementation of the peace process. This supports a realistic mandate and empowers the international military and police to deal with serious militant and criminal threats.

6. *Primacy of the peace process.* Achieving viable peace requires that the peace process be the guiding directive of all action taken by both international and local actors. The resolution should say that the international mission "supports those who support implementation of the mandate and opposes those who do not." While international actors may be impartial to the parties, they should not be neutral about bad behavior that obstructs the peace process.

7. *Removal of obstructionists and parallel power structures.* Anticipating that some powerful, entrenched rival factions will seek to obstruct the peace process through either violence or illegal parallel power structures, the resolution should empower the UN transitional authority to use "all necessary means" to remove such obstructionists who by their actions oppose the peace process.

8. *Cooperation by indigenous parties.* To create an obligation to support the peace process, the resolution should include a demand that all parties cooperate fully with all aspects of the peace process.

9. *Support by states and nonstate actors.* To create an obligation to support the peace process, the resolution should include a demand that all states and nonstate actors support implementation of all aspects of the resolution and cooperate fully with the efforts of the UN transitional authority.

10. *Unified political direction.* Maintaining coherence in political direction among all international actors in the mission is essential. The resolution should empower the UN transitional authority to be the sole provider of unified political direction to all actors within the international presence, without interfering with "command authorities" of various entities, including the multinational military force. The transitional authority should control the political process to transform local power.

11. *Control of civilian implementation.* To ensure central direction among all entities operating within the international civilian presence (which usually includes independent multilateral and regional organizations), the resolution should explicitly empower the UN transitional authority to control implementation of the entire international civilian presence operating in the territory.

12. *Composite civil-military objectives and mutual support.* To set conditions for unity of purpose and mutual support between the civilian and military components of the intervention, a provision should direct both components to establish joint mechanisms for planning and coordination and to work toward composite objectives in a mutually supportive manner.

13. *Specified responsibilities for transformation.* To bolster the components of the international presence, the mandate should outline specific responsibilities of both the civilian and the military components within the mission. Because transformation involves political compromise, demobilization, a secure environment, rule of law, institution building, a legitimate political economy, and economic development, the mandate should specify all of these transformation tasks. The mandate should also specify other pressing matters such as human rights, humanitarian relief, freedom of movement, and border control.

14. *Discretion on transfer of authority.* To ensure that institutional safeguards are in place and functioning properly before the transfer of governance functions to local officials and indigenous institutions occurs, the mandate should authorize the UN transitional authority to both grant and remove this transfer according to local and indigenous compliance with standards for performance.

15. *Multiyear duration of the mission.* To avoid the adverse consequences of a premature exit, the resolution should send the message that the international community is committed to a long-term effort and will (in the words of Resolution 1244) "establish the international presence for an initial twelve months, to continue thereafter unless the Security Council decides otherwise."

◆ ◆ ◆

Appendix B

DESIGN CONSIDERATIONS FOR AN INTERNATIONAL MISSION

There are a number of design considerations for an international mission. The list below assumes a model that brings together a civilian UN interim authority and a green-helmeted military MNF as genuine partners to achieve viable peace.

1. *Genuine civil-military partnerships.* The fundamental design principle is to create a genuine partnership between the UN interim authority and the

MNF military command. This tight partnership must be embraced by a consensual international policy, the UN Security Council mandate, the attitude of UN officials and MNF commanders, the mission's public posture, and daily collaboration on activities within the civilian and military operation. From the outset the Security Council, together with the sponsor of the military coalition (such as NATO), must establish a common policy of genuine cooperation and mutual support between civilian and military commands of the mission. To bolster this policy consensus, the mission's civilian and military leaders should convey solidarity by their example and personal remarks. Moreover, the mission's public posture should reflect this tight association to the locals. Finally, in their daily activities, both military and civilian officials within the mission should collaborate continually in managing the transformation process.

2. *Mission strength.* A UN transitional authority and its partner MNF component must be properly sized to supervise and enforce implementation of the peace process. Although many considerations will influence a mission's size, in most cases a country's security environment, population size, geographic extent, and number of provinces drive the mission's size. Countries with a larger population dispersed in several provinces where local security is poor require a greater international presence involving international military troops, police officers, and civilian officials. This critical design issue is easily misjudged. Without adequate forces and competent civilian personnel, the risks of a failed transformation effort increase dramatically.

3. *Aligned deployment footprint.* The deployment footprint of the intervention is another core design factor. Habitual working relationships between MNF subcommands and UN civil administration subsectors are essential to achieving coherent mission policy implementation across the countryside among all factions. It is essential that the military's internal boundaries match up exactly with those of the civilian mission's administrative sectors—and these common boundaries should align with the host country's internal boundaries from the provincial level down to the district or municipal level. In addition, the headquarters of the military and the civilian components should be co-located at least down to the provincial level. Common civil-military boundaries and co-location of headquarters facilitate effective oversight of the peace process, efficient joint military and police operations, and consistent reporting on indigenous activities.

4. *Unified political direction.* An SRSG should be the highest international civilian official in the country and head of the international civilian mission.

Ensuring that all efforts of the international intervention are integrated to achieve a common purpose, the SRSG must be the single political director giving unified political direction to both the military and civilian components of the intervention. Unified direction ensures that the primacy of the peace process governs all aspects of transformation. Although the MNF commander should continue to receive military commands from a higher military authority, political direction regarding the implementation of the peace process must come from the civilian SRSG, who serves as custodian of the peace process. Unified political direction, without impinging on national command prerogatives, ensures proper application of Carl von Clausewitz's admonition that military actions (as well as parallel civilian efforts) should advance the political aim.

5. *Coalition integration.* A useful approach in mission design is to clarify the principal coalitions of the mission to guide the "division of labor." Transformation calls for an intervention to implement a range of diverse activities that include military security, humanitarian relief, law enforcement, civil administration, democratization and institution building, human rights and civil society, and economic reconstruction, among others. Mission structure is a key design factor in making progress, and past operations suggest that these coalitions are best integrated according to a pillar structure that operates under the political direction of the UN mission leader.

6. *Mission pillar structure.* The pillar structure helps organize each of the major activities under a competent lead nation or international organization such as the OSCE. Headed by a capable lead nation or organization, each functional pillar should work under the direction of the SRSG. Moreover, each pillar should rely on the leadership, capabilities, and expertise of the lead nation or organization, and that leader should partner with the pillar's other contributors as implementation proceeds. The rationale for a pillar structure is that it ensures effective organizational management of various complex mission areas and mobilizes international coalitions over the long run to sustain the transformation to viable peace.

7. *Integrated executive leadership.* The UN-MNF mission should have an executive committee that formulates the policy and strategy of the UN transitional authority. An executive committee normally consists of the mission's senior civilian heads of each pillar and the MNF military commander. Meeting regularly and chaired by the SRSG, the executive committee provides a topmost mechanism for each senior "cabinet official" within the international mission to negotiate policy priorities for the

transitional authority, thereby facilitating coherence in provisional governance. The executive committee steers policy through a strategic mission plan, sets near-term mission objectives, and tracks progress in transformation. The committee also oversees the preparation of the mission's next state plan and sets up "tiger teams" on short notice to prepare integrated action plans to address urgent problems needing integrated civil-military action by the mission.

8. *Director of operations.* The executive committee's policies should be implemented through an integrated strategy across the mission. To ensure coherency of action, a civilian director of operations should be empowered to implement an integrated strategy of transformation. This strategy should fuse intelligence, political mediation, military support, training and education, law enforcement, and public information efforts across the mission. The interim authority's strategy of transformation must embrace a holistic approach that needs daily focus by several key components of pillar structure. An empowered director of operations, who is either the deputy special representative or a named director of operations, should report directly to the SRSG, who is the custodian of the peace process.

9. *Co-located headquarters and operations centers.* Any international mission manages a host of daily activities that carry forward a coherent strategy of transformation. Day-to-day oversight of these diverse civil-military efforts is essential to effective peace implementation. Management can be achieved by establishing a consolidated operations center for the mission. Drawing on the military's natural skill in establishing operations centers, the first step is for the overall mission to create common space for such a center inside the mission headquarters. Obviously, key leaders in the mission would welcome such consolidation, especially the civilian director of operations, the police commissioner, the military commander, and the public affairs officer. A common operations center may also be useful in headquarters at the provincial level. Hence, an integrated communications architecture can establish a network of operations centers across the mission that facilitates collaborative planning between civilian and military officials.

10. *Mission planning group.* As they posture themselves to prepare for future mission priorities, the SRSG and the director of operations should be assisted by a mission planning group that consists of senior planners from each pillar of the mission, including the military. The role of the mission planning group is to ensure integration of crucial transformation activities across the mission. Integrated planning among the pillars facilitates

coherency of action in building viable peace. A key document that the mission planning group produces is a strategic mission plan for the transformation to viable peace, a plan that is updated regularly.

11. *Joint civil-military planning structure.* Because intrusive military security operations can have a dramatic impact on civilian transformation efforts within the intervention, a joint planning structure that merges military and civilian mission planners should be established to work closely on sensitive planning for forthcoming security operations. This joint planning structure brings together planners of the military commander and the civilian director of operations to ensure effective civil-military integration in planning security operations.

12. *Three core joint planning activities.* Planning is an essential activity that is performed by the joint planning group to anticipate requirements in the transformation process and promote unity of effort across the intervention. Planning efforts should be consolidated to produce three planning documents:

- A *long-range strategic mission plan* captures the strategy for the transformation of power. It clarifies the intervention's overall aims, key priorities, and a long-range strategy to achieve the transformation to viable peace.

- A *next-state (vs. an "end-state") plan* focuses on an important near-term (two to four months) turning point or desired intermediate outcome in the transformation process and addresses the following:

  - An unbiased characterization—in plain civil-military terms—of the key features of the desired "next state" for the mission

  - Composite civil-military objectives and the coherent strategy to achieve them

  - Key pillar tasks—precisely what needs to be achieved in political mediation, security, economic reconstruction, basic needs, and so on—that are central to achieving the desired next state in the transformation process

  - Measurement of progress in the transformation

  - Pillar action plans

- *Integrated action plans* for urgent challenges are prepared by tiger teams as directed by either the executive committee or the director of operations.

13. *Information management system.* The mission's leaders need timely and relevant information on how the transformation is progressing. The civilian component's chief of staff is normally responsible for establishing an effective information management system. The range of information requirements includes accurate reporting of day-to-day progress, early warning of local crises and emergencies, assessments of developments within the social and political landscape, and critical information on key transformation benchmarks. The phone and the fax machine are inadequate in meeting these requirements. An international mission needs capacities such as an information management unit, a user-friendly internal communications system, relevant databases, standard field reporting, and collaborative tools that extend the reach of the mission via the Internet. All these capacities must be put in place in the early weeks of the mission despite austere working conditions.

14. *Unified public affairs mechanisms.* A final design issue is a unified public affairs and public diplomacy campaign by all elements of the mission, including the military command. All press activities should be joint civilian and military events in which key actors within the mission present a unified approach. The public diplomacy campaign should draw together both civilian and military capabilities to advance the mission's political influence and help shape favorable public attitudes for transformation. These activities have to be integrated with the coherent strategy for transformation as envisioned by the director of operations.

NOTES

1. The likely minimum duration of five years is presented in chapter 9 of the extensive RAND study *America's Role in Nation-Building: From Germany to Iraq* (Santa Monica, Calif.: RAND, 2003), 166. Its primary author, James Dobbins, served as the Clinton administration's political director for several peace implementation efforts in the 1990s. This study contains many insights that are consistent with those presented in this book.

2. Reflecting policymakers' repeated calls for flexibility, the generic process presented in this section evolved through more than forty interagency planning efforts since 1994, beginning with the Haiti intervention. The Clinton administration conducted these interagency planning efforts according to Presidential Decision Directive 56, Managing Complex Contingency Operations. The directive was an outgrowth of the lessons learned from the 1994 intervention in Haiti and was championed by then deputy assistant secretary of defense Michele Flournoy. Although a first step, the Haiti planning effort established several building blocks for planning and managing future complex contingency operations, namely the Executive Committee (ExComm), a political-military plan, an interagency rehearsal, an after-action review, and interagency training activities. These innovations strengthen unity of effort by harmonizing the diplomatic, military, political, humanitarian, public security, and economic dimensions of an intervention and formed the core of the PDD-56 political-military planning process, which was first attempted in late 1994 for the UN peace operation in Eastern Slavonia and formalized in May 1997.

3. Amid the unprecedented eruption of internal wars during the 1990s, the "art and science" of advance planning evolved as seasoned political-military planners prepared for interventions to end fighting in Africa, Asia, the Balkans, the Caribbean, and Central America. Because policymakers earnestly demanded flexibility in these crises, interagency planners came to realize that political-military planning needed distinctive concepts and special terms to capture what "policy planning" was all about and to differentiate it from "agency planning," which is designed to write a detailed campaign plan.

4. The authors of this chapter produced a so-called generic political-military plan and distributed it widely on the Internet as an educational aid. A "living document," it has been updated periodically since 1995, when it was produced. The "Generic Pol-Mil Plan" can be found on the Web sites of the U.S. State Department and the National Defense University.

5. Our model incorporates lessons learned from several interventions, including Kosovo and subsequent operations. Although no such process can ever be viewed as an ideal solution, our approach carefully integrates the many policy-planning tasks into a cogent process to set a firm foundation for any international intervention. One can consider our model a "95 percent solution." This interagency policy-planning process was built on pragmatism and seasoned by experience. Policy planners saw that the advance planning process needed a distinctive lexicon for its products that embraced a new set of concepts that facilitated realistic policy option development and plan development. Therefore, they crafted and titled documents with special names: comprehensive situation assessment, mission analysis, strategic projection, and strategic approach. The evolving process also encouraged an emerging terminology that promoted clear thinking among planners, terms such as "strategies for transformation," "mission areas," and "instruments of government action," among others. All these emerging concepts were important to laying a solid foundation for writing an eventual pol-mil implementation plan for an intervention.

6. A related policy-planning evolution involved crafting an intrusive strategy for the intervention, or what we call the "strategizing process." This approach relied on a small working group of designated agency officials to fuse intelligence assessments of key protagonists in a crisis, the intervention's desired policy ends, and the available instruments of government action. The resulting pol-mil intervention strategy, often crafted through an iterative process, became a core feature of the political-military plan for the intervention.

7. A key lesson from past interventions is that traditional agency "tools" alone were often inadequate for dealing with the emerging problems presented by actual conflict situations of the 1990s. Typical instruments such as military peacekeeping forces, diplomatic pressure, sanctions, law enforcement, or war crimes prosecution were found to have limited effects when employed separately in achieving a transformation of power, especially when used to influence hard-bitten rival faction leaders or defiant nonstate actors. Moreover, these crises presented new problems that fell into gaps between traditional agency instruments. Therefore, each agency instrument, such as military force, had to be adapted in new ways and integrated with other instruments to respond effectively while avoiding unintended consequences arising from these adaptations.

8. Many advance planners and intelligence analysts, having grown up in the comfort of modern America, have never experienced the gruesome fighting and depravation that are characteristic of heartbreaking ethnic conflicts such as Kosovo. Many are intuitively weak in imagining on a personal level the powerful pressures that militate against ending civil war. Despite our hopefulness that fighting in Kosovo would end in June 1999, peace implementation began amid an unfinished war.

9. See Paul Collier, "Economic Causes of Civil Conflict," in *Turbulent Peace: The Challenges of Managing International Conflict,* ed. Chester A. Crocker, Fen Osler Hampson, and Pamela Aall (Washington, D.C.: United States Institute of Peace Press, 2001), 143–162. See also David Keen, *The Economic Functions of Violence in Civil Wars,* Adelphi Paper 320 (London: International Institute for Strategic Studies, June 1998).

10. See Barbara F. Walter, *Designing Transitions from Violent Civil War,* IGCC Policy Paper no. 31 (San Diego: University of California, Institute on Global Conflict and Cooperation, December 1997). This thoughtful research report addresses the question, Why do factions return to war after signing a peace settlement?

11. Roy Licklider presents a complete discussion of these pressures in "Obstacles to Peace Settlements," a valuable contribution to the extensive book *Turbulent Peace,* 697–718. Licklider's comprehensive work carefully notes the various research efforts on this subject.

12. Stephen J. Stedman introduced the problem of "spoilers" to a peace process in his article "Spoiler Problems in Peace Processes," *International Security* 22, no. 2 (Fall 1997): 5–53.

13. This is a major conclusion of a thorough study funded by the Office of the Secretary of Defense (OSD PK/HA) titled *Effective Transitions from Peace Operations to Sustainable Peace* (December 1997). This comprehensive study, conducted by DFI International under the direction of B. Blechman, W. Durch, and T. Stukey, discusses at length several of the issues highlighted in this section.

14. Lieutenant General Anthony Zinni (USMC), "Lt. Gen. Zinni's Twenty Lessons Learned for Humanitarian Assistance and Peace Operations," *CNA 1995*

Annual Conference Proceedings: Military Support to Complex Humanitarian Emergencies (Alexandria, Va.: Center for Naval Analysis, U.S. Department of the Navy, 1995), 17.

15. Both sides must participate in the discourse. Policy planners need to provide a generic set of issues that encompass a comprehensive situation assessment for the potential crisis. In return, these issues need to be incorporated in routine intelligence reporting at the beginning of a planning effort. In particular, a small group of political and psychological analysts should provide a policy-relevant faction leader analysis describing the important factors that can have leverage on key rivals in the crisis. In addition to this analysis, an informative and credible political forecast is critical in helping policymakers understand the difficulty of the situation, how the crisis could unfold, and what it would take to channel future events in a favorable direction.

16. A crisis-planning scenario helps policymakers understand the dynamics of the conflict and clarify trends to watch that will shape the success of a desired transformation. Prepared by an interagency policy working group that includes intelligence community officials, a crisis-planning scenario also helps policymakers appreciate the full scope of the crisis, thereby identifying a wide range of mission areas needed to transform power.

17. Organized by the NSC staff, several small interagency teams are established to complete this multiagency analysis of the looming crisis. For example, there will likely be teams for humanitarian relief, military security, political transformation, civil administration, police and justice, political-economic activities, and human rights, among others. Agency planners on these teams draw on the expertise of the intelligence community and prospective partners in the intervention, including multinational and multilateral organizations. The key is to begin the advance planning effort as an interagency enterprise at the very beginning.

18. As a crisis looms on the horizon, the baseline mission analysis must be completed in a matter of days in sufficient depth to clarify the considerations related to the policy questions of the anticipated intervention. This means that a mission analysis has to be timely, rigorous, realistic, and, moreover, relevant to the policy questions at hand.

19. Each mission area team should provide a report of these issues in standard format to the NSC staff. A policy working group should then prepare a comprehensive mission analysis document that can stand alone as a baseline analysis for the anticipated intervention. The interagency mission analysis effort does not end at this point, however. In fact, it should continue well into agency planning efforts as they unfold.

20. See Major General Michael G. Smith's thorough book, *Peacekeeping in East Timor: The Path to Independence* (New York: International Peace Academy, 2003). Smith identifies thirteen factors that were critical to the UN Transitional Authority in East Timor.

21. Without a credible justification at the outset, an intervention will not be likely despite the human suffering associated with an internal conflict. A compelling practical necessity for intervention often has political, security, moral, and domestic implications for potential contributors to an operation. When all four issues imperil several governments, including perhaps a major power, a potent imperative will likely bring a quick end to the crisis. In some emergencies in distant lands, however, busy government officials often have little appreciation for the adverse consequences of inaction absent outside media coverage. In these cases, a key part of the advance planning effort is to determine how the crisis would affect potential contributors and supporters, and then design an active diplomatic campaign that brings together concerned governments that can offer a range of essential capabilities necessary to conduct successful operations for a sufficient period to assure viable peace.

22. The support of leading regional powers is essential in gaining required access, entry, and collaboration for an intervention. In addition to making their own sizable contributions to the operation, regional powers usually influence smaller governments and important nonstate actors within the region to join in supporting the operation. Moreover, regional powers can play a key role in shaping a robust consensus within relevant regional organizations in support of the intervention. Taking an even broader view, one sees that leading regional powers can be very influential within international crisis response organizations, such as the UN Security Council, as members and vocal advocates. Simply put, regional powers cast a long shadow, and advance planners should find ways to leverage those powers' influence for the benefit of the intervention.

23. In most cases, there is more than just one influential regional power, making it prudent for pol-mil planners to establish an informal diplomatic mechanism, such as a "core group," in partnership with interested major powers to build close cooperation for a common approach to the transformation of power in the affected state. Driven by pragmatic considerations, this small group of influential governments can usually forge a policy consensus for managing the crisis and serve as the catalyst for decisions made by other international and regional organizations as the peace implementation effort unfolds.

24. See Timothy D. Sisk, *Power Sharing and International Mediation in Ethnic Conflicts* (Washington, D.C.: United States Institute of Peace Press, 1996), which was sponsored by the Carnegie Commission on Preventing Deadly Conflict.

25. *Statement by the Chairman on the Conclusion of the Meeting of G-8 Foreign Ministers in St. Petersburg,* May 6, 1999 (Toronto: University of Toronto, G8 Information Centre, 1999).

26. An international mission will usually rely on neighboring states for operational assistance in undertaking key transformation efforts. Such critical assistance usually includes placing diplomatic pressure on noncooperative factions and obstructionists, sharing intelligence on obstructionist operations, controlling cross-border military operations, stopping arms shipments and terrorist infiltrations, ending hate radio broadcasts, apprehending war criminals and fugitives from the law, and promoting legitimate economic activity in the region at the expense of organized criminal trafficking of diamonds, drugs, contraband, stolen property, and abducted women. Furthermore, neighboring states can have an important role in many other major priorities indirectly related to the transformation of power, namely the return of refugees, sanctions enforcement, or the granting of basing and transit rights to deploying military forces of international actors.

27. Transfomration is most difficult when criminal or armed nonstate actors enjoy near-complete freedom to conduct cross-border operations in the region. Therefore, neighboring states are the key to containing such operations. However, because they are often reluctant to confront these transborder threats or lack the capacity to do so, policy planners must develop strategies for working with each particular state in meeting its obligations. Another initiative is to impose a Security Council sanctions regime that specially focuses on obstructionist transnational activities, fortifying government action to control borders. In addition, the international military mission can help by conducting border security operations to interdict illegal cross-border activities and channel normal traffic through border crossings that are monitored by customs and immigration officials. Finally, the international mission will need an organized-crime unit that has reach across the region to enable law enforcement officials to contain this threat to the peace process.

28. Adding to its legitimacy, the Security Council resolution should rely on other key documents that help shape the international consensus for the intervention. In particular, a regional organization's statement of principles for a political solution and a multinational military coalition's statement of purpose are important precursors to a mandate because such documents demonstrate international resolve and commitment to the peace process. Moreover, acceptance of these regional declarations by the host nation and local parties adds considerable weight to the authority of the international mission.

29. The Security Council's mandate sets favorable conditions for political and operational cohesion among the various international actors, including its green-helmeted military force. Operative provisions of the resolution assure unity of direction and the primacy of the peace process. Given the broad scope of international activities involved, designating the SRSG as the single political director of the entire intervention permitted the SRSG to function as the custodian of the peace process and to make decisions without outside micromanagement.

30. The Security Council benefited from a hard lesson learned from earlier missions in the Balkans: compared with the failed civilian implementation effort in Bosnia, where the UN high representative had little authority to implement its peace process, the UN Transitional Authority in neighboring Eastern Slavonia was very successful largely because the UNTAES transitional administrator was vested with extensive powers under Chapter VII of the UN Charter by the Security Council. This lesson encouraged writers of Resolution 1244 to bestow substantial political and executive powers on UNMIK's SRSG (many of which track closely with the fifteen points listed in appendix A to empower the UN civilian authority to implement a peace process).

31. Four considerations usually shape a realistic military role for a peace implementation mission: the security needs of the peace process, the possible armed threats to its implementation, the political will of potential troop contributors, and the tactical capabilities needed to operate successfully in the physical environment of the affected country. An acceptable role for the military has to be crafted by interested governments working with the UN Secretariat. This consensus can often be delineated as specified military tasks in a Security Council mandate for the mission. This consultation process serves to refine a realistic military contribution to the peace process, nurture coherence among potential military contingents, and shape a political consensus among nations to mount a forceful intervention to secure a peace.

32. The security dilemma challenge is presented thoroughly in Barbara F. Walter and Jack Snyder, eds., *Civil Wars, Insecurity, and Intervention* (New York: Columbia University Press, 1999). See the chapter "Civil War and the Security Dilemma" by Jack Snyder and Robert Jervis, 15–37.

33. Snyder and Jervis, "Civil War and the Security Dilemma."

34. Obviously, the United Nations or the World Bank will have to establish a trust fund to collect donor contributions, and the UN mission will have to administer funds in a legally sufficient, transparent, and effective manner to ensure continued support by participating members and donors. Note that measures must be taken to ensure that corruption and bribery do not imperil effective and legal use of these funds by the international community. The leading nation or organization of each coalition will have to establish a financial management capability and a budget for supporting its coalition operations.

4

The Custodian of the Peace Process

Jock Covey

A FTER THE UN SECURITY COUNCIL mandates the establishment of a peace operation, the UN secretary-general selects a prominent international statesman to run the mission as the special representative of the secretary-general (SRSG). The SRSG thus becomes the custodian of the intensely political process behind, for lack of any better name, the peace process.[1] Success in achieving a viable peace will be determined, in part, by how adroitly the custodian guides the transformation of conflict among rivals in the postwar period. The fate of the mission also will be determined by the way the custodian maneuvers to overcome the tensions and shortcomings within the international community that in theory supports the mission. Substantial international support cannot be taken for granted. It will require prodigious effort and skilled statecraft to mobilize and maintain.

A custodian must carefully husband the mission's power. The international civilian presence initially will be very weak. It will be quickly challenged by local forces intent on derailing the peace process in order to maintain their power. The custodian would be wise to bring civilian and military components of the mission together promptly as a coherent team to advance the peace process without delay. The key to this is aligning the efforts of all components of the mission with the "primacy of the peace process." This is one of the major topics developed in this chapter, as well as one of the core themes of this book.

In addition to integrating the mission's internal components to implement the peace process, the custodian must ceaselessly mobilize international resources and political support. The Security Council mandate notwithstanding, a multitude of competing interests will come into play. Many international actors will seek to sway the mission, among them the member-states of the Security Council, the usual "friends group" of interested powers, the UN Secretariat itself, various international financial and humanitarian institutions, and relevant regional organizations. Aside from the custodian, none of these actors will have the success of the peace process as their solitary purpose. Thus did the United Nations Interim Administration Mission in Kosovo (UNMIK) find itself embroiled in a contest among much larger forces, each focused on its own institutional interests. To preserve and advance its assigned mission as custodian of the peace process, UNMIK adopted the perspective and often the behavior that a weak little country would adopt under similar circumstances.

POSTURING THE MISSION

Enshrining the Primacy of the Peace Process

The principle that the political process must guide decision making within a mission became starkly apparent in Bosnia as Serb hard-liners were attempting to muscle Biljana Plavsic, president of the Republic of Srpska from 1996 to 1998, out of power. Plavsic's record before and during the war was unenviable, but her postintervention role was constructive. Commanders of the NATO-led Stabilization Force (SFOR) believed it essential to the effectiveness of their mission and the security of their own troops that the former warring parties see the international military as an honest broker aloof from politics. As Momcilo Krajisnik, the Serb member of Bosnia's joint presidency, and his circle began to close in on Plavsic, SFOR felt its neutrality required that the contest be treated as just another intra-Serb spat.

At this point, Washington proposed to NATO headquarters in Brussels that it adopt a more rigorous standard: support the peace process and oppose those who seek to obstruct it. Within hours, this simple rule of thumb was translated into the SFOR commander's intent and passed down to subordinate units. This new concept immediately legitimated the role of SFOR in preventing Krajisnik's coup against Plavsic. Thereafter, it was clear to all concerned—would-be spoilers as well as risk-averse commanders—that the international military would no longer be neutral about the peace process. The importance of this seemingly small conceptual adjustment cannot be overestimated.

Two years after this policy shift, as the international community went into Kosovo, most military commanders and civilian officials understood their roles under UN Security Council Resolution 1244: the mission would be evenhanded with those who basically cooperated with the peace implementation process and would actively oppose those who obstructed it. The concept became a guiding principle for planning and performing daily business. UNMIK officials and commanders simply needed to ask, Does this situation advance or impede the peace process? If it was the latter, the default position was to act.

It was fortunate that the Kosovo Force (KFOR) started with a core of British officers at headquarters level and with General Michael Jackson in command. Nearly every British officer over the rank of captain had served in Northern Ireland and understood without NATO guidance the need to "support those who support the peace process." Jackson, in addition, had commanded the British in Bosnia and understood the concept perfectly before it was ever written down. That said, however, other conditions also were necessary for this principle to be more than a well-intended slogan.

Most important, the custodian must have a mandate to oversee and control implementation of the peace process. In Bosnia the senior international civilian official, known as the high representative, was denied such authority by the drafters of the Dayton Peace Accords and was limited to coordinating and advising. He was systematically prevented from giving instructions even to other international civil agencies. This was not the only reason for painfully slow political progress in Bosnia, but it was a major contributing factor.

In Kosovo, in contrast, the Security Council empowered the SRSG to exercise executive authority, under Chapter VII of the UN Charter. The mandate ensured the mission's fundamental legitimacy and provided ample authority to pursue our responsibilities in transforming Kovoso's conflict. While UNMIK could in no way insert itself between KFOR and NATO, Resolution 1244 was all a shrewd custodian needed to shape military and police activities to create consequences for those obstructing the process leading to a viable peace.

Second, the custodian needs a robust political strategy, as outlined in chapter 5, which calls for active engagement with all parties to the conflict. This involves encouraging them to rethink their interests in ways that could be compatible with the peace process. Influential faction leaders who are willing to take risks to support the process need to be protected. The custodian should make his expectations for proper behavior known at the outset, and then continually urge faction leaders to meet these expectations. None can be permitted to opt out or exercise a de facto veto.

Finally, any peace process requires popular support. In Kosovo we learned to work through faction leaders to encourage their followers to support the mission in an open manner and to renounce obstructionists' actions that were aimed at thwarting the peace process.

Thinking Like a Little Country

International officials seldom adopt an appropriate strategic outlook before embarking on a mission. Once appointed to an international assignment, they march into the field to implement what they have been told is their mission. Unfortunately, many actors are eager to tell them what their mission is, while none can possibly understand it as well as the custodian soon does.

In Kosovo it was clear that we were not independent from New York, but we recognized that we could not execute the extraordinary mission if we rigorously adhered to instructions from the UN peacekeeping office. Instructions would come too late or not at all. They would be diluted or rendered hazy by the conflicting demands of Security Council members, or they would be countermanded by some element of the Secretariat, such as the legal adviser or the political office.

Key capitals also attempted to address their own interests, either through senior officials seconded to the mission or by leveraging the material resources they provided, through strenuous diplomatic pressure in the Balkans Contact Group or via the resident diplomatic mission. Other international organizations, such as the UN High Commissioner for Refugees (UNHCR) and the Organization for Security and Cooperation in Europe (OSCE), also had nearly independent standing and considerable international clout and did not hesitate to lobby for their own institutional interests every bit as bluntly as did contributing capitals.

Our solution was to think like a little country that can service its national interests only by working through others. This notion meant that UNMIK could develop its own "foreign policy." Governments typically determine their foreign policy priorities through a standard planning sequence that starts with an unsentimental appreciation of their country's overriding national interests. From these inherent first-order interests, one can derive the nation's critical security issues and goals. On that foundation one erects policy objectives of sufficient clarity that they can be used to guide action plans. The rest is nearly mundane—deciding how best to achieve these objectives, how to measure progress, what resources are necessary, and so on. This is garden-variety foreign and national security planning, but it provides a surprisingly flexible framework that can enhance the custodian's effectiveness in making progress toward viable peace.

In Kosovo we essentially did what any little country would do when constrained and overshadowed by bigger powers pursuing their own overriding agendas. This involved building working relationships with those powers for the specific purpose of pursuing the interests of the mission. We consulted widely, trying to determine who would and who would not be helpful on each issue, aiming to construct a mosaic of strategic alliances.

The "little-country" approach did not in any way suggest sovereignty or autonomy. It was simply an intellectual construct that provided a useful perspective on our otherwise anomalous situation. It lent our efforts to transform conflict in Kosovo the kind of rigor that a national security policy perspective provides. This concept was an absolutely central insight for us, without which we would have been adrift in a tempest.

We also understood that this perspective was unavoidably at odds with the ethos of the UN and a bit in conflict with the expectations of the various capitals that seconded each of us in part to advance their respective national interests. We learned, however, to balance these competing imperatives. When sending people on international missions, a capital that does not allow its secondees at least this much freedom is simply asking too much and, by so doing, undercuts its basic interests in the mission's success. In Kosovo it also helped that the UN Secretariat issued few instructions and little advice. Nor did we often seek guidance, knowing that the Secretariat would itself be driven—consciously or not—by institutional interests that often would be at odds with the custodian's singular responsibility to advance the peace process.

Forging a Unified Civil-Military Partnership

In Kosovo the civilian and military pieces came together in part because of the failures in this relationship in Bosnia.

In Bosnia the Dayton agreement delineated the military role with exquisite specificity. The role of the civilian custodian, however, was little more than a sketchy afterthought. More important, one finds in the Dayton peace agreement only a single mention of coordination between the civilian and military components. Moreover, this coordination was not mandatory—effectively, the military could decide whether it wished to attempt any coordination at all. As a result, senior civilian and military leaders rarely shared information or plans, let alone coordinated their operations. This obvious gap was intentional, designed by the Pentagon to ensure that the success of the military mission would not in any important way depend on the performance of the civilian mission. Success for the U.S. military was initially defined as the exit of U.S. forces within one year. By insulating itself so effectively from the civilian component, however, the military ensured the failure of both.

By the time of the Kosovo mission, the Security Council recognized the consequences of disconnected military and civilian operations. As a result, the council directed that these components coordinate closely in Kosovo and work toward shared goals in a mutually supportive manner. The good personal chemistry between SRSG Bernard Kouchner and General Michael Jackson was a major asset, but it was even more important that the two approached their work with similar visions of this critical partnership. They both appreciated that the initial focus had to be on the military mission. With lives at risk, the KFOR commander had to make authoritative decisions about military matters. They also understood, however, that KFOR could not succeed in its overall mission without the political process succeeding over the longer term. The military commander had to contribute unstintingly to the political effort to achieve the common goals of the mission. Collaboration was both in the mandate and in the mind-set of the mission's civilian and military leadership.

Constructing a Joint Civil-Military Planning Framework

With a mutually supportive relationship established between UNMIK and KFOR at the outset, the foundation was in place for another major advance: the creation of a joint planning framework, in which military and civilian planners could employ a shared methodology to align military operations with the political objectives of the mission.

In the early stages of the Bosnia mission, joint civil-military planning was negligible. The high representative and the NATO commander were briefly forced to cooperate in managing the turnover of Serb-held suburbs of Sarajevo early in 1996, but for the most part, even the most rudimentary coordination was accomplished only informally during much of the first year.[2] Both sides did gingerly cooperate on security during the visit of Pope John Paul II. The intense coordination required to support the first election was accomplished in large part by having the military simply take over much of the planning and practical arrangements. Overall, the military command in Bosnia was fearful that it might in some way appear to be taking instructions from civilian officials. In fact, the military's reticence made even senior-level meetings too fragile for substantive attempts at integration. Little took place other than the sharing of nonsensitive information.

In Kosovo, however, we sought from the beginning to achieve a joint planning framework. We aimed not just for a willingness to talk; we needed concrete, joint, routine processes for planning objective-driven operations. Our solution was to meld the conventional national security–planning paradigm (i.e., the interests-goals-objectives cascade mentioned previously) with the military's time-driven and sequenced approach to operational planning.

Some of this joint planning was done simply to trace our shared civil-military priorities. The product was essentially a descriptive planning matrix familiar to military planners. This matrix merely depicted the multitude of civilian and military activities already in motion, with associated time lines and the actors responsible for each item. The simple process of mapping this jumble of activities built a sense of unity and laid a foundation for more meaningful integration later on.

By the time serious and complex security challenges arose, a joint planning framework had taken shape. UNMIK civilian planners worked with their KFOR counterparts on operational plans, sharing assessments, taking briefings, and articulating requirements. This "jointness" was easier for some militaries to accept than others. British forces found it easiest, and U.S. commanders eventually followed suit. The French remained distinctly uncomfortable with civilians of any nationality working inside their secure planning facility. Nonetheless, such joint planning teams demonstrated their ability to produce a single document prescribing integrated civilian and military activities. This was a major breakthrough, especially for transforming hard-line power in Kosovo.

Effective integrated planning was essential to the successful seizure of a dangerously polluting Serb-operated lead smelter in August 2000. Located in the Serb-dominated region north of Mitrovica, the Zvecan smelter had begun to pour vast plumes of toxic lead emissions over the surrounding area, including Mitrovica.[3] Belgrade effectively controlled the smelter, and its operations subsidized Serb hard-liners while enraging the ethnic Albanian population. UNMIK and KFOR planners met to clarify the issues at stake, beginning with interests and aims. For various legal and political reasons, the French, who commanded that sector, built their rationale on the pollution issue. Nominally, the French aim was to shut down the lead smelter because its continued operation posed an unacceptable health risk. At the same time, UNMIK envisioned a larger strategy of asserting UN authority over territory north of Mitrovica. As the custodians, we sought to leverage the military operation to accomplish the removal of Milosevic's stalwarts who were responsible for operating the smelter and also for other forms of obstructionism throughout northern Kosovo.

These differing aims converged in an integrated civilian-military plan that would close the plant in the short run, eliminating further lead pollution, while in the longer run also offering inducements to the Serb workforce in the plant to cooperate with UNMIK in cleaning up the toxic environment. In addition, to ensure that Belgrade could not retaliate for seizure of the plant, the integrated plan called for extensive security operations that would effectively assert a far greater degree of international authority throughout the north.

Every aspect of the joint UNMIK-KFOR plan was tested against a simple standard: Does it support the larger strategy? Joint civilian-military planning is standard practice in home capitals, but for the United Nations and NATO this was a new experience.

Underlying the process is a fundamental lesson: civilian and military actors must understand one another's requirements. Civilian political managers must grasp the military commanders' need to frame the mission in concrete, achievable terms. It is naive of civilian officials to see the military as inflexible and risk averse. Military commanders carry heavy responsibilities for the lives of their troops. They are not going to put their young men and women at risk without knowing what is to be achieved, what the consequences are, and that the likely gains will plausibly outweigh the costs. If the civilian custodian cannot present a relevant objective that is clearly achievable in a reasonable time with manageable risks, then the civilian cannot expect to have a military partner.

The supporting military commander has a reciprocal obligation to sustain critical aspects of the political manager's strategy. If the process of political transformation calls for pursuing incremental gains, cultivating ambiguity among the conflicting parties, neutralizing militants, and sustaining demobilization, then the military commander will need to adapt operations to these political aims. From the custodian's perspective, this is not just a series of operations implementing an exit strategy. It is a long process of transformation that can succeed only over time and often by indirection.

GUIDING THE MISSION

Strategizing for a Viable Peace

Given a mandate that seeks a viable peace, the custodian must develop a realistic strategic approach for conflict transformation that balances several considerations. First, a realistic assessment must be made to determine whether local war-hardened power structures are likely to work against the mission in order to protect their narrow, illegal equities. Then the custodian must assess sources of power, credibility, and leverage, as well as other resources that can influence key actors to join the peace process. Strategizing involves balancing these considerations to determine the magnitude of the transformation required to forge a viable peace.

The advance policy planning for the postwar period in Kosovo that was completed in Washington, Paris, London, Bonn, and Rome in the spring of 1999 before the NATO bombing campaign ended made an especially significant contribution. With this front-end work completed a few weeks before the mandate was adopted, senior officials in the UN Secretariat had a solid foundation for conceptualizing how to build a mission that could implement a peace process leading to a viable peace. The Secretariat's initial plans proved to be about 80 percent applicable to what was required in the first months of the mission.

As KFOR was deploying into Pristina in June 1999, a UN advance party was also moving in to begin shouldering UNMIK's responsibilities. This advance civilian cadre did a superb job of performing assessments and starting the strategizing process for transforming conflict. Within thirty days of the passage of Resolution 1244, the UN secretary-general was able to publish a realistic concept of operation for UNMIK that would prove effective well into the peace process.[4] When SRSG Bernard Kouchner and I arrived in July, we relied heavily on this solid foundation. Obviously, we had a long way to go to become operational and credible to the people of Kosovo, but this advance planning was crucial for us to begin establishing facts on the ground so essential for making headway toward a viable peace without delay.

Another critical feature was UNMIK's Joint Planning Group (JPG). The UN Secretariat created the JPG to work for UNMIK's leadership to prepare a broad strategy to accomplish mission objectives, integrate UNMIK's components, and bring capabilities to bear on the major emerging challenges to the mission. It gave us a small, effective planning asset that was close to the leadership to identify decisions that had to be made early to avoid operating continuously in a crisis-response mode. As our leading representative in the UNMIK-KFOR joint planning structure, the JPG was essential in bringing together the military and civilian efforts. It kept reminding all of us of the larger strategy. This perspective was very important to the staff, which also had to cope with urgent matters, especially recurrent murderous assaults on the Serb population. With the JPG occasionally engaging UNMIK leadership, we could step back briefly and put our discrete efforts in the broader perspective of conflict transformation.

The makeup of UNMIK's leadership team was also an essential feature. Bernard Kouchner headed our team, and his personality of passionate politician inspired the rest of us as methodical managers. The team's mix proved beneficial, not only for substantive reasons. Kouchner sometimes had to be rescued from his passion because he would get discouraged when progress seemed stalled, as would other team members. At these critical moments, those of us who were the methodical types would assemble the team for a strategic discussion. Instead of focusing on current activity, we revalidated the mission's vision and confirmed our objectives for the near term. We carefully analyzed what specifically was restraining us and why. It was during those strategic discussions, often undertaken in the depths of despondency, that we thoroughly reexamined what we needed to do to advance the peace process.

Developing Mission Policy

There is a distinction between policymaking and policy implementation. The JPG did policy implementation. It determined at the strategic level how to accomplish our broad mission. Part of the JPG planning effort also involved identifying policy issues that we needed to address so plans could be developed in a timely fashion. Determining what those policies should be is a policymaking process. In Kosovo we learned that it was nearly impossible to make policy, as we understand it from a national perspective.

Policymaking on internal matters is one area where the little-country model did not work. It was not possible to bring together the European Union (EU), the OSCE, the UNHCR, a group of UN civilians, and senior NATO military officers to have a policymaking discussion on controversial and complex issues and expect to get agreement. Instead, policymaking in the UN system requires a search for consensus at the lowest common denominator, especially because it involves melding value judgments. In UNMIK there were strenuous discussions about what should be done, and even after policies were seemingly determined and articulated, people would disagree and argue endlessly about options instead of taking action. This is a trap that an executive branch official would not normally fall into when operating in a national policymaking setting. But in a UN setting, where the components of the mission are responsive to decision-making authorities elsewhere, reaching consensus on policy regarding a controversial issue is nearly hopeless.

Yet the custodian must find a way to resolve controversial matters, so we did "policymaking in reverse." We would shape actions based on our instincts of where the peace process ought to be headed rather than determine the policy up front. In some instances, we may have had only an inchoate sense of what the guiding policy should be. As time passed and people started asking us the basis for our actions, we would make statements that evolved into, "Oh, that's our policy." In some cases we knew from the beginning where we wanted to go to transform conflict, but in other cases an action just felt right. We began to articulate a policy that described the actions we had already taken, distilling the policy after the fact. This was unavoidable in the UN system because seeking to establish policy at the outset would have created paralyzing opposition before we could even get started.

In making policy in reverse, the custodian needs to be careful. When some staff members are doing something illogical, they should be stopped or the effort should be reshaped to be beneficial. Ultimately, everything we did had to work in harmony with the peace process. That was our prime directive, and even small decisions had to be assessed against that guideline. When we acted on our instincts, we always did so with a sense of where the peace process needed to go to achieve transformation. Even though we may not have had a conversation about that very often, and even though in many cases we were busier taking action than thinking about it, we kept checking our actions against the imperatives of the peace process. This prevented policymaking in reverse from going too far off course.

TRANSFORMING CONFLICT

Building the Mission's Credibility and Power

At the outset of the mission, when the custodian is weakest, the mission is likely to be thrust into confrontations with local war-hardened power structures that have little interest in a meaningful peace process. Differences in the way these initial challenges were handled in Bosnia and Kosovo illustrate the importance of quickly fusing civilian and military leadership to demonstrate unity and strength, especially when dealing with potential obstructionists.

In Bosnia residents of Gorazde (a Bosnian enclave southeast of Sarajevo) could reach other Bosniak territories only via a narrow road subject to frequent attack. Civilian buses were regularly stoned, resulting in injuries to passengers, and there were reports of travelers disappearing. To some, it looked as if the security promises of the recently negotiated Dayton agreement were collapsing. Without consultation, High Representative Carl Bilt stated in a press conference that these attacks were a serious security challenge and that he expected the NATO-led Implementation Force (IFOR) to provide protection along the road. IFOR commander General Leighton Smith immediately responded in a separate press conference that NATO troops were not in Bosnia to do police work, and he demanded to know why the UN civil police were not yet in place. Dayton was at that point barely three weeks into implementation, and the world was already witnessing an open quarrel between the civilian and military components of the international presence. This exacerbated the underlying security challenges and set a pattern that would plague international efforts in Bosnia for years.

In Kosovo there were serious security problems in Pristina right from the start; Serbs were being forced out of their homes and often murdered. Any effective UN police force was months away from being in place. As in Gorazde, the credibility of the entire mission was at risk. In this case, however, the senior civilian and military leadership, Bernard Kouchner and General Michael Jackson, coordinated closely. KFOR units, chiefly British, used a mix of roving patrols, checkpoints, crowd control, surveillance, and quick reaction to buy time for the UN team to initiate a political process and deploy an international police force. UNMIK Police and KFOR planners jointly mapped a deployment sequence that would link military and police activities and transfer responsibility for conventional policing incrementally as UN capabilities grew. KFOR progressively shifted to backup positions and usual military-style duties in support of the police. This set the stage for joint operations as the mission progressed.

The British military was adept at joint military-police operations, having seasoned its forces and honed its model over the years in Northern Ireland. UN police planners had a different model in mind, but we quickly agreed to the British approach, both as a practical matter and to bolster confidence in the joint approach to secure Kosovo's environment. The climate of recrimination that was such a burden in Bosnia never developed in Kosovo. From the custodian's perspective, this tight UNMIK-KFOR partnership formed at the outset gave the mission substantially more power to influence Kosovo's transformation.

Making Judgments and Tough Calls

The combined assets of KFOR and UNMIK gave the custodian an enormous security force. A prudent custodian thinks of the mission as weak, however, or at least is very judicious about employing force. It can be somewhat like trying to drive a powerful car on ice—the power is rather theoretical because the traction is so poor, and as the car gathers speed, it is increasingly difficult to stop or change direction. A modest view of one's powers can be crucial when confronting hard-liners who seek to derail the peace process.

Some notorious thugs had held command positions in the KLA during the conflict and emerged afterward as virtual warlords, using intimidation and more coercive means to assert near-dictatorial control over their home regions. One such figure, Sami Lustaku, was believed to be responsible not only for terrorizing Serbs but also for murdering Albanians who were thought to have collaborated with the Serb regime before the conflict. UNMIK Police and prosecutors were intent on jailing Lustaku, but actionable evidence against him was thin, and no witnesses were likely to come forward. In some cases of this nature we had exercised UNMIK's administrative authority of "executive detention" to arrest a suspect considered especially dangerous so that investigations could be conducted without intimidation of potential witnesses.

In this case, however, we made a considered decision—in consultation with KFOR—not to go forward until we had built a rock-solid case and had also built up a robust civil, military, and police infrastructure in Lustaku's district. In spite of complaints that UNMIK was afraid to deal with warlords, the decision was a good call. The situation proved that for a prudent custodian, it is never enough to do the right thing; the right thing must also be sustainable.

Maintaining a Positive Outlook

There were often times when it was difficult to make progress, or there would be a setback and nearly everyone at headquarters would lose hope. It would take hours to energize those in the inner circle who were down emotionally. After the third or fourth such experience, those of us at the top agreed that we could not all be dejected at the same time. We recognized that someone always had to retain a positive outlook and work to revive our spirits because trouble would emerge repeatedly every day. A custodian must appreciate that this is part of the emotional roller-coaster ride involved in a peace mission and ensure that someone always remains upbeat to pull the others along.

CULTIVATING INTERNATIONAL SUPPORT

Sustaining Security Council Consensus

The custodian of a UN mission is empowered directly by the Security Council. Therefore, a major contributing factor to a mission's success is the custodian's effectiveness in capitalizing on the Security Council's intent, direction, and commitment to the mission. We recognized that we had several supporters on the Security Council, particularly France, the United Kingdom, and the United States. Each of these nations had responsibility for managing support for UNMIK within the council.

Russia was different. Russia and Serbia have a shared historical legacy, and Serbia relied on Russia to protect its interests in the Security Council, especially in sustaining Belgrade's sovereignty over Kosovo. Because UNMIK potentially threatened Serbian rule, the Russians did everything they could to harass UNMIK, and frequently they went beyond harassment to a kind of viciousness that was rather deflating. This involved derogatory inquiries into UNMIK's activities, which caused the UN Secretariat in New York to scurry around, ask many questions, and make never-ending requests for information about our operations. We would try to answer the Secretariat's questions, but it took valuable time and staff energy to provide coherent answers. Doing so became a hindrance to our operations.

The Security Council's open debates, often contentious owing to scathing Russian complaints, proved confusing and disheartening to some of our own staff. Those who were not American, British, French, German, or Italian frequently wondered whether UNMIK's mission was really a worthy effort because the Russians kept proclaiming that we were improperly executing the mandate. A few thought the Security Council itself questioned whether we should be in Kosovo at all.

A custodian needs to understand the dynamics of the Security Council and the pressures its members respond to. We realized that the UN Secretariat could not affect the Security Council one bit. Rather, the UN staff receives its guidance from the Security Council. The Russians exploited that very effectively to impede our operations. Once this became clear to us, we adopted the little-country perspective and campaigned for help from key nations on the Security Council such as the United Kingdom, the United States, and France. We urged them to take control of the Security Council on behalf of UNMIK.

We could not ignore the Russians because they wielded too much power, so we organized a monthly briefing session with the Russian mission in Belgrade. Unfortunately, these regular updates had no effect whatsoever on Russian behavior in New York. In the Security Council and other forums, the Russians were every bit as harsh as before, but our efforts in Belgrade did produce a positive impact. Other Security Council members recognized that we were doing everything possible to address Russian concerns. This led them to conclude that at least UNMIK was not part of the problem.

A custodian should pay attention to the Security Council, particularly when a permanent member dislikes the mission and pressures the UN Secretariat. The custodian must find friendly supporters on the council to help sustain a favorable consensus for the mission. Beyond that, the custodian's ability to sustain Security

Council unity is very limited, even though it is a key factor to the success of the mission.

Dealing with the UN Secretariat

Staff members of the UN Secretariat believe that the mission operates through them. However, that is not how Resolution 1244 was written, and even if it had been, we would have had to find alternate channels to get things done. As in any complicated government bureaucracy, a mission cannot allow itself to be trapped in any one channel. In our case, we opened other channels to advance the interests of the mission, and that had the favorable effect of making some Secretariat staff uncomfortable. They had the choice of either moving forward with us or being bypassed. Most decided to accept the situation and work with us. Ultimately, we did not have to treat the Secretariat as friend or foe, but we could not allow ourselves to be completely and singularly dependent on its control. Secretariat staff members must understand that the custodian always can find some way to get business done without them.

Because the Secretariat could easily have become politicized, particularly given persistent Russian harassment, we had to ensure that it focused on our key goals and retained objectivity. However, the Russian representative sought to use the Secretariat to debilitate us and impede the mission. In response, we went directly to the Russian representative in New York and we invited the Secretariat staff to join the meeting. Here, in contrast to other forums, this well-known Russian official was perfectly pleasant and reasonable as we explained everything we were doing in the mission in great detail. Witnessing his complete turn-around, Secretariat staff members saw that the Russian's blistering speeches in the Security Council were simply performances on a stage. Most of all, they recognized that we would not be persuaded in the future when they implored, "Don't you understand that the Russians won't accept this or that?" We had un-masked the actor and neutralized one of our major hindrances.

The UN Secretariat is a dynamic entity. It has many hundreds of well-intended, hardworking international public servants. This organization is a mission's lifeline, certainly administratively, and it casts a long shadow throughout the international system. However, a custodian must see the Secretariat for what it is: dependent on the Security Council and General Assembly for its very life. From these bodies, the Secretariat receives its budget, its mission, and its prestige. A custodian must appreciate this landscape in New York and then understand that the interests of the Secretariat and those of the mission may not be compatible.

Lobbying the United Nations' Budgetary Committee

UNMIK's budget was vulnerable. Because we were responsible for the administrative functions of a government, we had unusual budgetary requirements that typical UN missions do not. In addition, we faced Russian and Cuban objections because they did not support our mandate. So they tried to hinder the mission by radically reducing our substantial budget requests, making it a highly politicized exercise.

We carefully planned our budget presentation to the UN Advisory Committee on Administrative and Budgetary Questions (ACABQ), which consists of members from eighteen countries. This committee approves the operating budget request of all UN peace missions for the UN General Assembly. Usually, UN missions have their chief administrative officer prepare the budget request and send it to the UN for review. When a mission's budget comes up for approval, typically the chief administrative officer goes to New York to answer questions from the committee, which then negotiates a unanimous consensus needed for a final decision.

We treated this UN process as requiring both rational justification and political campaigning. We needed to mobilize the active assistance of nations that supported UNMIK's mandate and trusted our custodianship of the process. It became the custodian's responsibility, therefore, to go to New York, present our budget, and gain approval before the ACABQ. Our campaign was worth every second of our time. The handful of nonsupporting members on the committee tried to cut anything in the budget request they objected to, such as establishing a new judiciary. Russia, Cuba, and two or three other countries were fundamentally opposed to the mission, either out of solidarity with Serbian interests or in reflexive opposition to whatever the United States favored, or both. Because the budget committee works on consensus, once three or four nations contest a certain point, other members of the committee tend to accommodate the noisy few. Essential to our campaign strategy, therefore, was to respond so strenuously and convincingly to scathing questions from our opponents that the other committee members perceived the naysayers' efforts as simply political and mean-spirited.

We saw the budget process as a backdoor political challenge to the mandate. Naysayers were not only seeking to inflict budgetary pain; they wanted to do operational damage to the mission. A custodian cannot allow that to happen, and we made sure that opponents could not exploit the etiquette of the ACABQ to wreck the mission. Our campaign was a little complicated, but no more complicated than a U.S. federal government agency's plan to win congressional authorization of its budget. The custodian must be prepared to garner adequate financial backing for implementing transformation efforts. It is a political process where hidden agendas can do grave damage to implementation of the peace process.

Courting Support from Major Powers

Any international peace operation needs a political consensus among major powers to drive the overall process forward. In the case of Kosovo, the so-called Balkans

Contact Group consisted of France, Germany, Italy, Russia, the United Kingdom, and the United States. Mirroring the political role of a "friends group" or a "core group" that had been formed to support other UN peace operations, the Contact Group served as the clearinghouse for political consensus building and policymaking for UNMIK.

The Contact Group was very useful to us. Favorable opinions of the Contact Group could bolster UNMIK's status and advance the peace process by demonstrating to the disputants that UNMIK had the support of the major powers. As a respected international forum for shaping a political consensus in support of the mission, the Contact Group was decisive in enabling us to move ahead with conflict transformation. We were not at all cynical about its role. When difficulties arose, we could turn to the Contact Group, describe our situation, explain our preferred strategy, and urge its support for our efforts. For the most part, it was a powerful and reliable advocate for UNMIK.

The Contact Group somewhat restrained Russian harassment of UNMIK. The Russians enjoyed being included among the major powers in this prestigious and influential international political body, and they did not want to jeopardize this status. While the Russian representative in New York was harsh and hostile, his counterpart in the Contact Group was by no means as strident or abusive. In short, the Contact Group performed a vital political role for the mission and made it easier for us to exercise our authorities.

The Contact Group also provided one more useful option when we were shopping for support for our little country. In addition to the Contact Group, we had the Security Council, the G-8, the EU, NATO, the OSCE, and individual nations. As we pondered how to advance an important initiative, we sought to determine which of these groups could help us the most.

Frequently, operating as a little country, we sought assistance from major powers. For example, when we were not getting necessary funds from the European Union, which was paralyzing our ability to begin building a functioning economy in Kosovo, we turned to the biggest power of all, the United States. We made sure the United States understood that the mission could fail if the European Union's funding support for legitimate economic activity was not provided quickly. We gave very stern warnings in January and February 2000. This energized key figures in the U.S. Congress, who scolded the Europeans for not meeting their obligations. This created some ill will, but from the little-country perspective, it was a substantial net gain.

Sometimes a situation required a variation on the little-country model. For example, early in the mission the United States greatly favored the development of a complete constitution for Kosovo. The U.S. objective was to move Kosovo incrementally toward quasi independence, avoiding an immediate resolution but ensuring that any progress was irreversible. This reflected the traditional

U.S. preference for a well-defined exit strategy similar to what had been attempted in Bosnia.

UNMIK felt that Kosovo was not ready for constitutional debates and that such contentious discussions would set back the political process. Instead, we embraced the principle of cultivating ambiguity about power sharing to reduce potential threats to Kosovo's political transformation. However, if UNMIK officials had directly disagreed with the Americans, then, like any little country, we would have put ourselves in a losing battle. To avoid this, we consulted with the other major powers—the British, the French, and the Germans—that were distinctly unenthusiastic about drafting a constitution at that point in the process. Next we encouraged Washington to pitch its idea to a meeting of the Contact Group, where we were only an observer. We didn't press the issue, but we asked group members to debate and try to sort it out for us. With that, a premature and unconstructive proposal was dropped without incurring the wrath of a superpower. By thinking and acting like a little country, we navigated the straits.

Dealing with NATO

General Jackson faced many of the same challenges that we did. Rather quickly he realized that we were maneuvering among nations and international organizations, all of whom believed strongly that they had a right to instruct us.

Obviously, he had a direct command relationship with NATO. Jackson also had nominal direct command over the five multinational brigades, and each of his national contingent commanders had the right to consult with their own governments whenever they chose to. Jackson remembered that this was used as a weapon in Bosnia to obstruct the NATO military command. There, General Michael Walker lost the aid of French troops for nearly two weeks at one point when they became offended and went into the national consultation mode. Walker tried everything to repair the situation, such as giving instructions, making requests, and even placing phone calls. But the French military commander would listen only to Paris and otherwise was on radio silence.

Because he was under the NATO chain of command, General Jackson couldn't use the little-country model. Nevertheless, KFOR benefited by having UNMIK think that way. The concept helped clarify what our national objectives should be and what our national security strategy should include. The military needed us to provide that perspective. This top-level strategic thinking helped us have a coherent discourse about where the UNMIK-KFOR team should be headed in transforming conflict in Kosovo.

Working with the United States

In working with the United States, thinking like a little country was essential. Fundamentally, we needed an engagement strategy to ensure that the United

States helped the mission remain viable through all its difficulties. This included garnering support from others for new initiatives and sustaining operations over the long haul. In most cases, the nature of the specific issue and the kind of support we needed from outsiders determined our strategy for working with the United States. When an issue emerged, we would develop a strategy for involving the Americans and making sure they could accomplish what was needed. Overall, the United States was our friend 85–90 percent of the time and was a complication about 10 percent of the time. Our guiding principle was that we should do no worse to the United States than what the Pentagon does to the State Department.

As the senior American in UNMIK, I often engaged directly with the United States, especially the State Department, to advance the interests of the mission. In one call I would be talking to a U.S. official as a friend, a colleague, a fellow American. Then in the next call, perhaps even to the same person, I might take on the role of UN representative and lobby for support. Obviously, if a long-time friend in the State Department demanded something harmful for the mission, a friendship could be lost. A custodian simply must not take instructions as if he or she were a Foreign Service officer. In Kosovo I did not experience anything like that. The U.S. government was committed to the success of UNMIK, and most officials I worked with had extensive experience in the Balkans. That said, U.S. officials treated me, a senior UNMIK official, a bit cautiously, perhaps as they would a Canadian diplomat: extremely close but not to be completely trusted. The relationship made each of us slightly ill at ease sometimes, but it was the correct way to do our business. I was thankful for the professionalism of the U.S. Foreign Service, whose officers were savvy about this relationship. Fortunately, it worked most of the time.

Dealing with the Financers: The World Bank, the European Union, and Donor Nations

UNMIK had an unprecedented requirement for a UN mission in that the mission had to constitute the foundations of legitimate economic activity to nurture Kosovo's transformation to viable peace. This economic dimension took us into the unfamiliar territory of national financial management and budgeting. This meant that UNMIK needed considerable financial management expertise and assistance from the outside world, including the World Bank, the European Union, and several donor nations. A major financial component had to be added to the normal development requirements for a typical UN mission. This was new for everyone—in New York, Brussels, the capitals of the G-8 finance ministers, and the mission. We all had to learn on the job.

One critical point we did not understand going into the mission was that the World Bank would not contribute because it can work only with a sovereign country. We were stunned to learn this. Because of this constraint, the World Bank was in the peculiar position of making prominent judgments from afar about what we were doing while contributing nothing to our enormous needs. It took some time for us to understand the implications of this deficiency and adapt our economic strategy accordingly. We devised an arrangement whereby the World Bank would provide us analysis and advice and help us look for opportunities to advance our mission. Then, as a respected global opinion leader, the World Bank would endorse and advocate what we were doing. Nevertheless, it was frustrating that it could not contribute in substantial ways.

This suited the European Union, however, because it wanted exclusive custody of the mission's economic component. UNMIK was in a situation similar to that of a government with a very strong finance minister who believes that the essence of governance revolves entirely around money. In some ways, the struggle with our EU-led finance component was similar to our struggle in Bosnia with the military. In both instances the predominant attitude was, We have our assigned mission. We have our orders. We know what to do. We are going to do it our way. The primary mission of our financial component was to introduce economic reforms to create a legitimate market system. In the end, we were not badly served by it. It was beneficial that the financial component rapidly erected a well-thought-out market-based economic system. It was unfortunate, however, that that process was not integrated with UNMIK's related efforts to transform conflict in Kosovo.

For the custodian of Kosovo's transformation, this was very problematic. UNMIK had to undertake political initiatives, while our financial component was independently pursuing economic reforms that were obscured from view. As a result, we did not reactivate basic utilities and services in a timely manner, which was costly for the peace process. After nine months of the mission, we realized that we were not developing anything economically but were attempting to reform an economy that did not exist. The immediate requirements were being overlooked. After our first year, there was substantial criticism that we did not have an economic development program.

The lesson for the custodian is that the lack of integration of this new component, the financial piece, created a great deal of unnecessary friction for the peace process. As far as EU officials were concerned, the UN political mission was operating on its own track. This precluded the custodian from gaining much leverage from the financial side to advance Kosovo's overall political transformation.

Obtaining Intelligence on Threats to the Peace Process

Usually, a little country has an intelligence apparatus to provide early warning of threatening events, but a similar approach would have been anathema in the UN system. A custodian must accept that he or she does not have an intelligence service in the mission, at least not in the sense that we are accustomed to in a national setting. The constituents of the United Nations, especially on the humanitarian side, would regard it as a direct threat, first to their morality and second to their personal security, to be associated even remotely with intelligence gatherers. Moreover, the mission could not keep a secret even if it had one.

Anticipating obstructionist threats is an important issue for the custodian, but it must be handled properly. Although the mission will not have an intelligence apparatus, this does not preclude quietly networking with friends of the mission, again acting as a little country. In the end there is a critical need for intelligence, and a careful custodian can quietly satisfy this requirement without undermining the mission's credibility.

In Kosovo governments were usually shrewd about providing us with intelligence. Each of the five nations responsible for commanding one of the multinational brigades was self-interested in seeing that UNMIK was successful. They did not want the UN mission basing its plans exclusively on another nation's intelligence, however. This afforded UNMIK some leverage with the bigger powers.

The intelligence services of each nation regard the others as second rate, believing their own work to be better. These self-interested views create a muted competition among nations that is very potent. In Kosovo the Americans and the French each knew that the other was willing to share intelligence—and shared some of their national intelligence with UNMIK, if only so that the mission would not operate simply on the strength of the other nation's intelligence. The British had a somewhat higher-minded view of the matter. They did help but were not quite as driven by competition. The Germans and the Italians also provided intelligence that their governments assessed as useful to us.

Leveraging Crises to Gain International Support

Part of being a successful custodian is to be opportunistic about leveraging a crisis to make progress. Experience told us that the UN recruiting and hiring system, for example, would be slow in meeting our initial staffing needs of hundreds of highly skilled experts to help run the territory. What we did not anticipate was that UNMIK would have a recurring personnel demand about twice a year. This was an unforeseen requirement that became apparent in the early spring of 2000 when a large part of UNMIK's civilian staff were due to depart as their six-month contracts expired. At the turnover rate we were experiencing, we were actually depopulating the mission. Given the three to four months necessary for UN recruitment and hiring, we needed to energize the process immediately. Working against us was the fact that Kosovo was no longer a major world crisis. In addition, new UN missions, such as East Timor and Sierra Leone, were diverting attention from Kosovo.

This was a disaster in the making. Instead of treating it as an administrative matter, we turned it into a political emergency. We consulted heavily with friendly nations. With the welcome top-down leadership of the UN deputy secretary-general Louise Frechette and substantial help from the British and the Americans, we used this emergency to convince the UN Secretariat to rewrite the UN books. In the end, we were able to conduct recruiting and hiring directly from the mission rather than depend on the standard UN system based in New York. No other mission had been afforded this authority, but we were in a crisis, and that allowed us to insist on being treated differently.

NOTES

1. Stephen J. Stedman introduced the concept of the "custodian of the peace process" in his groundbreaking article "Spoiler Problems in Peace Processes," *International Security* 22, no. 2 (Fall 1997): 5–53. Stedman broadly defines the custodian as the international actor, usually the United Nations, whose task is to oversee the implementation of peace agreements. Implicit in the custodian's role is the cultivation and protection of peace and the management of spoilers. Consistent with Stedman's view, this chapter's definition is more directly focused on the civilian leadership team of the UN mission. In the United Nations Mission in Kosovo (UNMIK), the manifestation of the custodian in 1999 included SRSG Bernard Kouchner, his deputy Jock Covey, and perhaps two or three of their closest advisers. This small, tight leadership team at the top of UNMIK guided Kosovo's peace process, directed international civilian efforts, implemented the mission's political strategy, and acted as the executive authority implementation of the UN Security Council's mandate. This chapter examines many dimensions of this team's actions as custodian of Kosovo's progress in transforming conflict to viable peace.

2. Later, a degree of coordination took place during senior-level civilian-military meetings held several times a week.

3. UNMIK, "UNMIK Assumes Responsibility for Operations at Zvecan Smelter," UNMIK/PR/312 (August 14, 2000).

4. *Report of the Secretary-General on the United Nations Interim Administration Mission in Kosovo*, S/1999/779 (July 12, 1999).

5

Making a Viable Peace

Moderating Political Conflict

Jock Covey

In July 1999 Bernard Kouchner, the new chief of the United Nations Interim Administration Mission in Kosovo (UNMIK), went to Rome to solicit the support of Ibrahim Rugova, leader of the Democratic League of Kosovo (LDK), in restoring the apparatus of government in Kosovo. As Kouchner prevailed upon him to return to Kosovo, Rugova listened in apparent discomfort, hinting at disparate concerns, including security conditions in Pristina. By the end of their confusing meeting, Kouchner had made no progress in convincing Rugova to come home.

It took months to understand what Rugova's fears were. Only later did UNMIK officials learn that shortly after the NATO bombing campaign ended, five of Rugova's bodyguards had been apprehended and tortured by Kosovo Liberation Army (KLA) operatives under the command of Daut Haradinaj. One had escaped, but the other four had been executed. As it turned out, averting a civil war between these rival ethnic Albanian factions would be one of UNMIK's dominant preoccupations.

THE CHALLENGE

The following discussion is intended to illuminate some elements of tradecraft behind UNMIK's behavior in the first eighteen months of its mission in pursuit of a viable peace. It is not a history of that period and does not even provide a complete list of the issues UNMIK faced. Other chapters in this book provide additional detail about key events. The aim of this chapter is to explain how UNMIK developed and applied some key tools and political strategies to transform conflict in Kosovo in hopes that other practitioners might adapt some of them to their own challenges.

The Political Context

Although the bombing ended in June 1999, a vicious confrontation between Kosovo's ethnic Serbs and Albanians continued. Serbs did not accept that they had been conquered—they felt betrayed. The triumphant Albanians thought that NATO's peacekeepers were denying them real victory and independence.

As NATO troops began arriving in early June 1999, nearly one hundred civilians were being killed each week, mostly Serbs. The KLA hunted down Serbs who had been involved in the war, as well as collaborators among the other ethnic communities, especially the Turkish and the Roma, and even ethnic Albanians they regarded as simply too cooperative with their former Serb oppressors. KLA extremists were determined to chase the Serbs out of Kosovo, using violence and terror when necessary.

In July, fourteen Serb farmers were murdered while working in their fields not far from Pristina. The massacre left Serbs with an overwhelming sense of vulnerability. No matter what they did, if they were outside the safety of their homes, it was open season. Many Serbs, feeling victimized, retreated inward. They had nowhere to go—Serbia was shattered, winter was coming, and no one would have them as refugees. Most of these traumatized Serbs just wanted to be left alone in peace. Some were ready to consider living under a regime dominated by ethnic Albanians, once again, as they had in the 1980s.

Other Serbs adopted a much more belligerent posture, insisting that all Serbs must stay and defend their land and legacy, even if it meant martyrdom. This aggressive, provocative minority welcomed confrontations with KLA militants. The war was unfinished as far as they were concerned; they were unrepentant for Serb atrocities in Kosovo; and they held NATO accountable for any compromise of Serb freedom of movement. Traditional Serb solidarity notwithstanding, they also attacked Serbs inclined to cooperate with the international community.

The Milosevic regime actively supported these hard-liners. Belgrade saw Mitrovica as the place to take a final stand against Albanian encroachment and encouraged Serb hard-liners in enclaves throughout Kosovo, providing financial support, food, and equipment. Serbs in Kosovo who might have considered accommodation were bullied and intimidated, or worse.

At the same time, a less obvious bitter struggle inside Kosovo was going on within the majority ethnic Albanian community, between the emergent KLA and supporters of Ibrahim Rugova's LDK.

During Milosevic's decade-long oppression of the Albanian community, the LDK had maintained a remarkably sophisticated parallel apparatus that had run schools and hospitals and provided basic public services for the Albanian community. In the early 1990s, however, some Albanian nationalists and student leaders began to see the LDK as a part of the Serb regime—and Rugova as its tool. Many of those angry student leaders (including young Hashim Thaci) eventually became key figures in the KLA. For them, the fact that Rugova met with Milosevic just before the war confirmed his role as a collaborator.

During the war, the KLA performed as an armed resistance movement, but it was a loose collection of secretive paramilitary bands operating nearly autonomously. In the immediate aftermath of the war, these paramilitary elements asserted their dominion over the countryside militarily, declaring the KLA the "provisional government" of Kosovo. They lacked the expertise and infrastructure to address the public's urgent humanitarian needs, however, and most Albanians were inclined to look once again to the LDK for support and guidance.

Over time, it became more and more apparent that this was not simply a heated political argument. KLA extremists would use any necessary means to displace Rugova and his LDK party apparatus—as well as to be acknowledged as heroes and the guarantors of Kosovo's future independence. KLA fighters saw the LDK's military arm, the Armed Forces of the Republic of Kosovo (FARK),[1] as nearly as much of an enemy as the dreaded Serb special police. Even during the war, the KLA had attacked the FARK. In the vacuum that followed, the KLA's ruthless campaign against the LDK continued.

Transforming Kosovo's political conflict was contentious. The international community had achieved consensus only at the highest levels of generality. There were major differences just below the surface of UN Security Council Resolution 1244—over the role of Serbs; the future of the KLA; the timing, content, and conduct of elections; the drafting of a constitution; the role of the Kosovo Force (KFOR) and the international police; the role and authority of UNMIK officials; the tension between order and human rights; and even which body of law should apply in Kosovo. Much of the international community was skeptical that the United Nations could handle such a challenge. The Organization for Security and Cooperation in Europe (OSCE) was openly resentful that it was not given the challenge. The European Union was unilateral in its economic prescriptions.

The UN Secretariat could provide little relief. Institutionally, it had to respond to the Security Council, the very source of the most intractable differences. Organizationally, the Secretariat was unable to field senior talent on a sustained basis. Politically, it was risk averse, and our internal "little-country" perspective would be considered seditious.

Without the support of key capitals, especially but not only those represented on the UN Security Council, UNMIK's mission would soon be whittled down. Funding would shrink, talent would drift home, and it would become harder and harder to draw on capitals for leverage with the parties.

The Objectives of the Political Strategy

Resolution 1244 articulated UNMIK's formal objectives: establishing an interim civil administration and making initial progress toward substantial autonomy and democratic self-government. If Resolution 1244 were taken at face value, the exercise of sovereignty would rest exclusively with UNMIK, and the exact shape of Kosovo's new political order and the degree of local participation would be left entirely to the discretion of UNMIK's political managers.

At another level, rarely addressed explicitly, UNMIK existed to service European security and cooperation. The earlier complications in East-West relations, the massive refugee flows into Western Europe, and the centripetal pressures within NATO were all intolerable. If UNMIK succeeded, as was hoped, it would lighten Europe's massive refugee burden and help revalidate the NATO alliance.

With winter coming and more than a dozen killings a day, the most urgent initial objectives for the UNMIK-KFOR team were to stabilize internal security and to mitigate dire humanitarian conditions. While that was under way, it was also assumed that UNMIK would literally *govern* Kosovo—and somehow gain the consent of the governed.

Kosovo's final status was left ambiguous, and responsibility for resolving it was left outside UNMIK's stated mandate. With the existential issue of the territory's eventual political status unresolved, and facing an internal power vacuum that was rapidly being filled through violent means, the mission would have to overcome powerful incentives for continued conflict in order to accomplish these objectives.

THE STRATEGY

Lessons Applied in Crafting the Political Strategy

Clausewitz

"Peacekeeping" does not adequately describe the challenge. Realistically, at the time that "peacekeepers" first enter a conflict, there rarely is a peace to keep—yet. The disputants generally enter the peacekeeping phase with all their grievances and wartime goals intact. Each intends to achieve under cover of the peacekeeping process what they could not achieve in armed combat. They stand Clausewitz on his head: for them, peace is just the continuation of war by other means.[2]

So it will be until the peacekeepers manage to transform the way the parties see their circumstances. The parties must come to understand and pursue their interests differently than they did when they went into the conflict. Like any political process, this is accomplished only over time, in stages, and often by indirection.

Ambiguity

A good idea presented before its time is wasted—rejected viscerally by the parties, never to be revisited. The parties enter the peacekeeping stage incapable of seeing beyond their wartime interests. They have been locked in a life-or-death struggle. They worry that they may already have given up too much just to achieve a truce. They are alert for any trick, any backtracking, any potential conflict with their values or aims.

To illustrate the point, recall that it took the Middle East peace process thirteen years to make the full circle from the Camp David Accords to a second (now poignant) appearance on the White House lawn. The parties could not in 1980 conceive that which they would accept in 1993. If U.S. mediators had told the Palestinians in 1980 that they would one day sign a document recognizing the right of Israel to exist and renouncing the use of terrorism—but still would not control the West Bank or Gaza—any Palestinian inclined to accommodate such a dangerous fantasy would have been subject to attack. They would not have been alone. No Israeli politician could have survived politically pursuing a vision of Chairman Yasir Arafat standing on the White House lawn as the de facto head of a de facto state of Palestine, side by side with Israeli leaders committed to final talks on the status of Jerusalem. Nor would the parties have been alone. If Congress had been briefed in 1980 that it would thirteen years later recommit to open-ended deployments of U.S. troops in the Sinai, it would have passed a law to prevent any such nonsense.

Ambiguity is the mediator's friend. The parties constantly demand clarity but for exactly the wrong reason—so they can judge immediately whether the process is headed in a direction they must reject. There is a fine balance between the minimal clarity needed to maintain the parties' confidence and the ambiguity that keeps the parties at the table, crafting ways forward in small increments. In this, ambiguity is an asset to be cultivated actively and yielded grudgingly.

This is not a matter of hiding predetermined or predictable outcomes. Mediators who try to guess the outcome of the process generally guess wrong. The circumstances are so complex and the interests of the parties are so layered that wise mediators keep their predictions to themselves to preserve credibility. Even innocuous predictions are seen as prescriptions—that is, something being imposed. The parties have already spent much blood and treasure to resist imposed outcomes. Why should they roll over for their new mediators?

Rhetoric

The term "multiethnic" appears repeatedly in the Dayton Peace Accords. It locked the international community into a concept widely celebrated but rarely achieved even in highly developed Western countries. Although most thoughtful observers knew that true multiethnicity was a fantasy in a setting like postwar Bosnia, much scorn was heaped on the peacekeepers for their failure to achieve it. This was confusing to the parties, demoralizing for the peacekeepers, and a distraction from the more realistic and meaningful objectives then facing the international community.

This lesson the international community learned well: terms like "multiethnicity" and "multiculturalism" appeared nowhere in Resolution 1244. Achieving an ethnic modus vivendi would be challenge enough.

Exit Strategies

In Bosnia a one-year deadline on NATO's military peacekeeping mission was declared before the peace process had even begun. Potential supporters of the peace process feared they would soon be left defenseless and were loath to take risks for peace. Hard-liners were confident they could wait it out, and they simply stonewalled or went underground. Extremist power structures were preserved in each ethnic community, intimidating those considering participation in the political process. When the United States and others finally admitted the failure of the one-year exit strategy, their critics had a field day, accusing them of both incompetence and dishonesty—further undermining long-term confidence in the intervention.

Sustainability

It was clear from the outset that it would take years to fulfill the spirit of Resolution 1244—to merge all parties into a constructive political process leading to a viable peace, to overcome the worst hard-liners, to deliver public security and establish a real police force, to create durable political institutions, to cultivate a functioning economy, and to construct a lasting foundation of a civil society. In addition, it was obvious that the massive initial level of effort would be unsustainable: contributing nations could not manage such extraordinary economic burdens, military efforts, or political risks over the long haul.

UNMIK, therefore, had an additional, unstated, but fundamental objective: to render its mission sustainable. Whatever UNMIK might accomplish in the short term, it had to lay a foundation for a mission that the contributing nations would be willing to support—financially, militarily, and politically—for years and years. To keep the international community engaged, UNMIK also had to quickly whittle political conflict down to something the contributing nations believed safe to support. Getting to viable peace expeditiously was essential.

In the near term, UNMIK would have to show enough progress in conflict transformation that governments could convince their constituencies that the intervention was wise. In the midterm (i.e., the twelve to eighteen months that the initial UNMIK leadership team expected to remain in Kosovo), UNMIK had to create a realistic and convincing way forward.

Coercion

Parties to a conflict in failed states have generally been hammered far more mercilessly than the international community could ever contemplate. That certainly was the case in Kosovo. KFOR had neither the troops nor the stomach to control the population by force. KLA leaders could easily rally their local communities in any confrontation with KFOR. Hard-liners in the Serb communities could do much the same, on astonishingly short notice. As critical as KFOR was for providing a secure environment within which UNMIK could pursue a political process, it could not as a practical matter impose the will of the international community on the people of Kosovo.

The Evolving Political Strategy

The political strategy recognized Kosovo's hard realities. Battle-scarred rivals were still deeply committed to their war aims and ready to use violence to achieve them. Achieving UNMIK's objectives would require a transformation of the parties' wartime objectives. Key rivals would have to see their interests better served by moving ahead with UNMIK. Kosovo's peace would become viable only when rivals embraced political aims consistent with the peace process. At the same time, Kosovo had pressing needs, including security, relief, and basic services, locating missing persons, and jobs. These urgent demands meant that a working coalition was needed to get things running to build confidence in the mission. Eventually, a new way to compete for power through peaceful means had to be introduced as suitable conditions emerged.

Nurturing Favorable Conditions

Resolution 1244 did not take the KLA into account. Although KLA commanders acknowledged that NATO had "helped" them defeat the Serbs, they felt KFOR was now preventing them from finishing the job (of driving the Serbs out). KFOR was also perceived as supporting UNMIK's efforts to avoid a KLA-led administration. While the KLA was never a particularly coherent organization, there was a consensus among its militant leaders that they should now be calling the shots.

There was no practical option to confront the KLA militarily. Angry, tough, and well armed, they had a very real capacity for melting back into the hills, where they had extensive stockpiles and supportive clan members. Milosevic's army and special police had failed utterly in that terrain, and there was no reason to believe that KFOR would do better, especially under the critical gaze of the

UN Security Council. KFOR might try to outlaw the KLA and contain it to just its traditional heartland, but such a move would have taken more military forces than KFOR had to prevent the KLA raiding at will from its sanctuary. In any case, the establishment of a KLA enclave outside the authority of KFOR and UNMIK would have been seen as a fundamental failure of Resolution 1244 and was as unacceptable in Washington as in Moscow.

In almost every other aspect of Kosovo's transformation, KFOR provided military support for UNMIK's political strategy. In this specific area, however, UNMIK provided political support to deal with an otherwise unmanageable military threat. Because there was no military option for defeating the KLA, it was critical to develop a political framework within which the KLA could be contained and ultimately disarmed. Thus, the novel idea emerged for transforming the KLA into the Kosovo Protection Corps (KPC).

The concept of the KPC as an unarmed but uniformed nonmilitary but not quite civilian humanitarian service organization appealed differently to various players. Many of the KLA's militant leaders were only dimly interested in performing civilian activities. They saw themselves as real soldiers and believed Kosovo would need an army when NATO inevitably withdrew. The political wing of the KLA—represented by Thaci—was interested primarily in how to use the threat of an ungovernable KLA to strengthen its political hand. The demilitarization of the KLA did not have to mean an end to dreams of a national Kosovar army, and it could provide a few years' employment for thousands of young men habituated to violence and untrained for most civilian work. If not a full solution, it would clearly buy time.

Most of the negotiating was done by KFOR for two reasons: the KLA respected soldiers and NATO's interests were most at issue. KFOR consulted UNMIK, because the KPC would have to succeed at least nominally as a part of the interim civil administration UNMIK was striving to set up. Key capitals were consulted within the NATO framework, however, not via the United Nations, where Russia would obstruct anything short of the complete obliteration of all remnants of the KLA.

It took the charismatic presence of General Wesley Clark, then Supreme Allied Commander Europe, to bring the KLA military leaders to closure. But it took the combined weight of London, Paris, and Washington to persuade the UN Secretariat not to block the arrangement. The United Nations could not accept the wisdom of the arrangement, and the Secretariat was for some time quite bitter toward UNMIK. In terms of UNMIK's little-country calculation, this was a small price to pay to avoid certain failure in transforming political conflict.

Although formation of the KPC did not eliminate the capacity of individual KLA leaders to make mischief with the political process, it delivered Thaci and the political arm of the KLA to the threshold of a new political framework. It had never been easy for Thaci to work with the KLA field commanders. Now he was no longer responsible for their performance, nor did he need to produce jobs for ex-combatants. Thaci and his circle were now free to focus on personal ambitions, as politicians do, within a framework that UNMIK and others could begin to shape for the peaceful competition for power.

In September 1999 the KLA began its conversion to the KPC. Just three weeks later, the Kosovo Democratic Progress Party (PDK) announced its formation as a party with Thaci as its president. Most of the regional groupings that had served as the KLA's political network were consolidated into the PDK, with the remainder gravitating to the Alliance for the Future of Kosovo (AAK) party of Ramush Haradinaj, the only other senior KLA leader who appeared to harbor political aspirations.

Overall, the demilitarization of the KLA was a key element in nurturing favorable conditions for moderating political conflict. Other efforts included improving dire humanitarian conditions, providing basic services, shaping public support for the peace process, and cultivating the acquiescence of influential local leaders.

Mediating Conflict Incrementally

From the outset, a key element of UNMIK's mediation effort was bringing a full range of leaders into a political process that would transform conflict. Initial progress toward establishing an all-parties council was encouraging. When even the most tolerant Albanian representatives were unable to repudiate the murders of fourteen Serb farmers, however, even the most moderate Serbs abandoned the process entirely.

With an all-parties approach impossible, UNMIK decided to focus on the Albanian rivals. The Serbs could not be expected to rejoin a political process until they were guaranteed greater security and a meaningful role. None of that would be possible until the Albanian rivals were part of a stable and effective UNMIK-led interim civil administration.

In these first months, the Albanian factions were too concerned about outflanking each other to work with UNMIK. Thaci was forceful and demanding but had little experience and no apparatus, and he had not demonstrated a credible commitment to anything like democracy. Rugova's LDK had far more adherents, along with years of experience in providing basic social services and running elections. The LDK was by nature passive, however, and Rugova was out of the country and mortally afraid to return.

UNMIK could not simply pick a winner. The PDK would not accept being sidelined; choosing the LDK would clearly initiate a civil war. Neither the majority of Albanians nor the international community could countenance simply anointing the PDK, so undemocratic was its image. If UNMIK were to make peace in Kosovo, it would first have to make peace among the Albanians.

The mediation process that UNMIK devised was initially intended to better align political and military tasks. UNMIK's five-step concept also proved flexible, however, as a strategic planning tool for transforming local confrontations to achieve specific outcomes. It also served as an analytic tool to help understand how receptive the parties might be or simply where the process stood.

At the risk of vast oversimplification, it can be said that most successful mediation processes run through five steps:

- *Establish contact.* Initial communications are often indirect, via the mediator or other intermediaries. The parties need not necessarily be in the same room, country, or frame of mind. These communications need not be substantive—it is often better if they are not. The importance lies simply in the fact that the parties have acknowledged the existence of each other.

- *Build confidence.* The first gesture is often unilateral. It is not a random act of kindness, and it does not commit the party to anything further. The gesture can be easily broken off or reversed, and does not, in itself, require either party to change position or conviction. If reciprocated, it can stimulate imagination, but gestures may be exchanged a number of times before either party is comfortable doing anything more.

- *View interests in a different light.* Parties can only act in what they believe to be their interests. The parties enter this process with the same interests they pursued in war. They can act differently only if they begin to see their interests differently. With confidence enhanced by reciprocated gestures, a mediator encourages the parties to take a fresh look at their interests. Often, a single leader on one side begins to respond to a drumbeat not heard before. It does not necessarily matter much what interest is served—political ambition, family interests, security for the next generation, or personal prosperity. It only matters that the leader begins to wonder if that interest might be advanced by dealing with the other party.

  Note that the process has not so far induced any tangible change in circumstances, and neither party has done anything to materially alter the terms of the conflict. So far, the process has consisted of little more than gestures and speculation. At best, it has generated a bit of hope and some constructive appetites.

- *Take risks.* A party to a conflict rarely goes toward peace intact. Some of its factions are always more intransigent than others. Often, the hard-liner feels that perpetuating the conflict is essential to security, influence, or personal prosperity. The party's leader reaching out to the rival party suddenly discovers that he has put himself at risk and may now have less to fear from the former enemy before him than from the hard-line friends he is leaving behind.

- *Consolidate.* If leaders on both sides feel they can manage the new risks they are creating, they are free to service their newly reassessed interests. Gains are somehow formalized—whether by shaking hands, signing a treaty, permitting free passage, exchanging prisoners, returning property, or perhaps just meeting again, this time in public.

Note also that the mediator may at this point face a backlash. Often, the effort of reaching agreement has exhausted all goodwill on both sides. The leaders of the two sides now must convince their respective constituents that they got the better of the other, even as they angrily fret that they gave too much to get too little. The mediator may be the only one feeling good about events—and not for long, because the cycle must start all over again to advance the process incrementally toward the mission's objectives.

It is also interesting to note the parallels between this five-step mediation process and the concept of five stages of grief (denial, anger, bargaining, depression, and acceptance). This parallel was entirely unrecognized at the time but adds a useful dimension. Many of the actors in such a drama are going through grieving processes—for lost loved ones, comrades, neighbors, homestead, territory, privilege, prestige, wealth, or ideals. A shrewd mediator will bear in mind that the capacity of the parties to reexamine their own interests seems to depend at least in part on their capacity to cope with many layers of losses.

The incremental nature of the process and the simplicity of a five-step approach made it easier for UNMIK and KFOR to work together, even at the lowest organizational levels. A local UNMIK official and company-grade KFOR commander might determine that opening a certain road—currently in a no-man's-land between hostile Albanian and Serb villages—could facilitate refugee returns to some area miles away. Having agreed on what they would like to achieve, they could walk backward along the five steps, working out what risks have to be taken by whom, and how KFOR and UNMIK might minimize and mitigate those risks. By then, it would be clear who would need to see interests in a fresh light, who would need to be encouraged by confidence-building gestures, and who would need to be put in contact in order to kick off the process.

This simple planning template turned out to have much larger utility in transforming political conflict. Applying it in a broad way to the challenge of creating an all-parties process gave UNMIK enormous strategic flexibility. Once the larger goal was clear, the smaller challenges were easier to assess and address. Anything that would advance the larger goal, even a little, was probably worth doing. And the five-step approach made it relatively simple to craft a viable ministrategy.

UNMIK's incremental approach reduced the need for a grand master plan for transforming political conflict. In settings such as Kosovo, detailed road maps are divisive and extremely labor intensive. They are also usually wrong. UNMIK's willingness and ability to work incrementally and opportunistically, conducting multiple step-by-step processes in many different places, at many different levels, concurrently, helped it take advantage of opportunities as they arose—and avoid being weighed down for very long by any one disappointment.

This point deserves to be underscored. No grand master plan could possibly have been agreed on in any of the forums available to UNMIK—neither the Secretariat, nor the Security Council, nor the Balkans Contact Group could have achieved consensus around any detailed plan—at least not in any time frame useful to UNMIK. Happily, UNMIK's little-country resources were too meager to attempt anything so ambitious. UNMIK thus learned one of its most important lessons: if it is clear where one must go, many paths can get one there. Small opportunities are readily exploited. False starts are easily abandoned. Progress accumulates without sacrificing ambiguity.

UNMIK's managing guidelines had now emerged in sharp relief:

- *Avoid early crippling failures*—such as by averting a KLA rebellion, preventing starvation or winter exposure, curbing ethnic slaughter, forestalling hostile popular sentiment against the mission, or restoring basic services through effective civil administration.

- *Make the mandate sustainable*—for instance, by establishing a viable all-parties political process, establishing a working interim civil administration under UNMIK authority, and generally building a climate of tacit consent for UNMIK's many other economic, legal, social, and security challenges.

- *Cement international support*—by achieving specific milestones championed by key capitals (e.g., drafting a constitution or holding elections) and reducing the burden on the international community (e.g., generating revenue or enabling KFOR troop reductions).

UNMIK would now fan out, pursuing its broad objectives on many fronts at the same time. Management of the central political challenges—constructing an all-parties process and assuring international support—remained highly centralized, drawing heavily on Bernard Kouchner's political gifts. Much of the rest of UNMIK's work was often more decentralized, however, and often entrepreneurial.

Building a Working Coalition

UNMIK needed to get an interim civil administration up and running without delay. This compelling task required that UNMIK make its own peace with each of the parties. Almost no one welcomed UNMIK or accepted its mandate to administer Kosovo. Insecure as they were, most Serbs rejected UNMIK viscerally. Many Albanians saw UNMIK usurping powers of governance they had bought in blood. Those with public-sector experience resented the notion that UNMIK would administer at all. "We are not a banana republic!" they snarled.

Progress was sought individual by individual, institution by institution: contact was made, confidence was built, interests were reconsidered, and risks were taken. Consciously or not, the five-step approach played out again and again. The mediation effort was not always initiated by UNMIK; UNMIK was sometimes approached rather aggressively by some other party or interest.

The Families of the Missing, for instance, were quite hostile at first, and UNMIK retreated, wary of insatiable demands. When the Families attempted to spring a major protest, however, Bernard Kouchner went to the marshaling point, personally led the march to UNMIK headquarters, and then mounted the steps to thunder that he was as outraged as they were at the lack of information about their loved ones, committing UNMIK to work with the Families to get as much information as possible. He was criticized for taking on responsibilities outside UNMIK's mission, and that commitment cost UNMIK much time and money over the next eighteen months. However, the effort neutralized in Kosovo a force that had been extremely disruptive in Bosnia and earned goodwill that paid UNMIK handsome dividends later.

Kouchner and UNMIK went through a similar sequence with virtually every significant Albanian player. Thaci was open to communication but was soon angry that Kouchner might also reach out to Rugova. Rugova, psychologically shattered by the war, was reluctant even to communicate. UNMIK negotiated security arrangements with KFOR so that Rugova could at least feel safe enough to be on the ground in Pristina. Only then could UNMIK begin exploring contacts between Rugova and Thaci.

It took weeks of communication, confidence building, and reassessment of interests to bring the two face to face. Each worried that meeting the other would diminish his standing with his own constituencies. The first meeting was ugly, but it was an increment of progress in itself.

The whole process was repeated just to get another meeting. Rugova was wounded and passively aggressive. Thaci was angry and impatient and acted out his insecurities aggressively. Neither believed he could work with the other—or should have to. Kouchner had to reestablish confidence with each separately, and then between the two sides.

To that point, UNMIK's mandate to administer was still highly theoretical —UNMIK lacked the working-level skills and the financial resources to actually run Kosovo on a day-to-day basis. UNMIK's credibility required it to promptly fulfill the administrative mandate of Resolution 1244 to show progress to an impatient and skeptical international community. And it had to accomplish that by political means, because coercion was not a practical option. UNMIK also had shed the expectation that it would directly administer Kosovo, because the international community could not begin to meet, let alone sustain, such a burden.

Ultimately, Thaci and Rugova joined a trilateral agreement with UNMIK that established the Joint Interim Administrative Structure (JIAS). The LDK's demonstrated capacity to deliver social services was put back into service, with the PDK creaming off an agreed-on portion of responsibility, all under an UNMIK umbrella. Crucially, they also agreed to dissolve any parallel party-based administrative structures not explicitly integrated into the UNMIK-controlled JIAS.

In the meantime, UNMIK quietly kept up communications with Serb moderates. Although the Serb moderates were deeply skeptical about the intra-Albanian peace process, the establishment of the JIAS served as an important confidence builder in itself. As the Serb moderates worked their way through a wrenching reexamination of their community's interests, they were hectored and threatened by Serb hard-liners. Ultimately, leaders representing a portion of Kosovo's deeply conflicted Serb population took a seat in the JIAS.

As a "little country," UNMIK could take some quiet satisfaction. Looking back at months of difficult mediation, the mission realized that progress had been remarkably steady. It had taken three months to get Thaci and Rugova into the same room and another three months to get them to sign the same piece of paper: the JIAS agreement. It took another three months or so to actually put the JIAS into operation as a functioning civil administration (e.g., with offices, organizations, staffs, and so on). Serb moderates entered the JIAS about three months after that.

The JIAS could well have taken other forms. Given other players, UNMIK might have achieved a JIAS-type arrangement more quickly, or done without it. But UNMIK had established a kind of interim civil administration, and that alone reassured capitals about UNMIK's prospects. It had not required direct coercion, although protection of the risk-taking parties proved to be a major undertaking. Burden sharing with the parties, especially the LDK, made the arrangement relatively sustainable. And it provided a reasonably stable platform for the elections that followed roughly three months later.

The experience also reinforced UNMIK's confidence in its overall strategic approach to transform political conflict—pursuing its overarching objectives through multiple, concurrent layers of opportunistic step-by-step ministrategies while consciously avoiding cumbersome and divisive comprehensive master plans.

Containing Obstructionism

Other challenges remained much less malleable. UNMIK was not able to bring Serbs north of Mitrovica into the process in a meaningful way. Those Serbs could not conceive that their cultural and security interests would be better served in an Albanian-led administration, and they preferred to struggle as an impoverished satellite of Serbia.

The future of Serbia was as far outside UNMIK's mandate as was the contentious issue of Kosovo's final status, but Milosevic's presence put UNMIK's entire mission under a pall. UNMIK repeatedly reminded key capitals that Resolution 1244 could only buy time. Albanians would tolerate limbo for only so long —three to five years in UNMIK's estimate. Any resolution of Kosovo's status required Serbs—led by Serbia—to reexamine their long-term national interests, and that could not happen while Milosevic and his ilk controlled Serbia. If the international community wished to avoid another round of conflict in Kosovo, the "Milosevic problem" had to be resolved, and promptly.

Highlighting this external factor was a natural little-country response, both to energize a solution to which UNMIK could not contribute directly and to avoid being scapegoated if the international community failed to act.

Obstructionism from internal forces was also a serious, yet predictable, threat to the transformation of conflict in Kosovo. It came from all sides, particularly in the beginning before mediation efforts could gain traction. Powerful war-hardened militants chose to oppose the peace process because it undermined their illegitimate power and illicit sources of wealth.

Thus, the establishment of civil administration and other institutions was not in itself sufficient to achieve viable peace. Entrenched power structures persisted in opposition. To prevent obstructionists from blocking Kosovo's political transformation, they had to be constrained and, if necessary, removed. Containment of obstructionism required a strong relationship between UNMIK and KFOR.

Coercive action was reserved for particularly egregious cases where UNMIK and KFOR could be confident the coercion would not fail. When necessary, UNMIK had authority to impose "executive detention" or employ a "preemptive strike," and working closely with KFOR, UNMIK could leverage the military's capability to defeat extremists and develop civilian policing capacity. These efforts are a primary focus of the next two chapters.

Channeling the Competition for Power

As political conflict moderated, UNMIK was able to make progress in transforming Kosovo's competition for power. Elections provided both an inducement to reexamine personal interests and an expression of the result. Rather than being viewed as a single culminating event, elections were regarded as part of the process of transformation. Working in partnership over several electoral cycles, international and local officials sought to channel the competition for power from bullets to ballots, at which point local officials could safely supervise elections themselves.

Some capitals preferred to move directly to national elections. UNMIK strongly preferred municipal-level elections first—to give the electorate experience and to season officeholders. The OSCE and most of the Europeans would not contemplate elections until they could be conducted perfectly—more out of concern for the OSCE's reputation than out of any consideration for transformation of political conflict in Kosovo. UNMIK strongly preferred the earliest possible elections at the municipal level, out of concern that delay would give time for behind-the-scenes thuggery to reshape the political battlefield at the local level. Some capitals—especially Moscow—saw elections as a troubling step toward independence and simply wanted to avoid them for as long as possible. There ensued a distracting multicornered contest to determine the timing and office level of the elections, in which Albanians played only a small role. UNMIK drew deeply on its little-country diplomacy and ultimately carried the day on the more critical point—municipal-level elections—and helped forge consensus on timing that proved satisfactory.

By the summer of 2000, the climate was increasingly favorable for elections: the demobilization of the KLA continued to hold; the interim civil administration was functioning; international civil police, bolstered by freshly trained Kosovar recruits, were beginning to stabilize the streets; and many Albanians were beginning to envision a better life. The parties were also behaving politically. Thaci, for instance, was in no rush to go to elections. When his PDK was established, it had little popular support, and he wanted time to build political machinery and popularity. Starting from an assumption a year earlier that he deserved power and would take it by force, he had come a long way.

When candidates kicked off their public campaigns, however, political violence spiked, raising concerns that the decision to hold elections might have been premature. UNMIK and KFOR had contingency plans to protect candidates and reacted quickly to stabilize the political climate—in part by applying intense personal pressure. The spate of incidents subsided within a couple of weeks, and campaigning continued almost uninterrupted. There would have been little UNMIK and KFOR could have done if the violence had persisted, as dispersed, clandestine, and personal as it was. The fact that it subsided so quickly suggests that the initial judgment was correct—a broad reassessment of interests really had taken place; most Albanians were now invested in a political process leading to a viable peace, leaving the thugs more isolated than many observers had expected.

Municipal elections came in October 2000, sixteen months after the war had ended. Voting proceeded in a remarkably calm fashion, with massive participation by Kosovo's Albanian electorate: roughly 700,000 of some 900,000 registered voters turned out. Kosovo's Serbs did not participate, however, and other ethnic minority voting was negligible. Rugova's LDK party won 58 percent of the vote, and Thaci's PDK won 27 percent. Twenty-one municipalities would be run by the LDK and six by the PDK, with the three largely Serb municipalities remaining under UNMIK supervision, as before. The PDK grumbled ominously but accepted the results and the offices.

The successful aftermath of this first election suggested that Kosovo, on the way to transformation, had moved in the direction of a viable peace. The fall of Milosevic shortly after the municipal elections in Kosovo contributed greatly to the climate for political progress. In provincewide elections the following year, UNMIK brought the minority Serb community into the process as participants in the provisional institutions of self-government.

UNMIK's strategy to transform Kosovo's political conflict evolved as progress was achieved. It did not unfold according to a detailed master plan. Instead, UNMIK adapted the strategy along five interdependent lines of effort: nurturing favorable conditions, mediating conflict incrementally, building a working coalition, containing obstructionism, and channeling the competition for power into nonviolent political processes.

PROCESSES AND RESOURCES

A political strategy proceeds not in isolation but in the context of progress in related efforts to establish public security, rule of law, and a legitimate and sustainable economy. Effective processes must be established to integrate these efforts, both among international actors, as discussed in chapters 3, 4, and 9, and with local constituencies, as described below.

Processes

Joint Planning in a Genuine Civil-Military Partnership

UNMIK needed to create joint civil-military planning mechanisms. Everything touched by the joint planning process had to be tested against the deceptively simple standard, Does this action advance larger political objectives?

A genuine civil-military partnership emphasizes the needs of both parties. As discussed in chapters 3 and 4, civilian political managers must grasp the need for military commanders to be given achievable missions. Civilian officials must also anticipate military requirements early enough to permit military planners to complete their deliberate planning cycle. On the military side, commanders must accommodate the political managers' need to maintain ambiguity and take an incremental approach to make gains in political moderation. Civilian officials and military commanders need to meet in the middle, not just to coordinate—they need to meet as genuine partners.

Consultative Mechanisms

Political managers need to maximize participation by all communities and parties within a diverse and conflicted political landscape. At higher levels, a formal consultative process including the leading factions can be useful. Obstruction must not be rewarded. For instance, if some leaders fail to participate (and a few may walk out in protest from time to time), minutes of meetings can be provided and implementation can proceed to the extent possible, keeping the door open to those who want to join. Once the JIAS was established, it was clear to most rival leaders that it was in their best interests to participate in deliberations with UNMIK about the direction Kosovo's interim administration was headed.

Resources

Interim Funding

The delivery of basic public services, such as water, electricity, and trash collection, is an urgent priority. Credibility and popular consent for the mission's authority will be at issue. UNMIK had to employ upward of fifty-five thousand local civilians to repair and operate utilities, provide care in hospitals, teach in schools, and so forth. Until it could establish internal sources of public revenue, such as customs fees or other local taxes, UNMIK had no means to pay salaries. Finance ministers in potential donor nations initially resisted direct grants to support its budget, arguing that it might "create a dependency." Had this resistance not been overcome, UNMIK would likely have failed.

Qualified Civilian Professionals

UNMIK's unprecedented mission to establish a civil administration created an immediate need for a large number of technically qualified professional civilian staff to provide policy oversight, operational direction, and training to local public servants. This was a severe challenge that the UN Secretariat was ill suited to address. UNMIK staffing levels remained alarmingly low throughout the first year. By the spring of 2000, when the standard six-month contracts were due to expire, UNMIK's capacity to supervise the JIAS was at risk. UNMIK used the crisis to persuade the United Nations to permit the mission to hire directly from the field rather than rely on the cumbersome system required by the UN Secretariat in New York.

Information on Influential Political Figures and Power Structures

A UN mission cannot operate an intelligence service, but it does need detailed information on influential political figures who have to be persuaded to join the peace process. Potential obstructionists must be carefully judged to find opportunities to bring them along as well. An accurate personality profile and background information about a political leader's sources of power are needed to understand the complex political dynamics within his or her party. UNMIK exploited the partnership with KFOR to gain some information, especially security-related intelligence. The mission also quietly leveraged the personal connections of members of the mission. However, the information passed along related chiefly to force protection and was rarely insightful or timely enough to assist UNMIK's mediation requirements.

Regulatory Authority Provided in the Mandate

One potent resource immediately at UNMIK's disposal was the power to issue regulations. Use of this authority was constrained by limitations on the capacity of UNMIK and KFOR for enforcement and by the finite ability of UNMIK's Office of Legal Affairs to draft and coordinate proposed regulations with UN Headquarters. Nevertheless, regulatory authority was adequate to serve as a powerful inducement for local political leaders to participate with UNMIK in dialogue and consultative mechanisms. Over time this authority was instrumental in putting many of the building blocks in place to complete the "intelligence-to-incarceration continuum" that ultimately was needed to begin dismantling the power bases of irreconcilable obstructionists.

CONCLUSION

When UNMIK began its mission in June 1999, neither the Serb nor the Albanian community had relinquished its war aims. The future political status of Kosovo remained a casus belli, although resolution of that issue was outside UNMIK's mandate. The withdrawal of Milosevic's repressive security forces had precipitated a second dimension of conflict: a vicious internal struggle for power among rival ethnic Albanian factions. Entrenched in both ethnic communities were criminalized, war-hardened power structures that implacably opposed the UN mandate,

Figure 5.1. Viable Peace: The Turning Point in Moderating Political Conflict

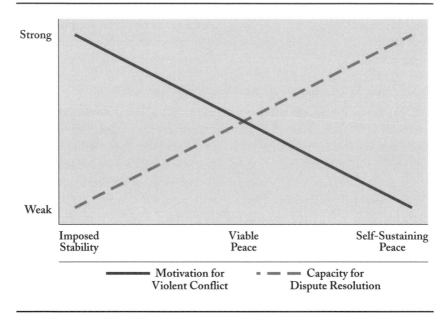

relying on violence, intimidation, and illicit sources of revenue to sustain their obstructionism. There was little peace to keep when UNMIK and KFOR entered the scene.

Within twelve to eighteen months, UNMIK had to make its mandate sustainable, avoiding crippling failures at the outset while working toward a broad measure of support for a political process leading to a viable peace that would take years to play out. It also had to cement the support of key capitals by reducing the massive military, economic, and political burdens that UNMIK represented.

UNMIK consciously avoided any detailed road map to drive its political strategy. Instead, the mission identified its most critical little-country interests in advancing the peace process and set about pursuing them through multiple, concurrent, and incremental efforts. Pursuit of these interests traced along several lines of effort, including nurturing favorable conditions for the peace process by demilitarizing the KLA, advancing an incremental mediation effort across the various layers of conflict, building a working coalition, containing obstructionism, and channeling the competition for power into nonviolent political processes. UNMIK generally avoided announcing goals, preferring to allow progress to accumulate. Above all, the mission sought to establish a loose framework for, and a climate conducive to, the economic, legal, social, and security activities that supported (and profited from) political progress toward a sustainable peace process.

As suggested in chapter 1, peace becomes viable when violence-prone power structures have receded and a balance of power has been constituted in favor of legitimate institutions of government. To accomplish this, the political strategy aims to reduce the motivations for continuing violent conflict while simultaneously nurturing the capacity of domestic institutions to resolve conflict peacefully. The thrust of UNMIK's political strategy was to help war-hardened rivals see their interests better served when they embraced political aims consistent with the peace process and pursued them through peaceful means in a legitimate competition for power. As portrayed in figure 5.1, viable peace is a decisive turning point in the transformation of conflict

- from intolerant, zero-sum confrontations in which incentives and payoffs for continued violence persist,

- to a system of governance where competition for power can be conducted through nonviolent processes.

Substantial progress has been made in Kosovo in the direction of a viable peace. Although the quest remains unfinished, the attainment of viable peace is within the grasp of those who continue striving to complete the process of conflict transformation.

✦ ✦ ✦

Editors' Postscript

As made clear at the outset of this chapter, the author's goal has been to illuminate aspects of UNMIK's activities during the first eighteen months of its mission. The following postscript, written by the editors of this volume, outlines developments that occurred after the author's departure from Kosovo.

Capacity for Dispute Resolution

During its first year, UNMIK established the foundation for political accommodation among rival Albanian factions. First, the two leading Kosovo Albanian leaders, Hashim Thaci and Ibrahim Rugova, were convinced to begin a dialogue, out of which emerged a power-sharing agreement—the Joint Interim Administrative Structure—intended to get an interim civil administration in operation.

The transition to democratically elected local governance began in ethnic Albanian communities with municipal elections in October 2000. Power began to be exercised by elected officials, as opposed to de facto parallel structures.

The political conflict between Kosovo's Serb and Albanian communities continued unabated, however, as epitomized by the divided city of Mitrovica. Public tensions and violence plainly revealed that conditions for moderating the white-hot Serb-Albanian conflict were not ripe. The demise of the Milosevic regime in October 2000 did, though, begin to open possibilities for broader participation in the peace process by Kosovo's Serb community.

The Constitutional Framework, promulgated in May 2001, articulated the governing competencies that would be put into the hands of the Provisional Institutions of Self-Government (PISG) and those that would be retained by UNMIK after general elections in November. UNMIK negotiated an agreement with Serb representatives that Kosovo Serbs would participate in the elections and in the new provisional government.[3] The evenly divided outcome of the election led to an Albanian-dominated coalition government made up of the LDK and parties formed by ex-KLA leaders.[4] With only 22 of the 120 seats in parliament and two ministries, Kosovo Serbs had a voice but no real power. Executive functions began to be transferred from UNMIK to Kosovo's provisional government, a process that was completed by the end of 2003, to the extent permitted under the Constitutional Framework.

Although these institutions provided the ethnic Albanian political class with experience in resolving issues among themselves, disputes over matters of concern to the Serbs were still handled as zero-sum affairs. This situation led to the withdrawal of the Serb coalition from parliament on several occasions and to a partial boycott of the October 2002 municipal elections.

The division of power between UNMIK and the PISG also irritated Kosovo's Albanian politicians and prompted periodic Albanian calls for a further transfer of competencies. Under the Constitutional Framework, however, authority over security matters, rule of law, and treatment of minority communities was to be retained by UNMIK pending the determination of Kosovo's final political status. Furthermore, any steps taken to transfer greater authority might suggest a tilt toward independence and could jeopardize the participation of the Serbs in the nascent political process. Thus, the longer Kosovo's political status remained in limbo, the greater grew the prospects for friction between UNMIK and the PISG over the transfer of governing powers.

Motivation for Violent Conflict

The international policy that was adopted to resolve this dilemma stipulated that the process to determine Kosovo's final status would be predicated on assurances of the preservation of the multiethnic composition of Kosovo's society. Articulated by SRSG Michael Steiner in April 2002, this "Standards before Status" policy identified eight core areas where benchmarks would have to be met: functioning democratic institutions, rule of law, freedom of movement, sustainable returns of the displaced, minority rights, economy, property rights, dialogue with Belgrade, and the conduct of the Kosovo Protection Corps. According to Steiner, "only the fulfillment of these standards will give the International Community confidence that Kosovo is ready for substantial self-government. The fulfillment of these standards is also necessary to remove the causes of future conflict—and to make Kosovo a normal European society."

While this policy was intended as a way to move toward resolution of the Serb-Albanian conflict, for eighteen months no plan was developed by UNMIK to promote attainment of the standards. Ambiguity about the goals that had to be met and the absence of a working partnership with the PISG to attain them created a widespread popular perception that this policy should really be called "Standards to Prevent Status."

In a bid to energize this process, U.S. under secretary of state Marc Grossman announced in November 2003 that progress would be reviewed in mid-2005. If sufficient advancement had been made by then, the diplomatic process of resolving Kosovo's final status should commence. In December 2003, UNMIK produced a refinement of Steiner's eight standards that specified the thresholds that would have to be met and provided indicators for measuring progress. UNMIK and the PISG worked in partnership to develop a joint implementation plan that would be reviewed on a quarterly basis by the Security Council and the Balkans Contact Group (France, Germany, Italy, Russia, the United Kingdom, and the United States) before the 2005 review date. The precise timing and nature of the process to determine Kosovo's final status remained to be determined, however.

The Unfinished Quest for Viable Peace

As the mission approached its fifth anniversary, continuing uncertainty over Kosovo's future generated increasing frustration among all communities, hindering attainment of a viable peace. Kosovo's undefined political status also deterred international investment, thereby contributing to economic stagnation. Together these conditions seriously eroded the strength of Kosovo's coalition for peace. Interethnic incidents in mid-March 2004 allowed extremist networks to incite demonstrators into a rampage, and for two days Serb communities and UNMIK facilities throughout Kosovo were besieged. However, while the toll in lives lost (nineteen), homes rendered uninhabitable (some seven hundred), and Serb religious sites desecrated or destroyed (thirty-six) was chastening, it was far lower than the very heavy toll in deaths and destruction exacted by the 1999 war.

As of late 2004, neither of Kosovo's internal political conflicts had yet been fully transformed into disputes that could be reliably resolved peacefully by its emerging institutions. Until Kosovo's political status is determined and accepted by Serbs and Albanians, peace will remain unviable, fragile, and dependent on extensive external involvement. UNMIK's mandate was to create conditions, including substantial self-governance, that would permit the status issue to be addressed in due course. The essence of UNMIK's political strategy to transform Kosovo's internal conflicts remains to support those who support the peace and to oppose those who oppose it. Ultimate success in achieving a viable peace, however, depends on the involvement of external powers to promote the resolution of Kosovo's final political status.

NOTES

1. As a rival group to the KLA, FARK was purportedly funded by former Kosovo prime minister Bujar Bukoshi. Also advocating independence for the province, it was the defense force of the parallel Kosovar government and was made up of Albanian Yugoslav former officers. See International Crisis Group, *Who's Who in Kosovo,* Balkans Report no. 76 (Pristina: International Crisis Group, August 31, 1999).

2. As Clausewitz famously declared in his 1832 classic study of war, "war is simply a continuation of political intercourse, with the addition of other means." Carl von Clausewitz, *On War,* ed. and trans. Michael Howard and Peter Paret (New York: Alfred A. Knopf, 1993), 731.

3. Agreement on Co-operation between Yugoslavia and UNMIK, November 5, 2001.

4. The Democratic League of Kosovo (LDK) won forty-seven seats, the Kosovo Democratic Party (PDK) thirty-six seats, the Serb Coalition Povratak (KP) twenty-two seats, and the Alliance for the Future of Kosovo coalition (AAK) eight seats. The National Movement for Liberation of Kosovo (LKÇK), the New Democratic Initiative of Kosovo (IRDK), the Justice Party (PD), the Albanian Christian-Democratic Party of Kosovo (PShDK), and the People's Movement of Kosovo (LPK) each won one seat.

6

Securing a Viable Peace

Defeating Militant Extremists—
Fourth-Generation Peace Implementation

Ben Lovelock

On June 12, 1999, as the first Kosovo Force (KFOR) contingent was prepar-
ing to enter Pristina, the capital of the province, KFOR commander General
Sir Michael Jackson made contact with the commander of the British battalion
there. "Pretty dodgy, sir," was the battalion commander's assessment of the situ-
ation. General Jackson asked how the commander intended to deal with the
chaotic situation that confronted him, and this prompted the battalion com-
mander to seek the general's advice. "Just imagine you're in Belfast," was General
Jackson's response. Instantly, the battalion commander fully understood how he
was to go about his mission.[1]

THE CHALLENGE

This battalion commander and others like him found themselves surrounded by
a state of near anarchy as the first elements of the NATO-led KFOR moved into
the war-torn territory. While they conducted a "relief in place" of Serbian security forces[2] in a largely successful attempt to avoid a security vacuum,[3] they found
conditions that were reminiscent of other conflicts they had experienced.

The Security Context

From the beginning, Kosovo's security situation was volatile and dangerous.
Although Serb military and police forces withdrew on schedule, KFOR found
Kosovo's public security institutions completely shattered. There were no police,
judges, or jails to provide law and order. The resulting "security gap"[4] provoked

a climate of lawlessness, fear, and apprehension. The crime rate mounted as wrongdoers attempted to take advantage of the fluid, lawless situation to steal property, burn houses, and extract revenge on Serbs and other minorities accused of collaboration.[5]

Amid this confusion, an inter-Albanian power struggle emerged to threaten Kosovo's internal security. Albanian paramilitary activity, ostensibly in the name of independence, became widespread as rival local factions sought dominance. While justifying its actions as meeting local security needs, the Kosovo Liberation Army (KLA) was quick to take on a public security role in an effort to seize power, consolidate its reach, and expand its hard-line power base. The KLA often acted in concert with rising Kosovar organized-crime networks that sought to exploit the vacuum in law and order.

After six months, KFOR's intensive security operations and the sheer size of the force had reduced direct threats to its military control. However, three persistent internal security challenges inhibited progress toward viable peace:[6]

- *Local interethnic violence within mixed towns and villages.* Ethnic majorities attacked their minority neighbors in assaults that primarily involved local Albanian retribution and intimidation against Serb and Roma families. Unsurprisingly, this intercommunal violence had an adverse effect on the credibility of KFOR as well as on the viability of the United Nations Interim Administration Mission in Kosovo (UNMIK).

- *Politically inspired violence by militant extremists.* Political violence emerged from two ongoing struggles for power in Kosovo. The most obvious variant involved largely Albanian militant extremists killing, terrorizing, and intimidating Serbs as part of an overall ethnic extremist strategy to drive Serbs from Kosovo. This form of violence became the most persistent threat to a secure environment in the early months of the mission. The second struggle for power was rather hidden, but no less murderous, involving a bitter inter-Albanian fight for exclusive dominance over Kosovo's political landscape. In this conflict, extremist militants of the KLA sought to eliminate the Armed Forces of the Republic of Kosovo (FARK), the rival Albanian paramilitary organization, through assassination and personal threats. Their objective was to assert sole KLA control over Albanian villages and towns. Both of these violent struggles severely undermined the peace process. As this political violence became more sophisticated over time, it required the UNMIK-KFOR team to develop more comprehensive civil-military responses to confront it.

- *Criminal violence and organized crime.* Criminal structures took advantage of the dire public security situation and weak government institutions. These increasingly well-developed organized-crime networks, running various forms of illicit trafficking of stolen goods, contraband, and women, were working together with the armed extremist groups mentioned above.

In addition to these internal concerns, KFOR faced difficult external threats. There was a potent, continuing military capability in the Federal Republic of Yugoslavia (FRY) that had to be deterred and, in extremis, defeated. This Serb military threat was countered to a degree by a safety zone within Serbia as part of the Military Technical Agreement.[7] Nevertheless, the threat could not be ignored; in some instances, it shaped the nature of the military deployments.[8] A further complication was the employment of paramilitary, militia, and covert units on both sides of Kosovo's boundary. For example, militant Serb extremists infiltrated Ministry of Interior Police from Serbia into Kosovo, while at the same time armed KLA groups infiltrated Serbia to support Albanian insurrections in the Presevo Valley of southern Serbia and in border communities of western Macedonia. In many cases, these armed groups were linked to Kosovo's organized-crime syndicates.

Analyzing these problems, senior KFOR and UNMIK officials recognized within the first six months that the fundamental challenge to Kosovo's transformation from bitter internal conflict to viable peace was gaining an upper hand against militant extremists and demilitarizing the political and social life of Kosovo. These extremists, both Albanian and Serb, used violence and armed threats in order to intimidate for political ends and so obstruct the peace process. Because violence remained extremely potent in Kosovo's society, the effectiveness of the UNMIK-KFOR security strategy would be central to making progress. Further, because these militant extremists had exploited the volatile combination of Kosovo's ethnic hatred, political tyranny, paramilitary violence, and organized crime to solidify their power, success of the security strategy would also hinge on progress in the three other strategies for transforming internal conflict examined in this book.

The Security Objective

In Resolution 1244, adopted on June 10, 1999, the UN Security Council gave KFOR a broad mission that included a range of intrusive and coercive military and public security tasks, which implied that a forceful approach was needed. These specified tasks were designed to establish from the beginning a secure environment in support of the peace process. They included:

- Deterring renewed hostilities, maintaining and where necessary enforcing a cease-fire, and ensuring the withdrawal and preventing the return into Kosovo of Serb military, police, and paramilitary forces

- Demilitarizing the KLA and other armed Kosovo Albanian groups

- Establishing a secure environment in which refugees and displaced persons could return home in safety, the international civil presence could operate, a transitional administration could be established, and humanitarian aid could be delivered

- Ensuring public safety and order until the international civil presence could take responsibility for this task

- Supervising demining until the international civil presence could, as appropriate, take over responsibility for this task

- Supporting, as appropriate, and coordinating closely with the work of the international civil presence

- Conducting border monitoring duties as required

- Ensuring protection and freedom of movement for KFOR itself, the international civil presence, and other international organizations

KFOR's mission was further defined by other significant agreements, including the Military Technical Agreement signed between KFOR and FRY;[9] the agreement between KFOR and the KLA, known as the "Undertaking of Demilitarisation and Transformation by the UCK";[10] and UNMIK Regulation 1999/8 establishing the Kosovo Protection Corps (KPC).[11] These documents formed the "mandate" of the international security presence, guiding the operations of KFOR and providing the basis for impartial actions in support of the various tasks—principally establishing a secure environment.

From the beginning, the Security Council concluded that Kosovo needed much more than a passive show of security in support of international civilian peacebuilding activities. As a result, the council directed that both the international civilian and military components operate toward the same goals in a mutually supporting manner. In addition, it empowered KFOR to secure Kosovo from outside threats, co-opt Albanian paramilitary leaders and remove the means for them to continue the war, and assert a credible security presence using robust peace enforcement tactics to establish peace and security. This broad set of objectives was envisioned within UNMIK's overall aim to nurture a nonviolent, promising outlook throughout the territory to promote the establishment of "substantial autonomy and self-government in Kosovo."[12] The expectation was that this would create conditions favorable to resolving Kosovo's final status; however, that matter was outside the scope of the mandate afforded to KFOR and UNMIK.

Armed with this powerful mandate, practitioners determined that Kosovo's peace process needed a robust, coercive security strategy so that the combined forces of KFOR and UNMIK, including the police, could wrest power from militant extremists over time. With an intrusive security strategy, they sought to break the ascendancy of extremist paramilitary leaders who used intimidation and physical violence to preserve their power. This applied particularly to former KLA commanders, but also to Serb paramilitary groups. Therefore, these officials adopted a challenging objective: defeat militant extremists and dismantle their illegitimate parallel power structures.

THE SECURITY STRATEGY

Lessons Applied in Crafting the Security Strategy

Many UNMIK officials and KFOR commanders were veterans of previous demanding UN and NATO peace operations in the Balkans. Still others—particularly members of the British Armed Forces who had served in Northern Ireland—had deployed into intrastate conflicts elsewhere and had mounted intrusive counterinsurgency-style operations to bring stability to conflict prone societies. Facing a rising threat to the peace process in Kosovo, these seasoned practitioners applied the following key lessons from previous experience.

Tougher Situations Require a More Coercive Approach

Between the deployment of the first peacekeeping mission mandated by a UN Security Council resolution, in 1957,[13] and the late 1990s, peace operations doctrine underwent three generations of evolution. None were explicitly intended to wrest power from obstructionists if necessary through the use of coercive force.

Initially, peacekeeping doctrine sought to deal, on agreed-on terms, with the aftermath of a conventional war between states. Postured to patrol demarcation lines in relatively benign settings, the early "Nordic," or "traditional," first-generation approach to peacekeeping embraced the three fundamental principles of consent, neutrality, and the use of force only in self-defense.[14] Missions were largely confined to the maintenance of cease-fire lines and zones of separation, or the delivery of aid, and Security Council mandates needed the consent of the states involved. Under the traditional approach, military peacekeeping and humanitarian assistance activities were normally conducted as separate activities with little, if any, coordination. These first-generation operations were not concerned with addressing powerful, war-hardened obstructionists.

With the end of the Cold War in 1989, the sudden emergence of ethnic war and internal conflict in failed states created "complex emergencies" involving humanitarian crises such as were seen in Bosnia in the early 1990s. These bitter internal conflicts made new demands on peace operations and, as UN missions sought to alleviate human suffering amid ethnic fighting, second-generation operations evolved.[15] Unlike earlier situations, these hostile settings were often dominated by unruly factions who violently manipulated the situation, forcing the adaptation of the core peacekeeping principle of using force only in self-defense. Faced with frequent attacks, UN force commanders adopted a more assertive military posture and employed rules of engagement granting a more flexible use of force, particularly in the protection of humanitarian aid.

Although this second-generation approach broadened the scope for the use of force, UN commanders still avoided armed combat against organized forces of the opposing factions. Because the ethos of traditional peacekeeping based on consent, neutrality, and limited use of force only in self-defense remained deeply engrained in the approach of many troop contributors, the more assertive second-generation approach did not provide sufficient stability in hostile settings, including those in the Balkans. Furthermore, the idea of a UN mission prevailing over powerful obstructionists to transform these internal conflicts to anything like viable peace was generally seen as well beyond the scope of second-generation missions.

By the mid-1990s, as critics questioned the efficacy of UN missions, peace operations doctrine began to evolve into so-called third-generation operations. As it considered the difficult challenges posed by internal conflict, the Security Council authorized UN peace operations only when rival factions demonstrated their consent to end the fighting by meeting specific obligations for a comprehensive peace process. But such consent was usually conditional; therefore, the military role was to create the necessary security conditions for others to do their work. As suggested by a contemporary British doctrinal publication, "de-escalation and resolution involves three overlapping activities: controlling the physical violence in a conflict; producing an atmosphere conducive to the promotion of co-operation; and identifying the underlying causes and symptoms of the problem so as to facilitate reconstruction and longer term settlement."[16]

This approach required military muscle together with a willingness to use it in order to leverage consent of the rival factions. Critically, the new doctrine was enabled by an important revision in thinking about the principle of neutrality. A more appropriate concept, impartiality, emerged, meaning that the military commander was obligated to defend and uphold the Security Council's mandate by using force, if necessary, and by putting pressure on the factions to meet their commitments to the peace process.[17] This ability to overmatch opposition in these operations was termed "peace enforcement."[18]

The deployment of more capable peace enforcement forces enabled the Security Council to direct UN missions to strengthen unity of effort between their civilian and military components. This third-generation approach called for a more diverse civilian component that featured, among other activities, an institution-building role and an international civilian police assistance mission coupled with a nascent administration-of-justice training activity. (These international efforts did not involve the exercise of executive law enforcement authority, however.) In practice, these civilian elements were employed in loose coordination with military forces and were referred to in the emerging doctrine as a "composite civil-military response."[19]

A major weakness in these operations, in practice if not in theory, was that the military component remained largely separate from the civilian component, including the international civilian police element. Hence, the overall civilian effort to address the underlying causes of the conflict was weakened because it was usually disconnected from military operations. Furthermore, while third-generation operations advocated using force to defend the mandate and applied the principle of impartiality as the key determinant to guide military operations, they did not envision the defeat of militant extremists who threatened the peace process.

Going into Kosovo, seasoned practitioners in both UNMIK and KFOR anticipated the daunting security threats that had been inflamed by the Serb-Albanian war. They concluded that the third-generation approach was, for the most part, highly relevant to the successful implementation of Resolution 1244. However, the military approach called for by the third-generation model appeared to be inadequate for a peace process threatened by the hard-core militants lurking in Kosovo. They saw that Kosovo's militant extremists, who were tantamount to insurgents, would derail the peace process if KFOR did not adopt a more coercive strategy in collaboration with UNMIK's civilian police. Obviously, UNMIK and KFOR leaders questioned whether national contingents had the requisite political will and necessary tactical training to confront Kosovo's extremists. Nonetheless, British military officers in particular, recalling their operations against armed extremists in Northern Ireland and elsewhere, sought to further develop third-generation peace operations doctrine. They focused on the judicious employment of force and impartiality, along with strengthening the civil-military relationship, in order to enable the defeat of Kosovo's militants who sought to derail the peace process through violence.

Counterinsurgency-Style Operations Are Effective against Militant Extremists

British and some other commanders in KFOR recognized that Kosovo's emerging security threats called for a counterinsurgency-style approach to military operations. As Tom Mockaitis argues,

> recent intrastate conflicts . . . and traditional insurgency have certain key characteristics in common. Both types often involve both regular military and paramilitary forces operating in difficult rural terrain or in the even more challenging environment of urban areas. Combat does not occur across clearly marked boundaries. . . . The belligerents will almost certainly

employ terrorism to enforce compliance amongst their own people and to
intimidate their opponents. To combat these threats an intervention force
may be required to do everything from conducting conventional military
operations to performing police duties. Internal war also disrupts the
infrastructure of a state, requiring a comprehensive, unified effort by military forces and civilian agencies to stop the fighting, provide relief to the
victims of war, and rebuild the institutions of civil society.[20]

Counterinsurgency operations[21] are intended to defeat terrorists, insurgents, and militant extremists who seek to use political violence to oppose or
derail a political process leading to greater stability. The requirement for a comprehensive response by a broad range of actors is among the many similarities
between counterinsurgency and contemporary peace operations. "The most striking feature of British counter insurgency," observes Mockaitis, "has been its unified
approach: soldiers, police and civil administrators worked together to provide a
comprehensive solution to the problem of civil unrest."[22] The requirement for a
comprehensive strategy and civil-military unity of effort was facilitated by appointing a director of operations who would chair an operations committee consisting of "the heads of the three [armed] services, the police, the principal officers
of the administration and the heads of intelligence and psychological operations.
. . . As soon as the situation permits prominent local political leaders and others
may be co-opted . . . so as to associate the local people with the conduct of the
emergency."[23] Political calculations must predominate in such circumstances, and
therefore, *political primacy and political aim* is a key principle that clearly subor-
dinates the military role to the government's overall aims.[24]

A critical tenet of counterinsurgency doctrine is that insurgents must be
separated from the population. As Brigadier Frank Kitson has remarked, drawing
on his experiences in Malaya, Kenya, and Cyprus, "it is in men's minds that wars
of subversion have to be fought and decided."[25] The concerted application of
available civilian and military instruments under the director of operations had
as its strategic goal gaining the support of the people. Separating extremists from
their potential supporters had to be a key objective during the conduct of military
operations as well as in the design of government programs intended to improve
the lives of the population.[26]

Another doctrinal feature of these coercive operations is the absolute requirement to develop intelligence in order to prosecute operations successfully. Kitson
warns that "the main problem in fighting insurgents lies in finding them."[27] He
stresses the need for tactical commanders to absorb background information in
order to make effective operational plans against insurgents. In this context, Kitson
introduced the notion of what today are termed "intelligence-led" operations to
find insurgents. He points out that "small units carried out 'framework operations'

until they could be reinforced . . . based on the idea of keeping a few troops in an area all the time to provide some continuity and protection to the locals."[28] This activity *fixed* the insurgent by denying freedom of movement while providing access to the population in order to *find* local intelligence. Intelligence and background information obtained by operating among the population leads to specifically targeted offensive operations to *strike* against insurgents. In a peace operations context, the application of these warfighting "core functions" of find, fix, and strike is directly derived from the counterinsurgency experience.[29]

In Northern Ireland these counterinsurgency concepts had been further refined in the battle against terrorists. With a focus on "military aid to the civil authorities," a committee structure directed activities at the operational level; military cooperation with the police was extensive at all levels, chiefly to support law enforcement by providing capabilities that a police force did not normally possess. This collaboration involved joint planning, joint command-and-control centers, and joint operations. On the ground, framework operations provided the essential backdrop for intelligence-led strike operations against the terrorists.[30]

Recognizing that a counterinsurgency-style approach was appropriate in Kosovo, British KFOR commanders drew on these lessons and exploited their long-standing ability to develop working relationships with the police. Having confidence in their collective experience, they determined that many counterinsurgency operations concepts, when adapted appropriately for a UN-mandated peace operation, could defeat Kosovo's militant extremists who threatened the peace process.

The Use of Military Force Requires Legitimate Civilian Authority

The application of military force in a peace operation may go beyond the provisions of the laws of armed conflict[31] and requires an appropriate civilian legal authority in order to provide demonstrable legitimacy in support of a peace process. Counterinsurgency doctrine usefully illustrates the need for soldiers to act within the law, "although terrorists and insurgents use lawless and violent methods . . . the security forces cannot operate outside the law without discrediting themselves."[32] Within a national context, the necessary legal framework to provide this legitimacy is typically derived from emergency powers. Such powers enable the mission's director of operations to exercise wide authority in conducting the necessary intrusive security operations legitimately. In Kosovo Resolution 1244 provided such legitimacy and specifically gave the UN special representative the necessary authority. The tasks given to KFOR by the resolution provided a rationale and authority for military action; however, the resolution implied that the KFOR commander should nevertheless seek the agreement of the special representative. Given that UNMIK was mandated by Resolution 1244 "to provide an interim administration for Kosovo," the special representative was empowered to act as the legitimate civilian authority for the use of coercive force.

In the Absence of a Defined End State, Strive for Interim Objectives

The absence of a defined end state is not an unexpected feature of peace implementation. An end state may be too hard to negotiate, or resolution of a deadlocked issue may be deferred to avoid igniting more conflict. Clearly, there were a variety of possible outcomes regarding Kosovo's final status, which left the ultimate end state ill defined.

The conventional military planning process seems to be confounded by this ambiguity. However, as the first KFOR commander, General Jackson, observed, "uncertainty is absolutely part of a soldier's job; not only should we not resent it, but we should learn to embrace it."[33] Dealing with such uncertainty entails envisioning an interim set of desired conditions to focus on in the near term.[34] In Kosovo this meant estimating the interim security conditions that would permit, in part, the demilitarization of political and social life. Envisioning an achievable near-term safe and secure environment, in conjunction with UNMIK, involved defining a range of conditions for the emergence of viable peace, or, as General Jackson simply stated, to "make things better."[35]

Demilitarizing Politics Is Critical to Stability

The transformation of armed groups and the reintegration of former fighters into civilian society are critical to removing the military option from rival factions. The Brahimi Report emphasizes that "demobilization and reintegration of former combatants—key to immediate post-conflict stability and reduced likelihood of conflict recurrence—is an area in which peacebuilding makes a direct contribution to public security and law and order. But the basic objective of demobilization and reintegration is not met unless all elements of the program are implemented. Demobilized fighters (who almost never fully disarm) will tend to return to a life of violence if they find no legitimate livelihood, that is, if they are not 'reintegrated' into the local economy."[36] KFOR and UNMIK applied a unique approach for clearing this extremely important hurdle, demilitarizing the KLA by transforming it into the KPC with a civilian disaster response function. This initiative was designed to establish suitable conditions for UNMIK's political process to move forward and to allow KFOR to maintain control over the former KLA.

The Evolving Security Strategy

The evolving security strategy integrated tried-and-true counterinsurgency methods with third-generation peace operations approaches within a comprehensive framework of civilian activities in order to act decisively in securing

Kosovo's transformation. This departure set an innovative course for peace implementation efforts in Kosovo, with the intent to create the necessary political-military conditions for viable peace.

The objective of the evolving security strategy was to secure peace by defeating militant extremists and to dismantle their divergent parallel power structures, and so directly to support the political aim. The key components of the strategy involved military commanders addressing the political dimension of their work through collaborating with the civilian leadership and adopting an assertive posture using a maneuverist approach. This then provided the basis for the mounting of decisive operations conducted jointly with international civilian police to find, fix, and strike against militant extremists.

The security strategy integrated doctrinal principles of peace operations and counterinsurgency operations as *fourth-generation peace implementation*. Undertaken within a Security Council mandate, this approach to peace implementation relied heavily on local intelligence for NATO-led "green-helmeted" troops to apply coercive force by conducting counterinsurgency-style operations with international civilian police officers at the direction of UN officials—a fresh, nononsense approach for securing peace in a tough situation.

The security strategy was founded on unprecedented collaboration between the special representative of the secretary-general (SRSG) of UNMIK, Bernard Kouchner, and the KFOR commander, General Sir Michael Jackson. Their tight bond set the stage for a truly comprehensive response. Unlike with Bosnia, where the military purposefully set itself apart from the civilian effort, the UNMIK-KFOR leadership determined to be one unified team. The basis for this approach was an appreciation, universally shared, that the military operation could not succeed without achieving substantial parallel progress in Kosovo's political transformation. Underwritten as policy by NATO, this approach was further manifested by General Jackson's outward commitment to SRSG Kouchner's personal leadership and priorities for the overall mission. Significantly, the policy was cemented by UNMIK and KFOR operational planners, who set up a joint civil-military planning structure for major security operations—these joint planning activities were performed shoulder to shoulder by civilian and military planners inside KFOR headquarters.

This approach produced a genuine unified partnership, a bond that proved to be substantially more than "unity of effort" and arguably only a step away from full "unity of command."[37] This relationship between the UN civilian leadership and the green-helmeted KFOR command can be termed a truly comprehensive response, and it served as the bedrock for all other efforts to prosecute the UNMIK-KFOR security strategy. In an effort to ensure that this unified partnership was replicated at all levels, General Jackson directed that such joint structures be established by all the multinational brigades of KFOR.[38]

The evolving fourth-generation security strategy, adopted by the British Armed Forces in particular, was not easy to undertake, but it was largely effective. The strategy included four central features that established a decisive military role in Kosovo's transformation:

- *Adopt an assertive posture with a maneuverist approach.* An assertive mental posture is needed by military commanders to anticipate potential trouble and to disrupt the extremists' overall cohesion and capacity to obstruct the peace process. Commanders need to adopt a maneuverist approach that turns chaos and disorder into an advantage by taking the initiative and placing violent extremists at risk.

- *Seek reliable local intelligence.* There is an absolute requirement to develop local intelligence in order to prosecute security operations successfully. By gathering intelligence among the people, military and police leaders can anticipate danger and, using intelligence-led operations, locate potential perpetrators and prevent them from doing harm to the peace process.

- *Mount framework operations in support of civil authority.* To bring violent paramilitary extremists to justice, military commanders must collaborate with civilian law enforcement authorities. Military commanders also should mount framework operations in close collaboration with civilian police forces in order to develop local intelligence to locate extremist threats, limit their freedom of action, and, when directed, defeat them before they can harm the peace process. The explicit activities of framework operations, drawn from the counterinsurgency paradigm, include *find*, by developing the necessary local intelligence to feed offensive activities; *fix*, by denying militant extremists freedom of action or movement while at the same time protecting essential friendly groups and facilities; and *strike*, by using coercive action against militant extremists to bring them under arrest or disrupt their activities.

- *Ensure joint military-police planning and action.* Effective framework operations call for joint military, special police, and civilian police operations from beginning to end. In mounting these coercive operations, soldiers, police, intelligence analysts, civilian officials, and public information experts must work closely together as an integrated team.

These central features of fourth-generation peace implementation were nested within the broader context of the UN peace operation and were underpinned by seven wider principles applied in both the civil and the military domains. Given that coercive military actions to find, fix, and strike at militants were part of the international community's current political, legal, and moral framework for UN peace operations, the principles, described below, set conditions for the legitimate implementation of the security strategy:

- *Act at the direction of legitimate civil authority.* In UN peace operations, only an appropriate civil authority can direct coercive operations against militant extremists. Authorized under Chapter VII of the UN Charter, Security Council Resolution 1244 vested UNMIK's special representative with executive powers to enforce compliance with the law.

- *Enshrine the primacy of the peace process.* UNMIK's civilian leaders and some KFOR commanders directed that overall priority be given to the primacy of the peace process as military, police, and civilian officials sought to secure peace. UNMIK's civilian officials made political, legal, and moral judgments regarding all coercive actions in support of the peace process. By applying this guiding priority, the military effectively harnessed its assertive role in defeating militant extremists to set conditions for Kosovo's transformation to viable peace.[39]

- *Pursue interim conditions for viable peace.* In determining the specific interim security conditions necessary for Kosovo's transformation, military planners were guided by Resolution 1244. Envisioning these interim conditions for viable peace enabled civilian and military leaders to set practical near-term priorities for civil-military efforts to be taken against threats to the peace process.

- *Design composite civil-military objectives.* UNMIK and KFOR senior leaders eliminated sharp distinctions between military objectives and civilian objectives by designing composite civil-military objectives that would bring about the interim conditions. Because these interim conditions became driving priorities for all officials, the composite civil-military objectives reinforced the need for a joint civil-military planning structure for operational planning and coordination to deal with Kosovo's multifaceted threats to the peace process.

- *Separate extremists from their popular constituency.* Substantial popular support for the peace process, including joint military-police operations against militant extremists, is necessary to get the job done without inciting adverse public disapproval and outright opposition. This involves winning the hearts and minds of the people and is best achieved by demonstrating that "peace pays" in tangible and material ways. When military commanders apply force, sustaining popular support requires applying only the *minimum amount of force necessary* to accomplish the mission.

- *Neutralize the threat of organized paramilitary conflict.* Substantially reducing the potential for organized paramilitary conflict, particularly by former KLA units, was paramount in managing down the potential for violence. Rogue KLA units could have thwarted the peace process by mobilizing and rearming former fighters. UNMIK and KFOR officials therefore sought to transform the KLA into the KPC to contain the threat of organized paramilitary conflict.

- *Operate within the law.* Civilian and military authorities must recognize that coercive operations can be undertaken only pursuant to the rule of law adapted appropriately for the conflict environment.[40] Not only is this standard important to the overall effort to build popular support for the mission; it was essential for setting an example to rising Kosovo leaders on how military and police powers should be exercised in an emerging democratic society.

These central features and principles of the security strategy set the stage for KFOR to carry out fourth-generation peace implementation to defeat militant extremists, or "all-or-nothing, total spoilers,"[41] who attempted to preserve their illegitimate power by derailing Kosovo's peace process. The key challenge was to implement this strategy effectively.

Implementation of the Security Strategy
Pursuing Interim Conditions for Viable Peace
In June 1999 KFOR commander General Jackson recognized that resolving Kosovo's final status was not possible at the early stage of the peace process; he saw the need to convey his perspective of Kosovo's future to his military commanders so that they could deal with the volatile situation on the ground. As KFOR deployed, General Jackson promulgated a set of desired interim conditions that conveyed his vision of what near-term conditions were important to attain:

> Kosovo is a province of FRY, under effective UN administration, with arrangements in place for local elections, with all refugees having returned to their homes, with ethnic communities no longer able to intimidate one another, with the UCK [KLA] de-militarized and reintegrated into society, with nominal FRY forces undertaking agreed activities within Kosovo, with a growing appreciation of the benefits of respect for the rule of law, with an independent UN appointed judiciary, and an effective UN civilian police force, with a recovering agricultural economic sector and opportunities identified for economic diversification, with increasing inward investment, and reducing inflation, thereby encouraging further normalization and improvement of conditions within Kosovo.[42]

General Jackson's projection of Kosovo's future provided a basis for a collaborative dialogue and planning process between KFOR commanders and their civilian counterparts in UNMIK about the direction in which Kosovo should be headed in the near term. It also energized efforts to establish composite civil-military objectives, leading to mutual clarification of near-term priorities.

Designing Composite Civil-Military Objectives

On achieving a consensus about the desired interim conditions, the UNMIK-KFOR team set about designing composite civil-military objectives to focus efforts leading to Kosovo's transformation. This meant avoiding sharp distinctions between military and civilian objectives. Thus, planners established civil-military objectives[43] to be achieved through joint UNMIK-KFOR efforts, an important evolution captured in fourth-generation peace implementation. Once they established these composite objectives, planners prepared operational civil-military plans outlining the many diverse tasks that various actors working together needed to complete.

The diverse tasks are illustrated by the equally diverse components that were necessary to achieve law and order in Kosovo, one of the conditions required for viable peace:

- Agree on a body of applicable law.
- Establish an effective judiciary.
- Agree on detention rules.
- Establish a detention review procedure.
- Establish an appeals procedure.
- Train forces and equip them for law enforcement.
- Set up a detention facility.
- Establish an international police force.
- Create joint policing procedures.
- Open a local police academy.
- Establish local police forces.
- Hand over law-and-order responsibilities to local police forces.

This list suggests that bringing about desired conditions for law and order involved a combination of sequenced activities performed by both military and civilian actors. No single actor could deliver the necessary conditions; instead, all had a part to play as well as an interest in the result. The list also illustrates that the military commander had to perform many roles in the establishment of law and order in Kosovo. General Jackson described achieving composite civil-military objectives as "weaving the strands of a rope,"[44] meaning that individual efforts must be woven together to create a composite response, thereby strengthening each actor's efforts.[45]

Enshrining the Primacy of the Peace Process

Resolution 1244 represented the Security Council's policy, and the custodian of this process was UNMIK's civilian leadership. Facing many destructive rivalries among various Kosovar faction leaders during the early stages of UNMIK's custodianship, Jock Covey, the principal deputy special representative of the secretary-general, asserted the principle, developed in Bosnia, of the primacy of the peace process—namely, "We support those who support the peace process and actively oppose those who obstruct it."[46] In practice, UNMIK's civilian leadership made practical political, legal, and moral judgments regarding all coercive actions that had to be taken to protect and advance the peace process. This included the determination of who should be regarded as obstructionists and when it was advantageous to confront them.

The principle of primacy of the peace process implied that implementation of Resolution 1244, as interpreted by UNMIK's leadership, would remain the overriding consideration unless the tactical circumstances, such as violence or threat to life, demanded otherwise. By applying this principle, UNMIK's civilian leadership effectively harnessed KFOR's role in defeating militant extremists, a key feature of fourth-generation peace implementation. This also implied that a non-confrontational posture toward obstructionists was inappropriate. UNMIK's political guidance was direct: the military was not to be impartial about the peace process; it was *for* implementation of Resolution 1244. This implied assertive action.

Primacy of the peace process also enabled UNMIK and KFOR's leaders to reconcile potentially confusing security dilemmas. A crucial limitation at the outset was that the international community simply did not have the capacity to respond in an evenhanded manner to every challenge to the peace process, particularly those challenges at the lower level that did not involve the use of actual violence. This is illustrated by the problem of enforcing the UNMIK regulation requiring a permit to erect war memorials, something that former KLA members were wont to do in a provocative manner adjacent to Serb enclaves. Consistent action to enforce this regulation across Kosovo would have placed UNMIK in the midst of a series of explosive confrontations that it was not prepared to pursue and could not win. Indeed, the result of assertive action in this case would have been an erosion of UNMIK's credibility and latent coercive power, an adverse outcome that would have jeopardized other objectives more central to the peace process at the time.[47] UNMIK's decisions on such matters required a degree of discretion among KFOR commanders over when to act, and they normally deferred to UNMIK's leadership.[48] This example highlights the essential relationship between political direction and military action to advance the peace process.

Adopting an Assertive Posture Using a Maneuverist Approach

It was not sufficient for KFOR simply to provide a secure context in which civilian elements could perform all other functions. This third-generation approach would have been a prescription for paralysis in the peace process. KFOR had to assume an assertive posture, in partnership with UNMIK, to neutralize militants. Major General Robert Fry, commander of Multinational Brigade (Centre) MNB(C) from August 2000 to March 2001, stressed the imperative to take active measures to shape the security environment: "If you are being supine you are tarred with the brush of failure."[49] Fry's commanders sought to secure peace through the discrete use of force and did not confuse "minimizing the use of force" with "not using force." The challenge was that it took time for UNMIK to be ready, in both political and practical terms, to fully exploit such a stance.

This assertive fourth-generation posture was achieved by adopting a maneuverist approach based on doctrine and previous experience.[50] The maneuverist approach accepts chaos and disorder and seeks to channel these to advantage. NATO's doctrine for peace support operations suggests that "they must seek to gain, and maintain, a position of advantage with which to influence the will and cohesion of opponent(s) or parties."[51] This implies an ability to maneuver in the physical dimension. As Fry has commented, "There is a great temptation in Kosovo to get tied up in static fixed tasks and forego the capacity to maneuver. [Our] pattern of patrolling and operations . . . has introduced a far greater dimension of maneuver. . . . [Our operations] create in the minds of the terrorists real doubt that they will be able to conduct terrorism and get away with it."[52] Patrolling on foot, among the population, in a purposeful yet relaxed fashion, paid dividends in this context and provided essential links with the community and knowledge of the situation together with vital intelligence.

Seeking Reliable Local Intelligence

Accurate local intelligence was an absolute requirement in mounting successful coercive security operations against militants. By tasking military and police patrols to gather intelligence among the people, planners could anticipate trouble. Then, by using intelligence-led operations, KFOR and UNMIK security forces attempted to locate and prevent perpetrators from doing harm to the peace process, rather than simply reacting to the adverse consequences of extremist violence.

An essential feature of fourth-generation operations, the quest for local intelligence was a necessary step forward, but intelligence activities were not easily accepted in this UN peace operation or within some national military contingents where second- and third-generation practices still ruled operational thinking. The Brahimi Report has addressed the almost systemic aversion to the use of intelligence in UN operations.[53] Nevertheless, gathering and sharing local intelligence among KFOR military commanders and UNMIK Police officials became a necessity in Kosovo, and it enhanced the effectiveness of security operations in ways not seen before in a UN peace operation.

Joint Planning and Action by Military and Civilian Police

Joint military and police operations were another key feature of fourth-generation peace implementation. Because UNMIK was mandated to govern, its civilian police force exercised executive law enforcement powers. Acting in close collaboration, military and police officials were able to help fill one another's critical capability gaps.

In general, the military role was to create conditions for successful police operations by providing intelligence, surveillance, security, and search capabilities that the police lacked, while the police provided the legal and evidence-gathering capabilities the military lacked. Credit for successful operations went to the police because it was their responsibility to maintain a close relationship with the population, and it was the police who would remain for the longer term. Not all international police officers appreciated the close association with the military that these joint operations required. However, in the near term, particularly in view of the uneven deployment of the police in the early months of the mission, the only way to establish an adequate security environment was through joint operations.

Campaign Planning to Achieve Desired Political Results

By early 2000 the British-led MNB(C) developed a campaign plan[54] based on General Jackson's intent to set conditions for permanent nonviolent political dialogue within Kosovo. Dialogue among Albanians and Serbs could certainly be thwarted by dangerous militant extremists from both sides. Thus, the coercive use of force would be necessary to establish an environment that would encourage moderation by leaders willing to take risks consistent with the peace process. Military planners focused on attacking the militants' center of gravity,[55] namely, "Serbian/Albanian willingness to use violence for political ends."[56] They developed key lines of operation to lay the foundation for military operations that were integrated with civilian activities to demilitarize the political landscape. These included:

- Securing the operation's own center of gravity

- Conducting local information operations

- Deterring aggression

- Neutralizing extremists

- Disrupting the transit of violence across the boundaries of Kosovo (in either direction)

- Ensuring the security of minorities

- Ensuring compliance with military-political agreements

- Breaking the cycle of impunity by assisting with the construction and management of an effective judicial and detention system

- Maximizing multinational strength

- Helping to establish viable municipal and regional administrative structures

- Establishing joint military-police command and control

- Facilitating credible elections accepted by all

- Providing access to schools, amenities, work, health care, and religion for all

- Assisting with the return of refugees and internally displaced persons (IDPs)[57]

This comprehensive approach incorporated composite civil-military objectives as planners steered clear of the narrower third-generation perspective that views some of these objectives as being well outside the military remit. Although the military was not the lead actor in many cases, even limited success would have a positive military security effect, contribute to the overall attack on the extremists' center of gravity, protect rising moderate political leaders, and so set conditions for improved political dialogue. In contemplating any military activities, MNB(C) planners applied the overarching yardstick consistent with the primacy of the peace process: "will this activity advance the political process? . . . if not, do not do it."[58] The "operational art" for military planning then became to collaborate with key civilian officials along these broad lines of operation to integrate military operations with civilian activities. This called for a sophisticated understanding of the contributions made by civilian and military actors in achieving the desired results implicit in a comprehensive approach.

In assessing the extremists' critical vulnerabilities, or centers of gravity, planners took two key aspects into account: (1) the physical dimension, or the extremists' actual military capability to commit violence, and (2) the moral dimension, or the extremists' resolve to use violence. Both aspects needed attention, and this is why the comprehensive approach proved useful. When attacking the extremists' center of gravity, military planners recognized that difficulties could arise because popular Serb and Albanian support for UNMIK and KFOR was fragile. This meant that without a comprehensive approach, planners would find it progressively more difficult to defeat the truly hard-line extremists in both the physical and the moral dimensions of the campaign.[59] In practical terms, MNB(C) employed intelligence offensively to concentrate a range of civil-military activities (including community life, security, and information operations) in order to have the desired impact on the willingness of both Serb and Albanian extremists to use violence for political ends.

Mounting Framework Operations to Secure Peace and Defeat Militant Extremists

The thrust of the security strategy was the removal of violent obstructionists who sought to derail the peace process. In implementing this decisive element, MNB(C) mounted framework operations to find, fix, and strike against militant extremists. This formed the main operative element of fourth-generation peace implementation. Most military resources necessary to mount framework operations were available relatively quickly; however, there was a limit to the effectiveness of purely military activity in the face of cunning militant hard-liners. While KFOR imposed stability and provided a power base, many civilian efforts in the rule-of-law arena were required to fill the void in establishing public security and administering justice for these militant obstructionists.

Finding. British commanders recognized that operations had to be conducted among the people in order to gain reliable local information and at the same time favorably influence the population. This approach needed a degree of sensitivity in its execution because, as Major General Fry has noted, "operations can only be drawn from links into the community—what you get from helmets and body armor is a physical barrier and a cultural barrier because you alienate the local community."[60] Furthermore, a fortress or enclave mentality driven by force protection concerns served to distance soldiers from what goes on "outside the wire."[61]

The military imperative was to operate continually among the people in order to gain an understanding of local social dynamics and other factors affecting the security situation, critical information that was not easily gained by technical means. This contact with the population had the added benefit of extending the influence of KFOR and nurturing the confidence of the people by relating to them and demonstrating that they were living in a more secure environment. Over the longer term, close collaboration among UNMIK, military, and police analysts clarified several important issues: cultural considerations, influential local leaders and personalities, local political dynamics, likely sources of political violence, activities of obstructionists, capabilities and vulnerabilities of the extremist organizations involved, and their links to local organized-crime groups. The output of this analysis became the raw material with which to develop fixing and striking options for subsequent action by UNMIK-KFOR.

Fixing. Military commanders used part of their resources to control and shape the operational environment and so to enable subsequent striking operations. On a day-to-day basis, this fixing activity limited the extremists' freedom to maneuver while protecting KFOR's freedom and reassuring the population.[62] This aspect of framework operations often yielded dividends through the arrest of suspects and the confiscation of weapons and other materiel by military patrols and temporary checkpoints.

In Kosovo fixing also applied on another level, that of demilitarization. A key aspect of the military mission was the delicate task of keeping the KLA in check. Hashim Thaci's "Undertaking" to the KFOR commander, which Thaci signed on June 21, 1999, provided for the demilitarization of the KLA after ninety days. Permanently removing the military option from KLA commanders and other Albanian warlords became a complex challenge for the UNMIK-KFOR team. Although many thousands of weapons were either surrendered or seized, the KLA effectively continued to exist as a quasi-military organization. In the face of the KLA's dogged resolve to win Kosovo's independence and become its national army, strategically fixing the KLA through this innovative approach was an essential interim objective.

If the KLA had not been fixed strategically, KFOR would have had a daunting security dilemma. Could KFOR have allowed the KLA simply to dominate the central area of Kosovo, much as it had done against the Serb police just a few months earlier? Or would KFOR have had to go into the hills to dig out these seasoned fighters? It was clear that most troop contributors to the NATO-led operation would not favor full-scale ground combat operations against these paramilitary fighters, who, after all, were heroes to many among the Kosovo Albanian population. NATO could not sustain its intervention unless the KLA could be made to demobilize.

The solution was to demobilize and then demilitarize the KLA by transforming it into the KPC, a completely civilian organization established to deal with humanitarian emergencies and other pressing civilian needs. An UNMIK regulation established the KPC:

> The Kosovo Corps shall be established as a civilian emergency service agency . . . the Corps shall not have any role in law enforcement or the maintenance of law and order. . . . KFOR shall provide day-to-day operational direction to the Kosovo Corps. The tasks of the Corps were: disaster response services, perform search and rescue, provide a capacity for humanitarian assistance in isolated areas, assist in demining and contribute to rebuilding infrastructure and communities.[63]

The KPC proved to be an expedient means of providing a practical alternative in an attempt to eliminate the military option from Albanian factional leaders. Perhaps it amounted to a "necessary fiction for a security purpose."[64] Nevertheless, the (former) KLA had been given a role in a future Kosovo, its visibility was to be maintained, a control mechanism was in place, and, arguably, it was strategically fixed until any different role might emerge at a later stage. The ongoing task for KFOR would be to provide guidance and meaningful activity for the KPC while dealing firmly with any transgression or noncompliance.

Striking. While many of the most powerful extremists were known to the UNMIK- KFOR team through frequent contacts with the population and subsequent intelligence analysis, the ultimate challenge was to disrupt their operations, seize their weapons, and arrest them through the law-and-order dimension. These striking operations necessitated the development of credible intelligence derived through finding and fixing operations, and then the conversion of this information to admissible evidence for use in the judicial process to secure convictions.

KFOR and UNMIK officials conducted joint military and police planning to strike judiciously at militant extremists as conditions permitted. Over time, striking included a range of operations, including "cordon and search" to seize arms and illegal materials, targeted arrests, confiscation of illicit financial resources, interdiction of smuggling, disruption of training bases, and dislocation of communications. These strike operations were carefully focused, using the most appropriate security element available. In several situations, the Multinational Specialized Unit (MSU), which belonged to KFOR, and the Special Police Units (SPUs), which belonged to UNMIK, were employed to leverage their unique capabilities for these types of operations.

In September 2000, following a spate of attacks perpetrated by extremist Kosovo Serbs, a British battalion conducted a strike operation to arrest a small number of suspected individuals inside the Kosovo Serb enclave of Gracanica. Planned and prepared over several weeks, this successful operation was entirely intelligence led and successfully removed a potent threat to the peace process. The coercive use of force required many supporting efforts. Officials appreciated that politically motivated violence could be manifested in a variety of ways, including orchestrated civil disturbances. Contingency operations, therefore, such as crowd and riot control, were also planned. Further, because the aim in striking was to neutralize extremists, plans for criminal investigations and forensics also became central to their incarceration. For MNB(C), the success of these strike operations required substantial political oversight and close intelligence-military-police planning, followed by skillful tactical employment of the mission's limited capabilities and resources to get the job done.

Putting It Together in Practice. A brief example illustrates the success of framework operations in Kosovo's countryside. During the spring of 2000, while on routine patrol, a British infantry sergeant observed *(find)* at a distance some suspicious activity just outside an Albanian town. The sergeant's report led British commanders to task units to conduct specific surveillance and reconnaissance activities in order to pinpoint what was going on and control the situation in the suspected area *(fix)*. These surveillance activities revealed a possible KLA arms cache. A subsequent cordon-and-search operation led to the discovery and seizure *(strike)* of a large number of arms that, under the terms of the KLA "Undertaking," were clearly illegal.[65] The political effect of the dramatic seizure of these arms was to force the former KLA chief of staff, General Agim Ceku, the leader of the KPC, to take additional actions to rid Kosovo of other weapons, lest he be incarcerated for allowing the peace process to be obstructed by supporting a continuing armed KLA presence in Kosovo.

This operation also illustrates the conceptual planning framework referred to as "close and deep operations" used by MNB(C). Usually conducted at battalion level and below, close operations are designed to manage and control the local operating environment by maintaining contact with the population and looking for possible threats to local security. Adopting an assertive stance, such operations help to improve the security situation and promote popular consent for military activities. The purpose of close operations is to find and fix. These routine activities, conducted among the people by regular infantry troops, often with local police, formed the bulk of the daily pattern of visible surveillance operations for most troops and civilian police officers. These close operations set the stage for conducting a deep operation, if it was deemed necessary.

A deep operation seeks to achieve a decisive effect on an extremist's center of gravity.[66] Usually conducted at brigade level or higher, and planned and executed by more specialized troops and police, a deep operation is intended to find and strike at extremists directly. Once authorized by UNMIK's civilian leadership, these strike operations sought to set favorable conditions by defeating obstructionists' willingness or means to use violence.

By the spring and summer of 2002 the removal of extremist lawbreakers began to become a reality. The political situation had become propitious for their arrest and conviction. Nearly three years after KFOR's initial deployment, SRSG Michael Steiner outlined his transformation priorities to the UN Security Council, on April 24, 2002. He emphasized the decisive growth of the rule of law through an effective police force and judiciary.[67] The UN mission was in a position, he reported, to move steadily toward viable peace in the law-and-order arena as the remaining elements of the intelligence-to-incarceration continuum were in place: "now we have the instruments, we have the judges, we have enough time to prepare . . . the judicial framework has been done . . . in 1999 we didn't have the means so it was not possible to do that in a legally sound way."[68] Arrest of hard-liners was therefore possible beginning in the spring of 2002, advancing Kosovo's transformation toward viable peace.

Separating Extremists from Their Popular Constituencies

When questioned on "the magic formula" for success, General Jackson suggested that "it is just there in our collective experience. . . . It is a mixture of a firm hand but appreciating that it is not a war—the battleground is in people's minds and therefore how do you engage with that?"[69] Popular support and legitimacy were primary considerations as framework operations were conducted; these operations among the people—*not* at arm's length from the people—required the active support of local communities. Extremists had to be isolated from their likely constituencies by winning popular support, as opposed to simply gaining passive consent.

Commanders sought to mold public expectations surrounding the conduct and impact of the military presence using information operations. Because information operations overlaid all military activities, they were seen as the principal firepower available. Information operations were intended to magnify the efforts of the police and military through the promotion of truthful information to target communities.[70] In this way, the cumulative effect of framework operations, both physical and psychological, was more likely to influence local communities to support the peace process. Popular support was also shaped by providing "carrots," such as assistance or aid to mollify the effects of the use of force in local areas. Civil-military cooperation programs were used in supporting the achievement of a security effect; the withdrawal of assistance, either threatened or actual, was another effective measure.[71]

The UNMIK-KFOR team, in an evolving partnership with Kosovo's own emerging security forces, sought to manage down the role of violence in Kosovo's struggles for power. The lack of clarity about Kosovo's final status, however, meant that Albanians and Serbs continued to view political interaction with each other as a zero-sum game, and violence remained an option. The murders of three Serbs in Obilic and Serb children in Gorazdevac in 2003 indicated that violence had not been wrung out of the interethnic equation. Assaults on leading Kosovo Albanian political figures early in 2004 suggested that violence was creeping back into the intra-Albanian discourse, as well. The discovery of a 4-kilogram explosive device outside UNMIK headquarters coinciding with the visit of the head of the Department of Peacekeeping Operations in the beginning of March 2004 turned out to be a harbinger of what was to come.

News accounts on March 16 that three children from a Kosovo Albanian enclave had drowned, and unsubstantiated and ill-founded assertions by the press of Serb complicity in their deaths, set the stage for a massive popular response. The transformation of this situation into a violent rampage against Serb communities and UNMIK facilities across the breadth of Kosovo had all the hallmarks of a conscious choice.

The riots of March 17–18, 2004, have been described in the secretary-general's report to the Security Council as follows:

> The onslaught led by Kosovo Albanian extremists against the Serb, Roma and Ashkali communities of Kosovo was an organized, widespread, and targeted campaign. Attacks on Kosovo Serbs occurred throughout Kosovo. . . . A total of 19 persons died in the violence, of whom 11 were Kosovo Albanians and 8 were Kosovo Serbs, and 954 persons were injured in the course of the clashes. In addition, 65 international police officers, 58 Kosovo Police Service (KPS) officers and 61 personnel of the Kosovo Force (KFOR) suffered injuries. Approximately 730 houses belonging to minorities, mostly Kosovo Serbs, were damaged or destroyed. In attacks on the cultural and religious heritage of Kosovo, 36 Orthodox churches, monasteries and other religious and cultural sites were damaged or destroyed. The places of worship that were attacked date as far back as the fourteenth century.[72]

The dominant factors that produced the upheaval of violence in March 2004 were mounting frustration and apprehension caused by Kosovo's uncertain future status. This issue had remained stalemated since the beginning of the mission, creating an opening for extreme nationalist and violence-prone elements to reassert themselves and seize the political initiative as soon as an opportunity presented itself. UNMIK, however, was not empowered to resolve this source of conflict. It could only attempt to nurture favorable conditions that would permit key actors in the international community to begin a process of negotiation to resolve the existential conflict over Kosovo's political status.

RESOURCES

Successful implementation of this security strategy requires a formidable collection of resources, the most notable of which are listed here, along with the shortfalls experienced in Kosovo.

An Empowering Mandate

KFOR's security strategy required an assertive mandate backed by political resolve to confront Kosovo's powerful paramilitary extremist groups. However, in practice coercive operations were hampered by differing guidance from troop-contributing governments to their deployed military contingents. Coercive operations against militants varied in application from area to area, and this became a factor in restricting coercive options and slowing the tempo of intrusive military activity.

Public Diplomacy

Given that Kosovo's transformation to viable peace rested in the hands of the people, perception management was central to making progress. With "the battleground [being] people's perceptions and attitudes,"[73] the arrival of the international community raised expectations to an unrealistic level. As a first priority the international community needed to protect and project its own credibility, promote consent for its actions, and show the population that life was improving and that "peace pays," thereby diminishing popular support for militant obstructionists. Persistent effort was (and is) required in this area.

Skilled Military Units

The strategy rested on military units skilled in both peacekeeping and counter-insurgency-style operations to deal with militant extremists. Soldiers had to have an agile frame of mind and additional skills to conduct low-level patrolling and surveillance activities among the people. In addition, the military training process needed to integrate military and police capabilities in ways that fostered mutual understanding and effective joint performance to conduct find, fix, and strike operations. As Christopher Bellamy observes:

> Experience of recent operations in Bosnia, Haiti, Kosovo and Sierra Leone suggests that peacekeeping is anything but an activity for wimps. . . . local populations have most respect for peacekeepers who are also unmistakably professional soldiers, robust in their manner and well equipped. However, if forces are too heavy-handed, or remain too remote from the local population out of concern for "force protection," they lose respect—and effectiveness.[74]

Intelligence

The security strategy called for multiple types of intelligence, including human intelligence and information obtained by surveillance and other technical means. Human intelligence was not easily obtained, however, partly due to the language barrier, but also due to the prevailing climate of fear.[75] Nevertheless, multiple sources were vital for purposes of corroboration.

Special operational capabilities were needed to deal with organized criminal networks and their linkages to local power structures. This included specialist reconnaissance and surveillance capabilities on hand to perform the find function against organized crime. These capabilities needed to be backed by a theaterwide communications architecture for sharing intelligence.[76]

Figure 6.1. Viable Peace: The Turning Point in Defeating Militant Extremists

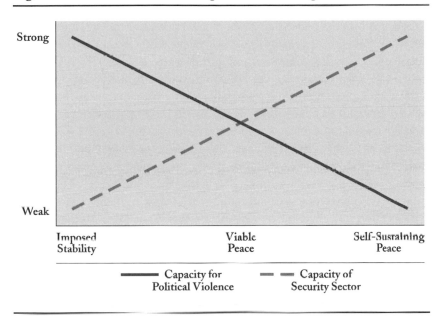

Specialized Troops and Police

KFOR needed to have specialized troops and police to conduct deep operations. The majority of operations tended to be static, close operations. Although useful in finding and fixing, these operations did not defeat militants who obstructed the emergence of viable peace. Deep capabilities were decisive to the military's success. This point is highlighted by a former KFOR commander, Lieutenant General Carlo Cabigiouso, who observed in 2001 that "the overall situation remains tense and the threat is such that KFOR still has to concentrate on its key framework tasks, the protection of fixed points, patrimonial sites and the enclaves."[77]

CONCLUSION

Kosovo's substantially improved security environment is evidence that the combination of peace operations and counterinsurgency-type principles in the fourth-generation construct have successfully enabled the military to play a decisive role in shaping the environment and defeating militant extremists in the quest for viable peace. Since June 1999, as a result of KFOR's efforts with the police, the power of Albanian and Serb militant extremists has been diminished. Despite this substantial improvement, viable peace remains elusive. The dominant reason for this is continuing indecision about Kosovo's political status. This political problem brings with it a negative impact on the prevailing security situation. Resolution of the status issue, however, is outside the mandate provided to UNMIK and KFOR. They do have a crucial role to play, though, in establishing conditions that are conducive to final-status talks.

In general terms, the security environment must be transformed, from a context that is dominated by armed groups with a capacity to use violence to destroy the peace, to a context in which armed groups are subordinated to a legitimate security sector, reintegrated into society, or marginalized. As portrayed in figure 6.1, viable peace is the turning point in the transformation of conflict when the capacity of the security sector prevails over the capacity of militant extremists to use political violence to thwart the peace process. As of 2004, this transformation had progressed but was not yet at the point where peace could be regarded as viable.

Capacity for Political Violence

For the most part, peoples' lives are better and freedom of movement has improved.[78] Numerous former KLA members involved in politically motivated crimes and some former Serb paramilitary personnel have been convicted or are awaiting trial. Areas where continued effort is required have nevertheless been emphasized in reports to the Security Council.[79] There continue to be incidents of violence with political overtones and ethnic unrest in the territory.[80] Significant caches of weapons have been discovered and seized in the border regions of Albania and Macedonia, indicating persistent illegal activities by armed extremists operating across Kosovo's borders.

Capacity of the Security Sector

Many of the policing roles initially carried out by KFOR are now in the hands of the civil authorities, and KFOR's role in these areas is diminishing as public institutions grow and strengthen. This has enabled NATO to reduce force levels. On the other hand, large amounts of contraband continue to transit Kosovo despite joint KFOR, UNMIK Police, and KPS patrols in border areas. Economic crime and corruption are also pervasive, but with increasing arrests made by UNMIK Police and the KPS. The KLA has been strategically, if temporarily, fixed through the medium of the KPC. Some KPC leaders continue to make statements portraying themselves as the nucleus of the future armed forces of a future independent Kosovo. Thus, the KPC still requires careful international oversight and direction.[81]

Addressing the security aspects of these persistent challenges to viable peace clearly requires continued endeavor. An integrated military-police posture to find, fix, and strike at criminal obstructionists as the decisive element of the intelligence-to-incarceration continuum continues to be needed. Troop contributors' restrictions on the conduct of coercive operations need to be removed, and additional specialized troops and police are required to conduct deep operations.

The Kosovo experience demonstrates above all that international security contingents must decisively address militant extremists disposed to use violence to thwart progress toward peace. Concurrently, and as a priority, the international community needs to protect and project its own credibility, promote consent for its actions, and show the population that life is improving and that "peace pays," thereby diminishing popular support for militant obstructionists.

Serious consideration needs to be given to the reality that many modern conflicts demand a fourth-generation approach if the international community wishes to bring about viable peace in countries where violence and armed conflict dominate life. The difficult and ambiguous challenges facing future military commanders in such settings demand a sophisticated grasp of effective security strategies as well as contributions made by their civilian partners to transform conflict to achieve viable peace.

NOTES

The opinions represented are the author's own and do not represent UK Ministry of Defence policy.

1. General Sir Michael Jackson (address to "An Integrated Approach to Complex Emergencies: The Kosovo Experience," a conference co-hosted by the UK MOD Joint Doctrine and Concepts Centre and Cranfield University, Eynsham Hall, UK, May 10–11, 2001).

2. General Sir Michael Jackson, "KFOR: The Inside Story," *RUSI* (February 2000): 13–18.

3. Brigadier William Rollo, interview by author, Bovington, UK, June 27, 2001. Rollo was Commander UK 4th Armoured Brigade on entry into Kosovo in June 1999. His brigade subsequently became the Multinational Brigade (Centre) (MNB(C)) and remained in Kosovo until September 1999.

4. See Robert Oakley, Michael J. Dziedzic, and Eliot M. Goldberg, eds., *Policing the New World Disorder: Peace Operations and Public Security* (Washington, D.C.: National Defense University Press, 1998), 8–16.

5. Lieutenant Colonel Richard W. Swengros, *Military Police Functions in Kosovo*, http:///www.call.army.mil/products/nftf/julaug00/swengros.htm (accessed March 9, 2001), 4.

6. Brigadier Richard Shirreff, interview by author, London, June 18, 2001. Shirreff commanded 7 Armoured Brigade, which formed the framework of MNB(C) from February to August 2000. See also http://www.unmikonline.org/press/mom/lmm160700.html (accessed February 2, 2003).

7. According to the Military Technical Agreement, the Ground Safety Zone (GSZ) was the territory within "a 5 kilometre zone that extends beyond the Kosovo province border into the rest of the FRY territory." Eleven days following the entry into force of the agreement, all FRY forces were required to complete their withdrawal to areas outside Kosovo and not within the GSZ.

8. The change of leadership in Belgrade has greatly reduced, if not removed altogether, this problem. The continuing requirement is to maintain a dialogue on mutual security concerns, not least the emergence of Albanian cross-border extremism.

9. The Military Technical Agreement was signed by KFOR and the governments of the FYR and the Republic of Serbia at Kumanovo, Former Yugoslav Republic of Macedonia, on June 9, 1999.

10. Hashim Thaci, commander in chief, Ushtria Clirimtare e Kosoves (UCK), signed the "Undertaking" on June 21, 1999.

11. UNMIK/Reg/1999/8, September 20, 1999.

12. UN Security Council Resolution 1244.

13. UNEF 1 was deployed to Egypt in the wake of the Suez crisis. It was "the first to be called a peacekeeping mission . . . it served as a precedent for all subsequent missions." Oliver Ramsbotham and Tom Woodhouse, *Encyclopaedia of International Peacekeeping Operations* (Santa Barbara, Calif.: ABC-CLIO, 1999), xi.

14. Ibid., 179.

15. See John Mackinlay and Jarat Chopra, *A Draft Concept of Second Generation Multinational Operations* (Providence, R.I.: Brown University, Thomas J. Watson Jr. Institute for International Studies, 1993).

16. *Peace Support Operations,* UK Joint Warfare Publication 3-50 (JWP 3-50), 1998, 2–4.

17. For a description of how this principle of impartiality was introduced, see Christopher Bellamy, *Knights in White Armour: The New Art of War and Peace* (London: Pimlico, 1997), 250–251.

18. See *Peace Support Operations,* JWP 3-50, 1-1; and *Peace Support Operations* NATO Allied Joint Publication (AJP) 3.4.1, July 2001, 2–4.

19. *Peace Support Operations* JWP 3-50, 2–5.

20. Tom Mockaitis, *Peace Operations and Intrastate Conflict: The Sword or the Olive Branch?* (Westport, Conn.: Praeger, 1999), 128–129.

21. For the purposes of this work, "insurgency" means "the actions of a minority group within a state who are intent on forcing political change by means of a mixture of subversion propaganda and military pressure aiming to persuade or intimidate the broad mass of people to accept such a change." See UK Army Field Manual, Army Code No. 71596 (parts 1 and 2), *Operations Other Than War: Counter Insurgency Operations, Part 1: The Concept and Practice of Insurgency* and *Part 2: The Conduct of Counter Insurgency Operations,* 1995, annex A, A-3 and part 1, 1-1.

22. Mockaitis, *Peace Operations and Intrastate Conflict,* 134.

23. UK War Office Code No. 9800, *Keeping the Peace,* January 7, 1963, 24–25.

24. UK Army Field Manual, Army Code No. 71596 (parts 1 and 2), part 2, 3-3.

25. Frank Kitson, *Low Intensity Operations* (London: Faber and Faber, 1971), 31.

26. UK Army Field Manual, Army Code No. 71596 (parts 1 and 2), part 2, 4-1.

27. Kitson, *Low Intensity Operations,* 99–100.

28. Ibid., 134.

29. *Peace Support Operations* JWP 3-50, 3–8.

30. UK Army, *Operations,* UK Army Doctrine Publication, vol. 1 (ADP 1), DGD&D [Director General Development and Doctrine] 8/34/46 Army Code No. 71565, June 1994, paragraph 0227.

31. However, NATO's peace support operations doctrine effectively dodges this issue: it was not possible to agree on a definitive text because national approaches to this issue vary. See *Peace Support Operations,* AJP 3.4.1, July 2001, 4B-2.

32. UK Army Field Manual, Army Code No. 71596 (parts 1 and 2), part 2, 3–13.

33. Jackson, "KFOR: The Inside Story," 14.

34. *The Military Contribution to Peace Support Operations,* UK Joint Warfare Publication 3-50, 2nd ed. (JWP 3-50), June 2004, 2-8–2-9.

35. Jackson (address to "An Integrated Approach to Complex Emergencies").

36. United Nations, *Report of the Panel on United Nations Peace Operations* ("The Brahimi Report"), A55/305, S2000/809, August 21, 2000, 7–8, http://www.un.org/peace/reports/peace_operations, 9.

37. This necessary partnership was also called for by external commentators at the time. See United Nations Association of the United States of America, *Peacekeeping at the Brink: Recommendations for Urgent International Action on Kosovo—a Report of the Project on Finding Solutions for Peace in Kosovo* (New York: United Nations Association of the United States of America, February 2000), 3.

38. Lieutenant Colonel T. C. G. Hunter, Royal Marines, discussion with author, December 4, 2002. Hunter was a KFOR planner in Kosovo from June to September 2002.

39. Jock Covey, interview by Len Hawley, San Francisco, November 6, 2002.

40. Ibid.

41. Stephen Stedman, "Spoiler Problems in Peace Processes," in *International Conflict Resolution after the Cold War,* ed. Paul C. Stern and Daniel Druckman (Washington, D.C.: National Academy Press, 2000), 178–224.

42. Major-General Andrew Ridgway, former chief of staff, Headquarters KFOR (lecture to the Higher Command and Staff Course, UK Joint Service Command and Staff College, March 15, 2001).

43. Ibid.

44. Jackson (address to "An Integrated Approach to Complex Emergencies").

45. The context for, and practicalities of, developing this approach have been examined in detail elsewhere. See Stephanie Blair, *Weaving the Strands of the Rope: A Comprehensive Approach to Building Peace in Kosovo* (Halifax, N.S.: Dalhousie University, Centre for Foreign Policy Studies, 2002).

46. Authors' workshop discussion, Washington, D.C., July 22–23, 2001; and Covey, interview by Hawley, November 6, 2002.

47. Colonel Mike Dziedzic, USAF (ret.), former UNMIK strategic planner, discussion with author, Washington, D.C., October 16, 2001.

48. Major General R. A. Fry, MBE, interview by author, Portsmouth, UK, July 16, 2001. Fry was former commander, MNB(C), from August 2000 to March 2001.

49. Ibid.

50. According to Lieutenant Colonel G. Messenger, "The maintenance of a manoeuvre capacity was a fundamental tenet of our operations in Kosovo—it made the difference." Lieutenant Colonel G. Messenger, chief of staff, 3 Commando Brigade Royal Marines, discussion with author, May 1, 2001. Messenger's brigade formed the framework of MNB(C) from August 2000 to March 2001.

51. *Peace Support Operations,* AJP 3.4.1, 6-2, 6-3.

52. Brigadier R. A. Fry, commander, MNB(C), quoted in *Jane's Defence Weekly*, September 27, 2000, 40.

53. UN, *Report of the Panel on United Nations Peace Operations.*

54. A better term might be "operational planning in the absence of strategic direction." It is difficult to see how a true "campaign planning" process can be adopted at brigade level. Nevertheless, the methodology provides a planning framework for the conduct of security operations.

55. Warfighting doctrine describes the importance of centers of gravity: "We should try to understand the enemy system in terms of a relatively few centers of gravity or critical vulnerabilities because this allows us to focus our own efforts. . . . However, we should recognize that most enemy systems will not have a single center of gravity on which everything else depends. . . . It will often be necessary to attack several lesser centers of gravity or critical vulnerabilities simultaneously or in sequence to have the desired effect." U.S. Marine Corps, *Warfighting*, Doctrine Publication 1, U.S. Marine Corps PCN 142 00000 600, June 20, 1997, 47.

56. Shirreff, interview by author.

57. These were subsequently reconceived as ensure security against external threat; provide secure internal environment (stop interethnic killing; protect key sites, mobile operations, and operations against crime [with police]); transform KPC (train on non-military lines, build infrastructure, raise its standing, ensure compliance, seize weapons); conduct civil-military operations (support infrastructure, hearts, and minds); and carry out information operations (overarching activity). Messenger, discussion with author.

58. Major R. Williams, former COS, 7 Armoured Brigade (lecture at Joint Doctrine and Concepts Centre, Shrivenham, UK, March 14, 2001); and Covey, interview by Hawley, November 6, 2002.

59. Messenger, discussion with author.

60. Fry, interview by author.

61. Colonel Vincent J. Goulding, "From Chancellorville to Kosovo: Forgetting the Art of War," *Parameters* (Summer 2000), http://carlisle-ww.army.mil/usawc/Parameters/00summer/goulding.htm (accessed February 19, 2001), 6.

62. Messenger, discussion with author.

63. UN, UNMIK/Reg/1999/8, 1

64. Jock Covey (speaking by telephone link at "The Quest for a Durable Peace in Kosovo: Evolving Strategies of Peace Implementation" conference, cohosted by the Association of the US Army [AUSA] and the International Institute for Strategic Studies [IISS], IISS London, UK, December 5–6, 2002).

65. Williams (lecture at Joint Doctrine and Concepts Centre, Shrivenham, UK).

66. See also NATO's peace support operations doctrine, which provides such a framework based on the warfighting model. AJP 3.4.1, 6-1 and 6-2.

67. UNMIK, Press Release UNMIK/PR719, April 24, 2002, www.unmikonline.org/press/2002/pr719.htm (accessed on August 28, 2002).

68. SRSG Michael Steiner, interview by Radio Free Europe, "UNMIK Must Accelerate Its Plans in the Wake of 11 September," September 3, 2002, http://www.rferl.org/nce/features/2002/09/02092002152308.asp (accessed September 3, 2002).

69. Jackson (address to "An Integrated Approach to Complex Emergencies").

70. Steven M. Seybert, "Shaping the Environment for Future Operations: Experiences with Information Operations in Kosovo," *Lessons from Kosovo: The KFOR Experience*, ed. Larry Wentz (Vienna, Va.: Command and Control Research Program Publications, July 2002), 311.

71. Messenger, discussion with author.

72. *Report of the United Nations Secretary-General to the Security Council, March 30, 2004,* S/2004/348 (April 30 2004).

73. General Sir Michael Jackson, interview by author, Joint Doctrine and Concepts Centre, Shrivenham, UK, February 14, 2001.

74. Christopher Bellamy, "Combining Combat Readiness with Compassion," *NATO Review* 49, no. 2 (Summer 2001), http:/www.nato.int/docu/review/2001/0102-02.htm (accessed August 9, 2001), 9–11.

75. Lieutenant Colonel E. Foster-Knight, former officer commanding 111 Provost Company Royal Military Police, interview by author, Joint Doctrine and Concepts Centre, Shrivenham, UK, July 5, 2001.

76. Ibid.

77. Lieutenant General Carlo Cabigiouso, "An Assessment of the Situation in Kosovo: A Commander's Perspective," *RUSI World Defence Systems* 3, no. 2 (July 2001): 123.

78. Kosovar community leader, conversation with author, Brussels, Belgium, September 11, 2002.

79. *Report of the United Nations Secretary-General on the United Nations Interim Mission in Kosovo*, S/2002/1126 (October 9, 2002), S/2003/113 (January 29, 2003), and S/2004/487 (June 11, 2004).

80. The potential for trouble remains, however: "Although the level of ... violence declined ... it could easily surge again." *Report of the United Nations Secretary-General on the United Nations Interim Mission in Kosovo*, S/2004/487 (June 11, 2004).

81. *Report of the United Nations Secretary-General on the United Nations Interim Mission in Kosovo*, S/2002/1126 (October 9, 2002), S/2003/113 (January 29, 2003), and S/2004/487 (June 11, 2004).

7

Safeguarding a Viable Peace

Institutionalizing the Rule of Law

*Halvor A. Hartz and Laura Mercean,
with Clint Williamson*

*Soon after the United Nations Interim Administration Mission in Kosovo
(UNMIK) took over the prison in Prizren, a local Kosovo Liberation Army
(KLA) chieftain swaggered into the international prison warden's office, threat-
eningly making demands and asking if the warden knew who he was. After
that failed to impress the warden, he returned the next day with some armed
friends. The warden told them to wait right there while he summoned the
Kosovo Force (KFOR) to detain them. They quickly disappeared.*

THE CHALLENGE

The Context

Far from sustaining the rule of law, public security institutions in Yugoslavia traditionally operated as instruments of state control. After Milosevic deprived
Kosovo of its autonomy in 1989, the Interior Ministry, police, court system, and
prisons, along with the intelligence apparatus, functioned as mechanisms of harsh
and humiliating subjugation of the ethnic Albanian community that made up the
vast majority of the population. Hundreds of ethnic Albanian police resigned,
and many were convicted en masse in show trials in 1991 and 1994.

For self-preservation, ethnic Albanians organized a parallel system of education and health care, with Ibrahim Rugova emerging as leader. Some former police officers organized the Union of Expelled Officers, which sought to call international attention to their oppressive treatment while also providing a covert intelligence network, headed by one of Rugova's relatives, that operated throughout the Milosevic period. Although Rugova's parallel "government" did not attempt to substitute for the Serb-dominated justice system, the informal code (or Kanun) of Leke Dukagjini[1] did provide a limited alternative for dispute resolution, especially in rural areas. Traditionally, when disputes would arise, clan leaders or other eminent members of society would be chosen to resolve the matter according to guidelines put forth in the Kanun. By 1989 these practices were confined primarily to isolated rural areas. The formal legal system provided little recourse or justice for Kosovo Albanians. Overall, the legal system was characterized by impunity for those in authority and avoidance by the powerless, to the extent that this was possible.

When Milosevic capitulated to NATO in June 1999, the agreement that ended the NATO bombing campaign required all security forces of the Federal Republic of Yugoslavia (FRY), both military and police, to withdraw completely within a few days.[2] A de facto regime imposed by the KLA rapidly filled the vacuum (except for the Serb-dominated pocket north of Mitrovica and a few enclaves where Serb internal security forces exerted a controlling influence). Although this caused a reversal in fortune for Kosovo's Serb and Albanian communities, the common denominator was an absence of the rule of law.

The KLA had been formed out of regionally based familial networks, and even during the war a bloody rivalry raged within the KLA to determine which clans would dominate in the postwar period.[3] One of the most prominent of these noncombat-related killings was the assassination of the designated minister of defense for a free Kosovo, Ilir Konushevci, in northern Albania in late 1998. When Serb forces departed, the remaining KLA commanders asserted their writ over their traditional localities. They regarded themselves as victors and Serbs as the vanquished, resulting in widespread brutality and the displacement of about half the ethnic Serb population.[4] Vengeance was not the only motivation. Those who had taken up arms also felt they were entitled to acquire the spoils of war. Forcibly vacated Serb dwellings were often occupied by former KLA combatants. Albanian ethnicity was no guarantee of respect for property, however, and much valuable real estate was expropriated by KLA members for personal use. Shopkeepers and small business owners were often compelled to pay protection money. Kosovo Serbs clustered in enclaves and in the three northern municipalities that bordered Serbia, where parallel power structures surreptitiously supported from Belgrade continued to hold sway. The most notorious situation evolved in

Mitrovica, where paramilitary "bridge watchers," supported by the Serbian Ministry of Interior and reputed to be involved in smuggling, prostitution, extortion, and protection rackets, operated with total impunity. They sought through various means to prevent UNMIK from extending its writ north of the Ibar River into the predominantly Serb portion of Mitrovica. These included the orchestration of unruly demonstrations and the intimidation of Serbs disposed to cooperate with UNMIK.[5]

The persecution suffered by Kosovo's Serb community obscured another conflict taking place simultaneously. The KLA leadership harbored intense hostility toward the parallel government that Ibrahim Rugova had headed during the previous decade. Thus, as the KLA asserted its claim over Kosovo's political and economic affairs, it was displacing not only the Serb regime. The erstwhile underground governing apparatus that Rugova and his supporters in the Democratic League of Kosovo (LDK) had presided over also came under deadly assault. In particular, this entailed settling a number of scores between the KLA and Rugova's paramilitary organization, the Armed Forces of the Republic of Kosovo (FARK). By July 1999 both the Serb administrative apparatus and the traditional Albanian parallel governmental structures had largely disappeared. A climate of lawlessness prevailed.

As refugees began streaming back to Kosovo, criminal gangs from Albania rushed in with them. The KLA had been reliant on its transnational criminal linkages for arms and as a resource base. Owing to the region's strategic location on the heroin-trafficking route running from Afghanistan into Europe, heroin shipments had been used to finance the purchase of weapons for the KLA. A lack of border controls after June 1999 allowed almost anything to be smuggled in or out, including drugs, cigarettes, alcohol, cars, and petrol. Cigarette smuggling became big business, both because of the high rate of cigarette consumption in Kosovo and because high taxes in Western Europe made smuggling into that market especially remunerative. Recurring reports linked ex-KLA leaders with illegal trade in cigarettes, alcohol, and petroleum products.

As late as June 8, 1999, the draft for UN Security Council Resolution 1244 did not specify which international organization would be responsible for police functions. The Organization for Security and Cooperation in Europe (OSCE) was bidding for the public security role on the strength of its recent experience with the Kosovo Verification Mission (KVM). The OSCE had already undertaken considerable advance planning, and the KVM continued to have a presence in Albania and Macedonia. The United Nations, which had largely been marginalized in the Balkans since the UN Protection Force had failed to prevent the massacres in the so-called safe area of Srebrenica and elsewhere in Bosnia in 1995, was seeking the opportunity to redeem itself in Kosovo. The United

Nations won the competition after the undersecretary-general for peacekeeping operations persuaded NATO leaders that the United Nations was the only organization with the capacity to field the thousands of police officers that would be required. He argued that the prior experience of the UN Secretariat with such tasks and its ability to recruit globally gave it crucial advantages over the OSCE. The United Nations assured NATO that it would assume responsibility for policing within three months.

Several formidable obstacles militated against attainment of this overly optimistic prediction. Chronic difficulties existed in recruiting capable police officers even for the missions already in existence. The demands in Kosovo, both in terms of the numbers and the functions involved, greatly exceeded those of any previous operation. The United Nations had never had to create an armed police force that would exercise full executive policing authority.[6] Nor was there any doctrine for this purpose or for the formed police units that would also be employed for the first time by the United Nations.[7] The United Nations was even less prepared to discharge the other functions that are essential to the rule of law, including operating a court system and a corrections service.

When Resolution 1244 was adopted, Kosovo was without police, judges, or jails to provide law and order. Even the basic infrastructure was lacking. Although the resolution called on the international military presence to ensure law and order, the real challenge was to *create* it in the first place out of an anarchic social environment. As William O'Neill observes in *Kosovo: An Unfinished Peace*, "Court buildings looked as if a plague of locusts had swept through, scouring the grounds for anything valuable and leaving broken windows and ripped-out electrical sockets in their wake."[8] The main prison at Dubrava, with a capacity for 1,200 inmates, had been bombed during the air campaign and was unusable. A massive public security gap awaited the international intervention.

The Objective

UN Security Council Resolution 1244 assigns responsibilities relating to the rule of law to both the "international security presence" (KFOR) and the "international civil presence" (UNMIK). Paragraph 9 charges KFOR with "ensuring public safety and order until the international civil presence can take responsibility for this task."[9] KFOR's mandate also includes "supporting, as appropriate, and coordinating closely with the work of the international civil presence."[10]

UNMIK's role is defined in paragraph 11 of the resolution. It is tasked with "maintaining civil law and order, including establishing local police forces and meanwhile through the deployment of international police personnel to serve in Kosovo."[11] In a July 12, 1999, report describing how this mandate would be implemented, the secretary-general stated that "two main goals will define UNMIK's law and order strategy in Kosovo: provision of interim law enforcement services, and the rapid developement of a credible, professional and impartial Kosovo Police Service (KPS)."[12] UNMIK's mandate also includes "protecting and promoting human rights."[13] Although the resolution does not explicitly mention the judiciary and penal system, these functions are implied, because UNMIK's duties include "performing basic civil administrative functions where and as long as required."[14] The July 12, 1999, report dealing with implementation of Resolution 1244 specifically cites "administration of courts, prosecution services, and prisons" as core functions of UNMIK's Judicial Affairs Office, and the revival of the judiciary and penal systems, along with the police, as vital to establishing the rule of law.[15]

As the mission progressed, the objective evolved as well. When Michael Steiner became special representative of the secretary-general (SRSG), he made the rule of law one of his top priorities. In his April 24, 2002, address to the UN Security Council, he stated, "We are also enhancing capabilities to effectively combat organized crime, terrorism, and corruption."[16] Steiner established benchmarks by which progress was to be measured. The performance standards expected of local institutions were impartiality, prosecution of suspected criminals, and a fair trial for accused. The context in which these institutions operated also had to be transformed; organized crime networks had to be disrupted and extremist violence had to be effectively deterred.[17]

Resolution 1244 does not define the "rule of law," but essential components are evident from the passages cited above. Public safety and civil law and order are specific concerns. Previously, political disputes in Kosovo had been resolved through the use of intimidation, coercion, and brutality. Institutions responsible for the rule of law (police, judiciary, and corrections) would have to begin functioning effectively and impartially if future disputes were to be resolved through peaceful rather than violent means. The emphasis on human rights in UNMIK's mandate expanded the purpose beyond "law and order" to include justice. For peace to be enduring, all parties to the conflict would need to perceive the judicial process as being able *and* willing to protect their fundamental rights, no matter which group happened to be ascendant politically. This is the most basic attribute of the rule of law—that no one can be immune from punishment for violating the law, no matter how wealthy, powerful, or dangerous the individual may be, and no matter what privileged group he or she may belong to. This is also the bedrock on which viable peace must be constructed in a society that has been lacerated by internal conflict.[18] These concepts were incorporated into the "Standards for Kosovo" issued by UNMIK in December 2003.[19]

THE STRATEGY

Lessons Applied

The international community had established a score of peace missions since 1989 that involved police or rule-of-law components. Several precepts stemming from those previous experiences, especially the mission in Bosnia, were influential in shaping the international response to Kosovo. The following were central to the strategy that evolved there.

- *Capacity building should be holistic.* One of the fundamental lessons derived from peace operations in El Salvador, Haiti, and Bosnia is that a holistic approach should be taken to establishing the rule of law.[20] In Kosovo, international planners generally understood that it would be necessary to develop local capacity not merely for policing but also for the judiciary, penal system, and legal code.

- *The mandate should provide adequate authority.* The Bosnia experience taught that the authority provided in the mandate must be commensurate with the magnitude of the task involved. The International Police Task Force (IPTF) in Bosnia was unarmed and had no authority under the Dayton Peace Accords to engage in law enforcement activity. Nor was any authority initially provided to discipline police misconduct or to reform the legal code, judiciary, or penal system. In contrast, Resolution 1244 endowed the SRSG with the equivalent of sovereign powers, which included the right to appoint and remove officials and to legislate by issuing regulations and revising the existing legal code. UNMIK Police had executive authority to enforce the law.[21]

- *International integration of effort is essential.* Programs and activities directed at institutionalizing the rule of law in Bosnia were fragmented among various autonomous organizations and programs. The creation of the pillar structure in UNMIK was a step in the direction of bringing greater coherence. Responsibility for training and capacity building was assigned to the OSCE. UNMIK Police were responsible for law enforcement and subsequently for field training and supervision of the graduates of the OSCE police school. Responsibility for re-creating and administering the local judicial and penal systems was assigned to the UNMIK Department of Judicial Affairs, which, in turn, was assisted and monitored by the OSCE. The need for KFOR to support and coordinate closely with UNMIK was specified in Resolution 1244.[22]

- *An international crowd-control capability may be necessary.* Implementation of the Dayton Peace Accords was difficult in the beginning because of a gap in capabilities between the NATO-led Implementation Force (IFOR) and the IPTF. IFOR was able to use lethal force, whereas the IPTF was unarmed. This left the mission vulnerable to civil disturbances. Ethnic extremists became proficient at exploiting this gap through the use of what came to be called "rent-a-mobs." Eventually NATO responded by deploying a Multinational Specialized Unit composed primarily of Italian carabinieri. The unit's nonlethal crowd-control capability and doctrinal understanding of how to deter and defuse public disorder helped to close this peace enforcement gap.[23] This experience led both KFOR and UNMIK Police to incorporate this type of "specialized" crowd-control capability in their contingents.

- *End dates are counterproductive.* The Bosnia experience demonstrated the futility of declaring an exit strategy based on elapsed time as opposed to the attainment of conditions conducive to peace. Indeed, declaring an intention to depart after a fixed period actually undermines institution-building efforts by encouraging political extremists and their allies in the criminal underworld to persist in seeking to sabotage the peace process. The mandate for Kosovo avoided this defect because Resolution 1244 does not impose a deadline on the mission.

- *Capacity building should lead directly to local "ownership."* UNMIK was expected to fill a void until local capacity could be developed. The conventional wisdom indicated that ownership should be transferred to local institutions as rapidly as possible to avoid creating a dependency on the international community. Unless qualified, however, this lesson could produce dangerous outcomes. Merely building institutional capacity is insufficient when violence remains the dominant political resource and illicit sources of wealth determine who governs. The timing of the transition to local ownership must be conditioned on both the willingness *and* the capacity of domestic institutions to overcome the threats to the rule of law in their environment. Otherwise, when the withdrawal of international security forces takes place, ownership of these institutions will likely pass to a criminalized political elite, making a mockery of the rule of law.

The Evolving Strategy for Institutionalizing the Rule of Law

While previous mandates have varied, never before had internationals been given law enforcement authority (i.e., executive powers) and made fully responsible for public security and the administration of justice. UN Civilian Police (CIVPOL) doctrine, called the SMART Concept (for support, monitor, advise, report, and train), was predicated on the existence of a local law enforcement establishment to work with. In the absence of a police force, as in Kosovo, a different approach was clearly indicated. As for judicial and penal reform, neither of the international organizations involved (i.e., the Department of Peacekeeping Operations of the United Nations and the OSCE) had any relevant institutional experience on which to base their approach. A strategy for implementing this unprecedented mandate was not developed as a result of extensive studies, research, or debate among experts and practitioners. Rather, new concepts evolved largely from field experience, emerging incrementally by trial and error in response to the exigencies of the mission.

Institutionalizing the rule of law was initially regarded primarily as a matter of *establishing capacity*. The assessment provided by the secretary-general on July 12, 1999, for example, states, "The security problem in Kosovo is largely the result of the absence of law and order institutions and agencies."[24] Because the institutions responsible for order, law, and justice had collapsed, international personnel would have to provide temporary substitutes. The need to take a holistic approach was generally recognized, but international capability did not exist to put this concept immediately into practice. By default, this meant that KFOR had to establish public order, provide detention facilities, and facilitate a rudimentary judicial process. For UNMIK, the overriding imperative was to field as swiftly as possible the personnel required to begin enforcing the law, administering the judicial system, and reestablishing the prisons. UNMIK eventually assumed full custody of law enforcement from KFOR. Subsequently, as recruits for the KPS were trained and had demonstrated their competence, UNMIK Police transferred increasing responsibility to the KPS. The relationship thus evolved from an international custodianship over law enforcement into a partnership with local counterparts. With the judiciary, in contrast, UNMIK rejected proposals to include internationals in the system and opted instead to rely totally on Kosovar judges and prosecutors. When the local judiciary proved incapable of dispensing equal justice to Kosovo Serbs, international judges and prosecutors had to be inserted into the process.

Thus, UNMIK's approach to establishing institutional capacity was inconsistent. Policing evolved progressively from international custodianship to partnership with the KPS. The judiciary, however, was given greater responsibility than it could handle initially, and internationals had to assert increasing control over politically sensitive matters.

One of the salient lessons evolving from Kosovo is that it is unrealistic to expect members of a previously subjugated and brutalized community to begin administering equal justice to members of a population that they identify with their former tormentors. Under these circumstances, the relationship between international personnel and the local legal profession should begin with international custodianship over cases of an intergroup or a politically charged nature.

As the mission in Kosovo progressed, the international community came to recognize that the initial concept of establishing institutional capacity and transitioning directly to local ownership would be insufficient. This was problematic because the context, in both the Albanian and Serb communities, was characterized by a dangerously high degree of overlap between criminal and political power. The transition to a local police force, judiciary, and prison system would not be conducive to the rule of law while forces hostile to Resolution 1244 were able to assert ownership over these institutions. Only after these political-criminal power structures had been dismantled, or at least dislodged, could the institutions responsible for the rule of law operate autonomously from destructive extremist and criminal interests.

The strategy evolved, therefore, beyond the establishment of institutional capacity to include *shaping the context* by disrupting, dislodging, and, to the extent possible, dismantling the extremist networks that were bent on obstructing and subverting the peace process. The deployment of specialized crowd-control units was necessary but not sufficient for this purpose, because their capability allowed a response only to the *symptoms* of obstructionism, not the means to address the *sources*. Toward the end of 1999, KFOR and UNMIK began to develop the full spectrum of capabilities—from intelligence to incarceration—that would allow them to dismantle rogue power structures. To prosecute high-profile and politically sensitive cases successfully also required the use of international judges and prosecutors, who, unlike their local counterparts, could be protected from intimidation and coercion by extremist elements in both of Kosovo's ethnic communities.

The final component of the strategy that has evolved is the introduction of *safeguards* to ensure that Kosovo's public security entities and overall judicial processes do not again become instruments of ethnic persecution or captives of political-criminal networks. The July 12, 1999, SRSG report to the Security Council on the concept for implementing Resolution 1244 stressed that "to strengthen the rule of law in Kosovo, UNMIK will develop mechanisms to ensure that the police, courts, administrative tribunals, and other judicial structures are operating in accordance with international standards of criminal justice and human rights."[25] Safeguards are needed to provide assurance that the institutional capacity developed by the international community will continue to function in a manner that is consistent with the rule of law. Functionally, this entails the capacity to observe performance (transparency) and to sanction misconduct (accountability). Structural safeguards within the state are part of the answer. These include open elections that permit transitions in power, judicial autonomy, and independent oversight bodies with effective disciplinary mechanisms for each institution involved. Safeguards in civil society, such as a free press, are also essential.

Developing adequate safeguards inevitably takes longer than the process of building institutional capacity. Domestic safeguards will be effective, moreover, only after the environment they operate in has been transformed, as described above. Thus, there is likely to be a gap between the completion of capacity building and the point when local ownership will be conducive to self-sustaining peace. International safeguards are needed to fill this gap. As SRSG Michael Steiner argued in a November 2002 speech in Berlin, even after Kosovo's final status has been determined, "we must safeguard these investments."[26] His proposal would have the European Union perform that function after the United Nations has completed its mission, much as has happened in Bosnia with the transition to the European Union Police Mission. As local safeguards mature and demonstrate their competence, the international role can diminish. This is a crucial difference between merely providing training programs and actually *institutionalizing* the rule of law.

The strategy for institutionalizing the rule of law has evolved beyond merely *establishing the capacity of the legal system*, therefore, to include a prominent international role in *transforming the institutional context* by depriving obstructionists of impunity and erecting *safeguards on performance* in the state and society—as graphically represented in figure 7.1. The timing of the evolution to local ownership should not be governed by arbitrary end dates or exclusively by the development of local skills. The international experience in Kosovo indicates that an environment capable of sustaining the rule of law is also a fundamental prerequisite, as are reliable domestic and internationally reinforced safeguards.

The evolution of these three components of the strategy for institutionalizing the rule of law in Kosovo is described below.

1. Establishing Capacity

In mid-1999 a largely unprepared international community was fully absorbed in the process of mobilizing personnel, funds, and equipment to establish the mission. In the midst of this process, basic strategic choices were made. Among the issues that confronted the UN advance team in Pristina, UN member-states, and UNMIK officials in the field were the following:

- Should international or local personnel be relied on to establish public order and re-create the judicial and penal systems? Which functions should the international community take responsibility for on an interim basis and which should be shared with their local counterparts? Are indigenous institutions capable of immediately performing any functions in a manner consistent with the rule of law?

- What law enforcement, judicial, and penal functions would KFOR need to perform and for how long? Where were detainees to be held? In the absence of a functioning court system, what would happen when the jails were full?

- How quickly could UNMIK assume responsibility for these tasks?

Figure 7.1. Viable Peace: The Turning Point in Institutionalizing the
Rule of Law

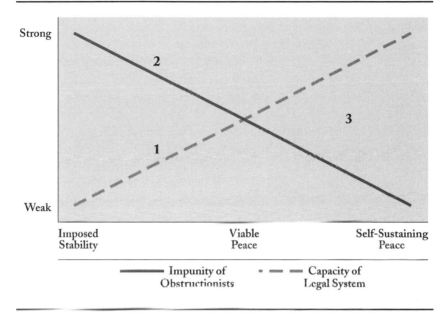

Note: The numbers 1, 2, and 3 represent the lines of action described in the following
sections: 1 = Establishing Capacity; 2 = Transforming the Institutional Context; and
3 = Safeguards on Performance.

- What body of law was going to be applied, and what revisions would be
  required?

- What resources and programs were needed to build indigenous capacity to
  establish the rule of law?

- How should the transition of responsibilities from KFOR to UNMIK and
  ultimately to the Kosovars be accomplished?

- What mechanisms were needed to ensure that the international community
  understood and took into account local cultural and contextual realities?

The responses to these questions were most often driven by the need to
respond to crisis conditions, by international political imperatives, and by the
absence of available resources rather than strategic thinking. Over time, several
key decisions had to be reversed. Through this process of trial and error, however,
the fundamentals of a strategy for establishing institutional capacity evolved.

The Police

Several factors limited the scope of strategic planning for the UN executive policing mission in Kosovo. The most basic constraint was time. There was no opportunity to conduct a premission field assessment. NATO's bombing campaign had ceased only a few days before the passage of Resolution 1244, when the law enforcement mission was assigned to the United Nations and police training was assigned to the OSCE. Planning in that context consisted of the UN Civilian Police Unit applying a factor of one police officer for every five hundred inhabitants to determine the number of international police required. That ratio, however, was based on presuppositions of a well-ordered society, not a war-torn land in anarchic conditions. It would take many months, moreover, for the member-states of the United Nations to mobilize even that underestimated number of international police.

Another barrier that had to be overcome was conceptual inertia. Previous international police missions had almost always been unarmed, and never had they assumed full responsibility for law enforcement. Because this was a total departure from the orthodox approach, there was little understanding that executive policing responsibilities would require much more than simply equipping police officers with pistols. When member-states sought to determine what "executive authority" implied, the initial response was merely to specify what a short-barreled pistol was. UN Headquarters saw no need to change any other basic requirements for CIVPOL officers. Thus, it was left to chance whether personnel with the range of specialized skills required by a major police force would turn up. The planning factors used to establish the level and type of support and equipment required were based on experience with missions in a traditional, nonexecutive role. This caused severe problems throughout the first year and longer because very basic equipment needed for public security and law enforcement, from handcuffs to automatic weapons for protection of dignitaries, was unavailable. As a result, UNMIK Police initially lacked the specialized personnel, equipment, and firepower required to perform some essential law enforcement and public order functions.[27]

According to Resolution 1244, KFOR was responsible for police functions until UNMIK was ready to take over, a process that required much longer than the three to four months that had been estimated. The United Nations had no strategy for executive policing, much less a strategy for how to share this responsibility with an international military contingent. In each of the five national zones of responsibility, KFOR military contingents applied different laws and procedures, in accordance with their respective national systems. As a result, many criminal charges initiated during this period later proved difficult for the judicial system to process.

Senior leaders of both KFOR and UNMIK recognized that their mandates (for security and for law and order, respectively) were inherently interdependent.

Effectively establishing mutually supportive operations between military and police contingents would eventually become a central focus in implementing both of these mandates. Because the British armed forces had already developed procedures for military-police operations in Northern Ireland, they approached the UNMIK police commissioner with proposals for Kosovo. The concept involved a staged approach to transferring law and order responsibility from the military to the international police. The first stage, termed "investigative primacy," indicated that UNMIK Police had assumed decision-making authority over criminal investigative activity. The second stage, termed "law enforcement primacy," referred to the full spectrum of patrolling, protection, and other policing activities.[28] The process of transfer of primacy was managed either across the entire area of responsibility of a multinational brigade (MNB)/UNMIK region or by individual municipality within the MNB/region. KFOR's Multinational Brigade (Centre) (MNB[C]), the British area of operations around Pristina, was the first to cede investigative primacy to UNMIK Police, in October 1999, followed shortly thereafter by the Gnjilane and Prizren regions. Coordination was established most efficiently in Pristina, and successful practices instituted there were adopted over time throughout most other regions. Over time, joint security planning groups were created at the central, regional, and municipal levels that managed the process of transferring responsibility in response to the circumstances in each locality. This coordination was well established in the field before ever becoming formally codified, largely because of the ponderous pace of consideration, both in New York and in Brussels, over the text of proposed agreements and protocols.

When UNMIK Police assumed full law enforcement primacy, one of the most difficult operational challenges for the police force was to overcome the prevailing culture of distrust of authority, especially of the police. This entailed reshaping the perception of the basic purpose of a police force from repression and control to assistance and service. The slow buildup of police forces worked against the mission. Early on, the omnipresent harassment and retaliatory crimes directed toward Serb and other minority communities created constant special demands that taxed UNMIK's limited security and law enforcement resources. This undermined the credibility of UNMIK Police within both the minority and the majority populations, because this often came at the expense of addressing regular policing needs. The bulk of the population, though initially jubilant, did not take long to become vocally concerned over the level of crime on the streets and to begin questioning UNMIK's capacity to control the situation.

The challenge of policing in an unfamiliar culture and language was compounded by a dispute that prevailed over the applicable law. In this context, international police were most effective when deployed in visible patrols on the streets of densely populated areas, often jointly with KFOR. To provide protection for

minority residents, fixed posts were used. Maximizing direct and personal contacts was essential not only to generate effective law and order during UNMIK's
executive mandate, but also to pave the way for the deployment of the KPS. The
basic preconditions for this were:

1. A minimum threshold of international police visible on the streets

2. Certainty that KFOR backup would be promptly available in instances of
   escalating threat so that police officers could address the public in a restrained
   and communicative manner

3. Constant reevaluation of the deployment patterns for the limited number
   of international police to maximize their psychological impact and impression of stability

In the early stages of deployment, a steady *increase* in reported incidents, whether
criminal or noncriminal, was actually an important success indicator.

The OSCE had expected to be given the mandate for policing based on its
extensive experience with the KVM. In anticipation of this, the OSCE had created
a planning team well in advance of the passage of Resolution 1244 that had conducted extensive surveys and developed a concept for reestablishing the police force.
This proved to be an important part of the success of the Kosovo Police Service
School (KPSS). Within weeks of receiving its mandate, the OSCE was recruiting experienced police trainers from member-states and establishing the KPSS.

The UNMIK police commissioner and the KPSS were under pressure to
begin training and graduating officers as quickly as possible. The first strategic
issue was to determine how the recruitment process should take place. The KLA
regarded the policing function as one of the spoils of war. As soon as Serb forces
withdrew, black-uniformed "KLA police" quickly appeared on the streets, carrying
handcuffs and armed with holstered pistols. The UN advance team decided that
it would be unhealthy to succumb to pressures to incorporate any group intact
into the fledgling KPS. In particular, recruiting existing paramilitary formations
such as the 1,500-member KLA police as a group was rejected. The UN advance
team insisted that everyone joining the new police force apply and qualify as an
individual. Former police experience would be considered an advantage unless
the applicant had been compromised by participation in criminal activities.

As part of the negotiation process, a phrase was added in the military
"Undertaking" committing UNMIK, when establishing new police services, to
give members of the KLA "special consideration in view of the expertise they
have developed."[29] An avid debate ensued among the leadership of UNMIK, the
OSCE, and KFOR concerning how "special consideration" would be defined in
practice. In July 1999 the SRSG informed the UNMIK police commissioner that

50 to 55 percent of police recruits should be from the former KLA, and this was adopted as an informal target, though never put in writing. From the perspective of the KLA leadership, this was understood to be a precise quota, the fulfillment of which would be a point of unrelenting insistence.

The political imperative of providing employment opportunities for the KLA fit uncomfortably with the mandate to develop a local police force that would contribute to institutionalizing the rule of law. UNMIK held the line regarding qualifications, however, and the majority of KLA applicants ended up being disqualified. A concession was made to allow members of the ad hoc KLA police force to receive priority review of their applications, which meant that the initial classes entering the KPSS had a substantial number of former KLA members enrolled. Pressure to accept the KLA into the KPS abated somewhat after an alternative source of employment was created in the form of the Kosovo Protection Corps. The 50 percent quota for former KLA members remained intact until the initial target of 4,200 KPS officers was achieved. Subsequently, when the strength was increased to 5,600, the quota for the KLA was dropped for that additional increment. By the end of 2003, some 38 percent of active KPS officers had come from the ranks of the KLA.

In Mitrovica KFOR's MNB North made an early strategic choice not to confront directly the parallel security presence operating in Serb controlled neighborhoods in the northern part of the city. The activities of the rogue Serb security force, euphemistically called "bridge watchers," were clandestinely supported from Belgrade. International police were, thus, faced with a different set of strategic options in northern Mitrovica than elsewhere. Consequently, this was the last area where UNMIK Police was able to assume primacy for law enforcement. This transition had to await not only the demise of the Milosevic regime but an additional two years, until late 2002, when UNMIK was able to obtain an agreement with authorities in Belgrade to unify Mitrovica under international administration. Under this agreement, members of the parallel local security force, or bridge watchers, could apply for entry into the KPS as long as their records (as maintained by KFOR and UNMIK) were clear of criminal activity and they were able to meet the basic requirements. As did former KLA members, bridge watchers had difficulty meeting these standards. The number of Serb KPS members operating in northern Kosovo gradually grew during 2003, and Serb KPS members began to be included in police patrols in north Mitrovica.

Judges and Prosecutors

Before the conclusion of the bombing campaign, the OSCE sent personnel from its KVM to the refugee camps in an attempt to identify Kosovo Albanian judges and prosecutors to help constitute a new judicial system.[30] The vast majority had not worked in those capacities since 1989, and the few who had were regarded as Serb collaborators. None were familiar with international human rights standards, nor could they be expected to be impartial in their treatment of Serbs accused of crimes after the trauma they had experienced. Thus, the OSCE prepared a plan for rebuilding the judicial system that involved the use of international judges and prosecutors along with members of the local legal community.[31] UNMIK, however, made the strategic choice to rely exclusively on local judicial personnel. The overriding factor was a feeling that giving international judges the authority to sentence citizens of Kosovo to imprisonment would smack of colonialism. Ultimately, however, international judges and prosecutors would need to play a prominent role.

On June 28, 1999, the SRSG established the Joint Advisory Council on Provisional Judicial Appointments to screen and recommend judges and prosecutors for an initial three-month period. International representatives held three of seven seats, with the remainder divided equally between Kosovo Albanian and minority representatives. Aided in part by the list of judges and prosecutors that the OSCE had developed earlier, the council appointed fifty-five judges and prosecutors under this provisional system before it was superseded in October 1999.[32] Because Serbian judges either fled or were soon intimidated into leaving, the vast majority of judges were ethnic Albanians. This cadre began functioning as a mobile court for the purpose of conducting detention hearings for the various KFOR MNBs. KFOR provided transportation, security, and makeshift courtroom facilities, in addition to performing investigations and holding initial detention hearings.

This emergency judicial system struggled to process the backlog of detention hearings that had built up in response to the wave of violence against Serbs throughout the summer of 1999. As a result, few cases were investigated. Under the civil law tradition observed in Kosovo, investigations were to be performed under the supervision of a judge; however, the number of judges available was insufficient to perform this vital function. Because little evidence was being developed, indictments were very rare. In December, this paralysis in the legal process reached a crisis point; after six months detainees had to be either indicted or released. The response by UNMIK was to draft a regulation extending the period of pretrial detention for serious offenses to one year.[33] KFOR dealt with this conundrum by adopting a practice called COMKFOR holds. Detainees in KFOR custody could remain locked up in spite of a judicial release order if the KFOR commander determined they constituted a threat to safety and security. This was regarded as a violation of judicial independence and the rights of detainees by the human rights community and provoked a prolonged confrontation, especially with the OSCE's Legal Systems Monitoring Section (LSMS). Although the merits of this action can be debated, it was indisputably an indication of the incapacity of the local judicial system to meet one of its most basic responsibilities.

In September the provisional Joint Advisory Council was replaced by an Advisory Judicial Commission (AJC). In another strategic choice that later experience would show to be misguided, Kosovo Albanian representatives were given control over the commission, with seven of the eleven positions.[34] In December 1999 the AJC began making longer-term appointments to all courts of Kosovo. By September 2000 the AJC had appointed 405 judges and prosecutors and the operation of the courts had been restored at all levels across Kosovo. Staffing the court system, however, did not equate to administration of justice, and placing ownership of the appointment process immediately into local hands did not constitute a formula for institutionalizing the rule of law. Kosovo Albanian members were inclined to make appointments on personal or political grounds rather than on the basis of professionalism. Nor did the AJC ever take disciplinary action to redress misconduct by its appointees (see below). The AJC did act, however, to remove the one Kosovo Albanian district court president who had been willing to conduct proceedings in both languages when Serbs were involved. The AJC fell into such disrepute that by December 2000 it had ceased to function, and its mandate was not renewed. It had overcome the shortage of personnel (judges, lay judges, judicial staff, prosecutors, court clerks, court administrators, etc.), but at a high price in terms of the rule of law.

Other fundamental deficiencies in judicial capacity also had to be overcome. Most amenable to resolution were physical shortcomings such as the condition of courthouses and the lack of basic office supplies.[35] More challenging and time-consuming to correct were the effects of Milosevic's discriminatory policies. Many Kosovo Albanian judges had been unable to serve on the bench for a decade. Additionally, entry into the legal profession had been effectively foreclosed by a combination of factors. Ethnic Albanians were not allowed to obtain a formal legal education after 1990, and during most of the Milosevic period it was not possible to take the bar exam in Kosovo or in the Albanian language.[36] Anyone who managed to overcome all these barriers and gain acceptance into the legal system was likely to be regarded as a Serb collaborator. Consequently, the pool of talent that was available to staff the justice system had diminished considerably by 1999.

UNMIK's early efforts to provide refresher training for judges and prosecutors, under the aegis of the OSCE-led Pillar III, consisted exclusively of seminars on international human rights standards. By February 2000 the OSCE had established a formal mechanism for providing continuing legal education seminars by creating the Kosovo Judicial Institute (KJI), staffed by respected members of the local legal profession together with international jurists.[37] Over time the KJI sought to address deficiencies in basic legal skills, but with mixed results. The OSCE also sought to establish a magistrate's school within the KJI and to make graduation from the school a prerequisite for appointment as a judge or prosecutor. The local legal community resisted this, however, because under existing law the only requirement that had to be met to perform these functions was to pass the bar exam.

Even as the qualifications of the existing cadre of legal professionals gradually began to improve, their numbers were simultaneously shrinking at a disturbing pace. It was often more remunerative to enter private legal practice or even to work as an interpreter or driver for UNMIK.[38] Thus, in addition to establishing a revenue base that would permit members of the legal profession to be paid a competitive wage, it was vitally important to replenish the profession by reinstituting the bar exam. Hundreds of prospective candidates had been deterred from taking the exam during the 1990s. It took until December 2001, however, two and a half years from the start of the mission, before agreement could be reached on the modalities for conducting the exam.[39] By May 2003 almost seven hundred aspirants had completed a refresher course at the KJI and taken the exam.[40]

Whereas the international community had taken full responsibility for policing at the inception of the mission, UNMIK initially rejected the use of international judges and prosecutors in the legal system. As a senior UNMIK official observes, "There was too much optimism. We thought, 'Let's appoint some judges, some good people, they have their freedom and they will be good and behave properly.'"[41] As a result, the international role was defined in very limited terms. Colette Rausch, head of the OSCE Rule of Law office (2000–2001)[42] notes: "Originally, it was believed that with some remedial training and assistance, the existing crew of former judges and prosecutors could be brought up to speed and function effectively."[43] As it turned out, the capacity for impartiality in dealing with Serb accused was severely lacking, and the overall quality of jurisprudence was deficient. The inability to retain Kosovo Serb judges or to provide defense counsel made justice all the more inaccessible for the Serb community.

Instead of a gradual process of diminishing international involvement, therefore, as was the case with regard to policing, international involvement in the judicial system had to increase. There was no other way to begin developing an impartial judicial system that could contribute to the equitable and peaceful resolution of disputes between Kosovo's ethnic communities. Equally vital was the need for international judges and prosecutors to play a decisive role in depriving violent obstructionists of their capacity to intimidate the judiciary and thereby thwart the peace process.

Penal System

Initially, UNMIK had no conception of what was involved in restoring the operation of a prison system. The initial Kosovo Consolidated Budget did not even
recognize the need to provide funding for the management of prisons. Once
again KFOR had to fill the gap. Even though this was an unanticipated requirement for most KFOR contingents, during the first phase of the mission each MNB
took responsibility for operating pretrial detention facilities. Because there was no
adequate jail in its sector, the U.S. military established its own detention center at
Camp Bondsteel, processing 1,800 detainees in the first year of operations.[44]
Among the factors that slowed the transfer of responsibility to UNMIK were the
need to locate and recruit professional expertise in penal management for this un
precedented international requirement; the delay in providing funds, especially to
repair Kosovo's main prison at Dubrava, which had been severely damaged by
NATO bombing; and the difficulty encountered by UNMIK officials in gaining
access to various penal facilities that KFOR regarded as high-security installa
tions and therefore placed off limits.[45]

Once UNMIK Police had become established in Pristina, it began operating the detention center there. In October 1999 UNMIK established the Penal
Management Division and began recruiting experienced local corrections officers to form the initial cadre for the Kosovo Corrections Service (KCS). One
month later, fifty-eight officers of the KCS under UNMIK supervision assumed
responsibility from KFOR for the prison in Prizren. In January 2000 the KPSS
began offering a corrections training course. By June 2000 UNMIK had rehabil
itated the main prison at Dubrava and restored it to use. This was a crucial accomplishment because due to the resumption of trials within the court system,
Kosovo's smaller facilities were full to capacity with sentenced offenders. At the
end of 2000, the prison population stood at 227, which was managed by a force
of six hundred corrections officials. By February 2001 the KCS, under Penal
Management Division supervision, had taken responsibility for all detention centers and prisons with the exception of the detention center at Camp Bondsteel,
which was used primarily for detainees held under KFOR authority (i.e.,
COMKFOR holds).

By default rather than design, the approach that evolved for the penal system closely resembled the path followed with policing. Initially, KFOR managed
all prisons and pretrial detention facilities, until UNMIK Police was in a position to
assume responsibility for some locations. As UNMIK's Penal Management Division was able to recruit and train local corrections staff, the KCS began to take
charge of the prisons, with international prison wardens providing supervision.
Thus, the relationship evolved from one of international custodianship to one of

partnership, with responsibility gradually being transferred as local KCS personnel were able to demonstrate both proficiency and adherence to professional
standards of conduct. This process was expected to culminate in June 2005 with
the transition to a Kosovar director for the KCS.

Applicable Law

Because Kosovo's final status remained undetermined, the selection of one penal
code over another became part of the continuing conflict. The existing "Serb"
code had no legitimacy with Kosovo Albanians because it had been used as an
instrument of brutal repression since 1989. This code also implied Kosovo's subjugation to Serbia and a reversal of ethnic Albanian aspirations for eventual independence. The penal code that had been used when Kosovo enjoyed autonomous
status before March 1989 was clearly the preference of Kosovo Albanians. Nevertheless, respect for FRY sovereignty was an overriding concern for the United
Nations.[46] Consequently, in July 1999 the SRSG issued Regulation No. 1, stipu-
lating that the law applicable in Kosovo would comprise "all the laws applicable
in the territory of Kosovo prior to 24 March 1999."[47]

   To administer this body of law—considered odious by Kosovo Albanians—
UNMIK decided to rely on recruitment of local judges and prosecutors. Because
the vast majority of judges were ethnic Albanians, they simply refused to apply the
existing "Serb" law. Until UNMIK reversed itself in December 1999, criminal trials
presided over by Kosovo Albanian judges actually applied the pre-1989 "Kosovo"
penal code.[48] In addition to amounting to open defiance of UNMIK's authority,
the fundamental legality of these rulings was in doubt. One remedy proposed by
UNMIK staff and endorsed by KFOR lawyers was to use UNMIK's regulatory
authority to establish a temporary code covering the most serious violent crimes
until the overall legal framework could be revised.[49] The United Nations was
unwilling to act until the issue reached the crisis stage, in December, when Regulation 1999/24 was adopted, reverting to the law in force in March 1989 when
Kosovo enjoyed autonomy.

   Although this was essential to end the judicial stalemate, there was a price
to pay. The international community was perceived as weak and vulnerable to
local pressure. The vanishing prospects for inclusion of Serbs in the judiciary
were diminished further. There was great uncertainty, moreover, about what the
pre-1989 laws actually were. Months would pass before the penal code and other
vital codes could be translated into English so that UNMIK police could be
trained on the law they were expected to enforce and UNMIK legal staff could
work with them. Instead of promoting peaceful resolution of disputes, the United
Nations' initial strategic choice about the applicable law had created an obstacle
that took almost a year to overcome. The Brahimi Report acknowledged that a

rudimentary international penal code and code of procedure should be developed.[50] This would at least provide an alternative for international authorities to use to avoid a legal vacuum at the inception of a mission in cases like Kosovo.

2. Transforming the Institutional Context

The early international response to the destabilizing waves of violence against Serbs and other minorities involved short-term surges in the security presence. Although it was critical to seek to deter and prevent interethnic violence, KFOR and UNMIK Police could not be in every location where they might be needed at all times. Beginning in the spring of 2000, UNMIK planners recognized that a strategy had to be developed that would *attack the sources, not just respond to the symptoms,* of interethnic violence and obstruction of the peace process.[51]

In areas populated predominantly by Kosovo Serbs, parallel power structures constituted a persistent threat. Mitrovica represented the most serious flashpoint owing to the dominance there of paramilitary bridge watchers who were responsible for the worst acts of violence perpetrated against UNMIK, including a grenade-and-sniper assault in April 2002 that injured twenty-six international police. Adept at orchestrating unruly demonstrations, the bridge watchers also used strong-arm tactics to resist deployment of Serb members of the KPS in northern Mitrovica, even after Belgrade had formally agreed to work toward their dissolution in late 2002.

For Kosovo Albanians, the challenge was both their vulnerability to lawless forces within their own community and the inevitable difficulty of administering equal justice to the minority population that was collectively identified with their former oppressors. A report issued in October 1999 by the Lawyers Committee for Human Rights documents the arbitrary nature of decisions by Kosovo Albanian judges in failing to prosecute an inordinate number of cases against suspected perpetrators of assaults on Kosovo Serbs.[52] Conversely, Serbs accused of similar offenses were often detained indefinitely without trial. In *Kosovo: An Unfinished Peace*, William O'Neill, UNMIK's senior adviser on human rights from August 1999 to February 2000, provides this assessment of the performance of the judiciary:

> Instances of bias against Serbs and other minorities among the Albanian judiciary surfaced early during the Emergency Judicial System and have continued ever since. . . . Albanians arrested on serious charges, often caught red-handed by KFOR or UNMIK police, frequently were released immediately or were not indicted and subsequently released. Meanwhile, Serbs, Roma, and other minorities arrested on even minor charges with flimsy evidence were almost always detained, and some stayed in detention even though they were not indicted.[53]

The collective effect was to subvert efforts to promote the peaceful resolution of disputes among Kosovo's ethnic communities. The institutional context was entirely inhospitable to the preservation of the fundamental rights of minorities, thwarting efforts to maintain the multiethnic character of Kosovo. Lawless forces remained untouchable in both the Kosovo Serb and the Albanian communities. These conditions would have to be transformed for peace to become enduring. Among the strategic choices that confronted the international community, therefore, were the following:

- What capabilities would UNMIK and KFOR need to have at their disposal to deal with criminalized power structures opposed to the rule of law and Resolution 1244?

- How could the capabilities of UNMIK and KFOR be integrated effectively to counter the major existing and emerging threats to the rule of law?

- How should the capabilities of the international community be integrated with the local criminal justice system and at what pace?

- What revisions to the applicable law were necessary to remove barriers to the collection of evidence?

- What was the proper balance to strike between ensuring international capacities to transform the institutional context in the shorter run and building the capacity of local institutions to be capable and empowered over the longer run?

- How should available resources be allocated between competing demands of countering extremist structures, providing a visible presence before the general population, and protecting special groups?

Criminal Intelligence

The first requirement was to identify the threats to the rule of law, including the major sources of interethnic violence. In early 2000 the Quint countries (i.e., Britain, France, Germany, Italy, and the United States) agreed to create a Criminal Intelligence Unit (CIU) within UNMIK Police in order to pool relevant KFOR intelligence with UNMIK Police information on the organized-crime threat. This seemingly commonsense proposition was confounded by an inherent reluctance to share intelligence, a lack of security clearances for many of the personnel initially assigned to the CIU, and a UN structure that was philosophically and bureaucratically unprepared to manage a criminal intelligence operation. As a result, it took nearly two years for the body to be established under UNMIK auspices. Over time, these challenges were addressed, particularly by the establishment of an institutional "firewall" between the CIU, which was staffed exclusively by the Quint countries, and the rest of the UNMIK Police structure. Another early impediment was the lack of a common vision among the Quint countries about whether this intelligence should be put to operational use in Kosovo. It was one thing for intelligence to start flowing into the CIU and back to home countries. It was quite another to convert this intelligence into actionable leads to guide the collection of evidence against threats in Kosovo. Ultimately, the need to supplement the CIU's efforts with a capability to gather criminal evidence was recognized, leading to the establishment of the Kosovo Organized Crime Bureau (KOCB) as the investigative arm within UNMIK Police for information developed by the CIU.

Criminal Investigation

Perhaps the most vexing challenge was to develop the evidence required to bring perpetrators of political violence to justice. UNMIK was hamstrung in its early efforts by obstacles in the applicable law.[54] Evidence gathered by covert means, such as video cameras or wiretaps, was not considered admissible. No provisions existed for granting immunity to witnesses or for protecting their identities.

Even after these deficiencies in the applicable law were overcome in 2001 and 2002 through the use of UNMIK's regulatory authority,[55] many standard investigative means remained unavailable. The United Nations opposed the payment of informants from UN funds, and it delayed the delivery of surveillance equipment for more than a year after the United States had provided funding for acquisition. Although a forensics lab was established after considerable delay, prosecutors remained reliant on witnesses. In spite of the creation of a witness protection program, resources were not available to operate it effectively, and thus witnesses continued to be vulnerable to intimidation. The justice system was unable to make adequate use of its authority to prosecute the most dangerous threats to the rule of law, therefore, because of a lengthy international failure to support it with the necessary resources.

Years passed before substantial progress could be made. In mid-2002 the UNMIK police commissioner reformed and expanded the nascent KOCB and forged effective working relationships with KFOR and the UNMIK Department of Justice (as the Department of Judicial Affairs was renamed when Pillar I was formed). The KOCB included specialists in various investigative disciplines, including the use of technical devices, supplemented as necessary by KFOR's surveillance capability. The integrity of the organization was maintained through the use of polygraphs and periodic surveillance on its own personnel. To facilitate the flow of prosecutable intelligence from KFOR, the UNMIK Department of Justice established a Sensitive Information and Operations Unit (SIOU). The purpose was to identify key figures involved in criminality and violent obstruction of the peace process, provide a mechanism for processing intelligence into a format usable in court proceedings, and secure their arrest. It was essential that lawyers assigned to the SIOU have the requisite security clearances from a NATO country.

Because UNMIK originally considered itself bound by a constitutional ban against extradition of citizens, Kosovo, in effect, became a safe haven for Kosovars who had committed serious crimes abroad. To begin addressing this, the Department of Justice negotiated bilateral arrangements with many of the most affected countries to provide records, access to witnesses, and financial support for translators so these fugitives could be tried in Kosovo. This allowed judicial proceedings to be initiated by UNMIK against criminals most wanted by foreign governments; however, it was only coincidental when this process could be used to build cases against dangerous criminals who were a strategic priority for UNMIK. In 2003 UNMIK took steps to amend the existing body of law to allow for the extradition of Kosovo citizens. Years of delay in putting this mechanism into effect deprived UNMIK of a powerful tool for ridding Kosovo of some of the most notorious criminal and extremist elements.

Prioritization and Planning

With the passage of time, UNMIK and KFOR developed an understanding of the various political-criminal power structures at play in Kosovo and the threat they posed to a sustainable peace. To confront this threat effectively, a process was needed to focus the limited resources of the international community decisively on the key figures involved. A key component of this strategy was to use intelligence resources already in place to identify potential high-value investigative targets. Two mechanisms were created in 2002 for this purpose. A Targeting (or Task) Coordination Group (TCG), which comprised the heads of the CIU, KOCB, SIOU, and KFOR J-2 (Intelligence) and the deputy commander of MNB(C), met every two weeks to assess the available intelligence and develop priorities. Its recommendations were presented to an Overview Coordination Group (OCG) chaired by the UNMIK police commissioner, with the director of the Department of Justice and the commander of MNB(C) also participating. The OCG met once a month to establish priorities for investigation and prosecution and allocate respective resources accordingly. Originally, this approach was confined to interaction between UNMIK and MNB(C), but it was so successful in bringing the most threatening criminal figures to justice that it was expanded Kosovo-wide, and the KFOR chief of staff replaced the MNB(C) commander on the OCG.

High-Risk Arrest

In the face of widespread attacks against the Serb population at the inception of the mission, it was clear that UNMIK Police would need the capability to counter a high level of violence. The UNMIK police commissioner drew on personal contacts to arrange for the early recruitment of a cadre of highly professional and experienced tactical police who specialized in high-risk arrests. These officers were called on frequently from the outset of the mission, usually with KFOR and UNMIK crowd-control units providing a wider security cordon while they carried out the arrest. Owing to the novelty of this type of mission, the United Nations was unprepared and unable to provide appropriate equipment and logistical support for this function for more than a year. The unit depended on ad hoc support from the contributing nations for appropriate weapons and other necessary equipment.

The professionalism of the UNMIK Police during the operation to take control of the lead smelter at Zvecan in the summer of 2000 so impressed British commanders that they actively sought to work with this specialized unit to deal with high-priority targets in their MNB. The proficiency of the high-risk arrest team was demonstrated throughout 2002 with the apprehension of more than sixty former KLA members suspected of involvement in a range of violent crimes.

Crowd Control

UN planners anticipated a need for a crowd-control capability based on the experience in Bosnia, where implementation of the Dayton Peace Accords had been stymied by orchestrated civil disturbances. As a result, UNMIK Police included ten formed police units, called Special Police Units (SPUs), each with 115 men and equipped with riot-control gear, body armor, and armored vehicles. KFOR also included a similar capability with its Multinational Specialized Unit (MSU).

It took almost a year before the SPUs began deploying to Kosovo. Initially, there was strong resistance at senior levels within UNMIK to the use of either the SPUs or the MSU in a crowd-control capacity, owing to the fragility of the peace process and uncertainty about how they would perform. As a result, the SPUs were used to supplement UNMIK Police, providing protection for Serb enclaves, support for the close protection and high-risk arrest units, prisoner escort, and point security for high-priority locations such as courthouses and UNMIK facilities.[56]

When UNMIK began arresting Serb bridge watchers and former KLA members wanted for murdering rival Kosovo Albanians during and after the war, the SPUs were an invaluable asset. These arrests provoked the sort of orchestrated civil disturbances encountered previously in Bosnia, including violent assaults on UNMIK police. The SPUs provided the capacity to control and defuse the situation. They were so successful in one of the earliest encounters that the demonstrators, KLA support groups from outside Pristina, eventually grew frustrated and turned to attacking city residents in downtown restaurants for failing to join the confrontation with UNMIK.

International Judges and Prosecutors

For successful prosecution of cases involving violent criminal and extremist forces, international judges and prosecutors were required, because they were not prone to ethnic bias and could be protected from local intimidation The need to involve international jurists in the legal process was raised at the inception of the mission and again within UNMIK in September 1999.[57] Several serious disruptions of the peace process eventually compelled UNMIK to begin incorporating international judges and prosecutors in an ad hoc manner into Kosovo's judicial system.[58]

The event that triggered the introduction of the first international judge and prosecutor took place in February 2000 near the divided city of Mitrovica. A deadly military-style assault on a bus carrying primarily elderly Serbs and children precipitated a Serb rampage against Kosovo Albanian residents living in the predominantly Serb portion of Mitrovica. During the skirmishing, armed members of the Kosovo Protection Corps were arrested by UNMIK Police and KFOR for firing their unauthorized weapons at French troops and Serb apartments. The ethnic Albanian judge involved in this case released the suspects the same day. This prompted UNMIK to act with unusual dispatch in promulgating a regulation authorizing the appointment of an international judge and prosecutor to the district court in Mitrovica with the authority to become involved in any case within the jurisdiction of the court.[59]

A few months later, Serb prisoners who had been languishing in jail without trial for a year went on a hunger strike, demanding that international judges be assigned to their cases. This precipitated the ad hoc appointment of international judges and prosecutors to be extended to all five district courts in Kosovo.[60] While UNMIK was scrambling to locate the additional eleven international judges and three prosecutors it estimated would be needed to process the hunger strikers' cases, further events made it evident that this "temporary" measure would have to be retained indefinitely.[61] UNMIK soon realized that two international judges would have to be assigned to each case: one for the investigation and another for the trial phase. With five district courts and the Supreme Court, this required the availability of a minimum of twelve international judges.

Even this number was insufficient to preclude the miscarriage of justice, however. At the district court level, judicial panels had five members. This meant that the single international judge assigned to the panel could simply be outvoted, which immediately began to happen. Serb defendants were convicted without sufficient evidence, and Kosovo Albanian defendants were released or acquitted regardless of evidence of guilt. Thus, instead of precluding the miscarriage of justice, the presence of an international judge had the perverse effect of appearing to legitimize patently unjust verdicts.[62] To ensure "impartiality, independence, and respect for human rights," therefore, UNMIK promulgated

Regulation 2000/64 in December 2000.[63] This provided for the formation of special three-member judicial panels—composed of at least two international judges—to hear high-profile cases, especially those involving interethnic violence, political violence, organized crime, or war crimes. The more difficult step was to locate qualified international judges and prosecutors who understood civil law, spoke fluent English, and were willing to confront the risks and rigors of the most difficult cases Kosovo had to offer. By July 2002 UNMIK had filled twenty-seven of the thirty-four positions it had created for international judges and prosecutors.

The practical effect of these "sixty-four panels" (in reference to Regulation 2000/64) was to create a division of labor between local and international jurists. On the one hand, the vast majority of proceedings remained entirely in the hands of the local judiciary. Politically sensitive cases, however, were dealt with by the sixty-four panels, and this was where almost all the attention of international judges and prosecutors was focused. Although this regulation was controversial initially, local judges later manifested their acceptance by asking international judges to relieve them of cases when external pressure and intimidation were too great to handle. Indeed, such concerns also caused local judges to decline to serve on many cases heard by the sixty-four panels, especially during the first year of their use. When their local counterparts did become involved in cases dealing with powerful criminal or political figures, international jurists found them to lack objectivity in weighing the evidence. When external influence, fear of social ostracism, or ethnic bias was not a factor, however, their conduct was professional and the relationship collegial. This suggests that as the institutional context is progressively transformed and extremist power structures are disabled, the relationship should also evolve toward greater partnership and eventually to greater local authority over the criminal justice system.

One issue that resisted effective resolution was the process for selection of cases to be handled by international judges and prosecutors. Although this was a topic of discussion from the early days of their incorporation into the local judiciary, the question was difficult to resolve because formal direction from the SRSG would have created concerns about judicial independence. Guidelines were eventually established for prosecutors in 2003; however, criteria for international judges remained informal. As a result, there was a tendency for the caseloads to become overcrowded with extraneous or inconsequential matters, which militated heavily against the ability of the OCG to establish priorities for prosecution.[64]

Close Protection Unit

In the summer of 2000, as UNMIK sought to introduce international judges and prosecutors into all five district courts in Kosovo, one of the main challenges was to provide for their security. As SRSG Michael Steiner would later warn the Security Council, "As we begin to make significant arrests against criminal gangs we should expect a criminal backlash."[65] In the same ad hoc fashion that the high-risk arrest team had been cobbled together, UNMIK Police created a small Close Protection Unit (CPU) to provide security for visiting international dignitaries and members of the Serb National Council who participated in the interim government. The addition of more than a dozen judges and prosecutors to their protection responsibilities in mid-2000, however, threatened to overwhelm the CPU's limited capabilities. UNMIK sought formal recognition of the unit from the United Nations in order to appeal for additional critically needed resources (e.g., automatic weapons), and it began allocating close protection teams according to the assessed level of threat. Over the next several years, international judges and prosecutors were seldom threatened. Instead, intimidation was directed at members of the local judiciary and at witnesses. Because international judges and prosecutors received a protection detail but their local counterparts did not, a disparity was created that was not conducive to partnership.

Incarceration

UNMIK was particularly ill prepared initially to provide maximum security for the prisoners who constituted the gravest threats to public order and the peace process. The majority of Serb suspects, including accused war criminals, were held in the predominantly Serb section of Mitrovica. Because the KCS remained unarmed until 2001, UNMIK police were assigned to operate that facility. Management of prisons is not simply another form of policing, however. A distinctive set of skills and specialized training are required to manage a prison adequately. Compounding this deficiency, standards were lax because UNMIK police tended to regard prison duty as a form of punishment. In August 2000 fourteen Serb detainees, many of whom were indicted war criminals, escaped from the Mitrovica jail. Subsequently, the Penal Management Division took over supervision of the UNMIK Police contingent there, providing training in basic prison skills and enforcing professional standards and procedures. At Dubrava, the largest prison facility, the SPU provided a minimum armed presence to prevent breakouts, but for a long time the Penal Management Division depended on a rapid-response agreement from KFOR to provide some deterrence against break-ins.

High-profile Kosovo Albanian detainees also required incarceration under tight international supervision. Although the U.S. military had initially considered the facility at Camp Bondsteel to be a stopgap measure and pressed UNMIK to relieve it of the burden, Bondsteel continued to serve for years essentially as a maximum-security facility for Kosovo's most politically dangerous suspects.[66] Cross-border subversion in southern Serbia and Macedonia in late 2000 and early 2001 demonstrated the continuing need for a facility secure enough to deal with the subversive and terrorist threat that menaced the peace, both inside and outside Kosovo. When the suspected ringleader of the February 2001 Nis bus bombing was apprehended, UNMIK officials determined that the risk was too great to use a local detention center. His subsequent escape from Camp Bondsteel revealed that military detention facilities that are designed for handling prisoners of war require various modifications to prevent such breakouts. Thus, even KFOR had to enhance its capacity in order to complete the last element of the intelligence-to-incarceration continuum.

In sum, KFOR and UNMIK would eventually have to acquire the full spectrum of capabilities—from intelligence to incarceration—to enable the dismantling of political-criminal power structures that were overwhelming threats to the rule of law in both the Kosovo Albanian and Serb communities. KFOR had vital contributions to make across the entire spectrum, which created a need to establish effective means of coordination, such as the OCG and Targeting Coordination Group. One of the most crucial gaps was in the capacity to gather evidence. While resources were important, it was just as vital for UNMIK to employ its regulatory authority actively to provide a suitable legal framework for this purpose and to establish an effective organizational structure in the form of the KOCB.

3. Safeguards on Performance

To ensure that the police, judiciary, and penal system actually serve the public interest, respect minority rights, dispense justice equally, and maintain their autonomy from corrupting political forces, effective safeguards must be developed. Safeguards entail the ability to observe the performance of these institutions (transparency) and to sanction misconduct (accountability). Ultimately, the citizenry must have channels for airing grievances and mechanisms for pursuing effective remedies.

Among the strategic issues that the international community grappled with as it sought to develop safeguards on institutions responsible for the rule of law were the following:

- Could Kosovars themselves be relied on to enforce standards of conduct, or would it be necessary for international personnel to play a custodial role until the institutional context was transformed and domestic safeguards could begin to function appropriately?

- What was the proper role for the SRSG during the period of international custodianship, and how was that role to be balanced against the long-term goal of establishing independent institutions to sustain the rule of law?

- At what point would domestic safeguards be able to ensure that the rule of law would continue to prevail?

Police

The SRSG's July 12, 1999, report to the Security Council describes the basic safeguards that would be instituted while the international community had custody of policing. It states that "critical assessment of the performance of KPS officers will be ongoing, and the Police Commissioner will retain full discretion, under the authority of the Special Representative, to dismiss or discipline KPS officers."[67] Oversight of KPS conduct was managed by UNMIK Police through the creation of a Professional Standards Unit staffed by carefully selected international officers at the central and regional levels. The unit served as the locus of internal investigations and continued to pursue expanded background checks on active KPS officers. The disciplinary authority retained by the UNMIK police commissioner proved crucial for the institutional development of the KPS. In 2003 nearly two hundred KPS officers were dismissed for misconduct or as the result of continued background investigations. Without the impartial authority of international police over KPS personnel during all phases of the service's growth, the KPS's effectiveness and reputation among the population would have suffered severely.

As the relationship evolved into a partnership and the KPS assumed leadership responsibilities, the emphasis was placed on "developing an effective and transparent command structure for the KPS in accordance with international standards of democratic policing."[68] Ultimately, once the KPS had demonstrated the capacity to assume full responsibility for policing, UNMIK envisioned transitioning to a "training, advising, and monitoring" role.[69] The empowerment of a permanent internal affairs structure within the KPS was one of the last planned stages in the transition to local ownership of policing.

Judiciary

International oversight of the judiciary was accomplished by the Legal System Monitoring Section (LSMS) of Pillar III as part of UNMIK's human rights monitoring mandate. Initially only a handful of LSMS monitors were assigned to each of the five judicial districts, where they began reporting on basic issues confronting the emergency judicial system, such as inadequacies in the detention process, lack of access to effective defense counsel, and the material shortcomings of the court system.[70] In August 2000 LSMS began issuing reviews at six-month intervals.[71] The first semiannual report was harsh in its condemnation of persistent deficiencies, such as the periodic use of lengthy pretrial detentions without suitable means of redress. Because this practice was largely attributable to other members of the international community (i.e., KFOR or UNMIK), this public rebuke provoked considerable controversy. Those responsible felt it would have been more appropriate to use internal avenues to address this concern. The report also judged the overall performance of local judges and prosecutors to be lacking in impartiality and their awareness of international human rights standards to be deficient.[72] On the other hand, LSMS reports credited the introduction of international judges and prosecutors into the legal system with curbing the ethnic bias of the courts. Similarly, the creation of the Judicial Inspection Unit to investigate allegations of judicial misconduct was applauded. Over time, international resources were progressively focused on many of the deficiencies identified by LSMS, such as access to defense counsel, leading to substantial improvement in many areas. Thus, LSMS served as a significant safeguard on the performance of the legal system. As Colette Rausch argues, "the fact that LSMS monitors are present in court provides the important function of making sure that those who are administering justice know that they will be held accountable."[73]

As noted repeatedly in LSMS assessments, access to defense counsel is an additional safeguard that is vital for ensuring fairness of the judicial process, especially for members of ethnic minority groups. During the early phase of the mission, no system was in place to pay for such services. Training for defense counsel in international human rights standards and assistance in case preparation were slow to materialize. Eventually, in mid-2001, the OSCE set up the Criminal Defence Resource Centre (CDRC) as an independent source for reference materials, practical training, legal research and drafting, and assistance in matters such as the safe transport of Serb defense attorneys.[74]

The reintegration of Serb judges and prosecutors into the legal system was another essential means of providing a long-term safeguard so that minorities could have an assurance of access to justice. The Department of Justice established a Judicial Integration Section (JIS) for this purpose in 2002 and began to work with Belgrade to recruit and hire some forty Serb judges and prosecutors. However, subsidies continued to sustain parallel judicial structures for Kosovo Serbs. By accepting contracts to work for UNMIK, Serbs risked the loss of these salaries and other forms of support. UNMIK shifted the focus of its efforts toward pressuring Belgrade authorities to eliminate these largely moribund parallel judicial structures, and during 2003 nine Serb judges and prosecutors took posts in Kosovo courts.

The initial mechanism created by UNMIK to involve the local legal community in preserving the integrity of the judiciary was the Advisory Judicial Commission. In addition to its role in appointing judges and prosecutors, the AJC was responsible for evaluating their work and, as necessary, recommending dismissal. The AJC consisted of eight local members (seven Kosovo Albanians and one Kosovo Serb) and three from the international community, which meant that the

Kosovo Albanian majority monopolized decisions. The AJC proved to be incapable of confronting the risks associated with disciplinary action. In an assessment conducted in February 2000, a team of U.S. government judicial specialists urged UNMIK "to establish a process to remove judges who abused their positions."[75]

Owing to the inefficacy of the AJC in fostering ethical conduct, UNMIK replaced it with the Kosovo Judicial and Prosecutorial Council (KJPC) in April 2001.[76] With five seats for UNMIK on the nine-member council, the majority shifted to the international community.[77] Given the nature of the threat to the rule of law at the time, it was necessary for the SRSG to act decisively to create a body that could deal effectively with the selection, discipline, and removal from office of judges, prosecutors, and lay judges.

To investigate allegations of wrongdoing, the Department of Justice established a Judicial Inspection Unit (JIU).[78] Additionally, UNMIK and the OSCE drafted a code of conduct, working in collaboration with the local judiciary. In the first four years of operation, the JIU initiated 458 investigations and submitted 41 cases to the KJPC for action (137 investigations remained pending). The KJPC recommended disciplinary action in 17 of these cases, including 10 dismissals. In addition to recruiting two international staff members, the JIU hired five local judicial inspectors to investigate allegations of misconduct, one being the national coordinator of the JIU. The greatest challenge impeding the transition to an expanded Kosovar role was ostracization of local staff among members of the small legal community. Moreover, understaffing of the international posts caused a backlog of cases.

The role of internationals in the reform of the Kosovo judiciary thus underwent a strategic shift between the inception of the mission in June 1999 and May 2001, when the KJPC and the JIU were created. UNMIK came to recognize that the local judicial community was vulnerable to influences that opposed the peace process and that this had rendered the AJC incapable of taking effective disciplinary action. The impression of mistrust that resulted when the KJPC replaced the AJC and the majority shifted to international representatives could have been avoided if this threat had been recognized and heeded when the mission began. UNMIK ultimately determined that to establish effective accountability for judicial and prosecutorial misconduct, it would have to play a custodial role within the KJPC and the JIU.

Penal System

Because Kosovo and East Timor represented the first cases where the United Nations had assumed responsibility for managing and reconstituting corrections systems, no principles or procedures existed to guide these efforts. Much more than training was required to instill an ethos in corrections staff that was consistent with the rule of law. Constant supervision while under international custodianship and reinforcement while operating in partnership were essential. This process could not be rushed. An early attempt to move toward local ownership by designating a Kosovar to be the deputy director for the KCS in early 2000 undermined the professionalism of the service, and he had to be removed. Subsequently, UNMIK took a phased approach to KCS leadership development, with those who demonstrated both ability and commitment to internationally accepted standards being selected for more senior posts.

One of the greatest safeguards that was built into the KCS was its multiethnic composition. As of 2004, some 11 percent of KCS personnel are Kosovo Serbs and other minorities. They serve side by side with their Kosovo Albanian colleagues in what has become one of UNMIK's most successful endeavors of ethnic integration. A well-run corrections system must also have "an independent oversight process or system including a willingness to accept international scrutiny."[79] Both internal and external systems of supervision and control were developed by the Penal Management Division.

It was essential for the international community to play a leading role in the creation of effective safeguards, beginning with long-term supervision of performance. Early attempts to transfer disciplinary responsibility to locals in the judicial and penal systems proved abortive and had to be reversed. Another common theme was the need for the international community to play a leading role in the operation of independent oversight bodies for each institution involved in the rule of law. This meant that the SRSG had to remain the ultimate decision maker to ensure the primacy of the peace process over lawless forces that were willing and able to subvert it. UNMIK and KFOR had to demonstrate that no one had impunity, no matter how well connected they might have been with dangerous elements of the ex-KLA or covert Serbian paramilitary and criminal enterprises. For transformation to take place, local members of these institutions must take increasing responsibility for disciplinary action. This will be proof that Kosovo is ready for ownership of its own institutions.

PROCESSES AND RESOURCES

Progress in institutionalizing the rule of law depends on effective processes to integrate the efforts of the full spectrum of international actors involved. The many relevant local constituencies must be brought effectively into the process as well. Interaction between international military and police contingents is treated in chapter 9. Other processes crucial to institutionalization of the rule of law are addressed here, as are the resources required to implement the three strategic lines of action described in this chapter.

Processes

Coordination within UNMIK

When the mission began in 1999, there was initially a three-way division of labor within UNMIK relating to the institutionalization of the rule of law. Law enforcement was assigned to UNMIK Police, which operated outside the pillar structure for two years. Pillar II managed the judiciary and penal system as part of its responsibilities for interim civil administration. Capacity building for the local police, judiciary, and penal system and monitoring of their performance were assigned to Pillar III.

In May 2001 UNMIK Police were integrated into a new Pillar I along with the Department of Judicial Affairs (which was renamed the Department of Justice), consolidating all administrative components of the rule of law (i.e., police, justice system, and penal management). The formation of the rule-of-law pillar had as its primary purpose the consolidation of functions that UNMIK would have to continue to perform for an indefinite period until Kosovo's final status was determined. Although it also encouraged greater functional policy coordination between the UNMIK Police and the Department of Justice, this was not the main purpose for the new pillar structure.

After Pillar I was established, the two major areas requiring coordination within UNMIK were the following:

- Integrating the training and capacity-building activities conducted by Pillar III with the administration of justice in Pillar I so that local personnel could eventually begin assuming those tasks

- Monitoring UNMIK's own performance by the LSMS of Pillar III

Capacity Building

Coordination on police training matters was effectively established in the field at the outset of the mission between the UNMIK police commissioner and the head of the OSCE-run KPSS. Coordination of capacity building for the judiciary, however, remained ad hoc. Those who were administering the justice system in Pillar I lacked a systematic means to provide input into capacity-building activities by Pillar III or to critique the training programs that were provided. Nor did the OSCE Rule of Law Division or KJI have a formal channel for discussing their institution-building concerns with Pillar I. Outcomes were personality dependent. As Colette Rausch observes, "When Pillar I was first created, panels were devised to address various topics, including institution building. OSCE was placed on these panels. Unfortunately, the panels went nowhere after a change of personnel."[80]

After the consolidation of the Department of Justice into Pillar I, a Legal Policy Unit was created to address long-term judicial and penal policy and strategy. The Department of Justice, like UNMIK generally, had been created on an ad hoc basis and had never coalesced into a coherent structure. The Legal Policy Unit made it possible for the department to take an active approach toward identifying problems within the justice system and developing solutions for them. The unit oriented at least some of the department's energies beyond the crisis response mode toward long-term objectives, including the preparation of a strategy for the transition to local ownership of judicial functions. The unit was responsible for ensuring that the department spoke with one voice in dealings within UNMIK, as well as externally.

Monitoring

Because UNMIK was responsible for performing and administering basic legal functions, the legal system monitoring process would inevitably reflect on UNMIK's performance in some fashion. The reports that the OSCE's LSMS began issuing, however, might not have become controversial had it not been for the fact that a fundamental, and perhaps unavoidable, policy conundrum was involved. The use of extended extrajudicial detentions by both the KFOR commander (i.e., COMKFOR holds) and the SRSG, without opportunity for independent review, ignited a sharp clash within the mission. A schism developed between elements responsible for establishing a safe and secure environment and those concerned with upholding human rights standards. Given the institutional void that UNMIK and KFOR were initially faced with, it was impossible to strike a balance between establishing order and preserving individual liberties that was acceptable to all parties.

Concerns over the detention issue simmered within the human rights community of UNMIK for some time. The publication of a report in 2000 by Pillar III converted it into a matter of public record. LSMS, having failed to prevail in internal debates within UNMIK, in effect resorted to becoming an external policy advocate by openly condemning the practice in its report. This had predictable results on working relationships within the mission, but it also led to efforts to improve the process by which these six-month reports would be produced. While protecting the independence of the LSMS, the OSCE also began to circulate the drafts in advance to the UNMIK agencies involved so they could comment and correct factual errors, making the report a more constructive document.

The issue of extrajudicial detentions persisted into 2001, however, especially when an insurrection in Macedonia created acute pressure on KFOR to prevent Kosovo from being exploited as a support base and sanctuary for cross-border subversion. This resulted in the detention of hundreds of suspected insurgents. In addition, the SRSG felt compelled to invoke his executive authority to order an individual detained in a particularly notorious case even after his release had been ordered by a panel composed entirely of international judges. The LSMS continued to denounce these detentions as unwarranted violations of judicial independence, especially because international police, judges, and prosecutors were an integral part of the legal system. The crucial missing element, however, was an inability to gather evidence or, in the case of KFOR, convert intelligence into evidence that could be admitted in court. The international community remained divided on this issue for several years, therefore, because a vital component of the intelligence-to-incarceration continuum was critically lacking.

Coordination between International and Local Authorities

The initial report of the UN secretary-general on June 12, 1999, noted, "It is clearly an essential requirement for the success of UNMIK that the people of Kosovo be included fully and effectively in its work. . . . Community leaders and professionals can make immediate and significant contributions in judicial affairs."[81] In practice, however, it became necessary to distinguish between activities in which the involvement of local professionals was necessary (e.g., matters dealing with the applicable law, culture, and capacity building) and those in which it was premature and even dangerous (i.e., confronting criminalized power structures).

Dual management under the Joint Interim Administrative Structure (JIAS) proved workable for normal administrative matters (e.g., budgets, refurbishment of courts, and the like). When international judges and prosecutors were brought into the system, however, it was not appropriate to involve the Kosovar cohead in such matters as the selection of cases for international judges to handle, the monitoring of the progress of these cases, hiring decisions, or the development of policy for their role. The international community had to take full custody of the process of addressing politically sensitive cases involving violent threats to the peace process in the form of war crimes, organized crime, extremism, and terrorism. Integrating judicial affairs and police under international supervision in Pillar I in May 2001 created a more appropriate organizational structure for dealing with these challenges to the peace process.

Local involvement was clearly required to reform the legal code as it was brought into compliance with international and European human rights standards. To accomplish this, a Joint Advisory Council for Legislative Matters (JAC/LM) composed of local and international experts was established in August 1999 to advise UNMIK on proposed legislation and to draft a new Criminal Code and a Code of Criminal Procedure. Initially, this process worked rather well, and the two codes were completed and presented to UNMIK in June 2001.[82] In spite of its early promise, however, JAC/LM began to suffer a loss of acceptance and was increasingly left out of the lawmaking process by UNMIK.[83] Ultimately, the process was completed entirely within UNMIK's Office of Legal Affairs, devoid of collaboration internally or externally, to the detriment of the final product.[84]

Accountability for Internationals

Accountability for internationals is especially vital because the essence of the rule of law is that no one should be exempt from punishment if he or she has been guilty of misconduct. Members of the international community should be held at least to the same standard of conduct they expect of local authorities. Kosovo provides a poor example because the influx of internationals was followed by the proliferation of brothels and trafficking in women. Part of the black market revenue that fed the criminal-extremist linkage, therefore, was provided by the international community. Establishing proper attitudes toward such behavior was a daunting challenge. UNMIK Police established a Code of Conduct, an internal investigative unit, and a disciplinary regime at the beginning of the mission. The UNMIK police commissioner regularly took disciplinary action, including repatriation. Member-states, however, occasionally thwarted disciplinary action against their personnel, and this seriously undermined UNMIK's credibility with the local population.

Resources

Pre-mission Planning and Mission Support Capacity

The preparedness of the Department of Peacekeeping Operations (DPKO) to assess the demands of Kosovo's executive policing mission conceptually, mobilize the resources required, and sustain the mission was far from adequate. DPKO's Mission Planning Unit was totally lacking in expertise on police matters, and with only a handful of officers, the Civilian Police Unit could do little more than manage personnel deployments. The expectation that UNMIK would be able to assume full responsibility for public security from KFOR after three to four months indicated a profound lack of understanding among decision makers in New York, Brussels, and Vienna of the requirements of an executive policing mission and the limitations on the capacity of the United Nations and its member-states to respond.

Mobilization of Qualified Personnel

In the estimation of Bernard Kouchner, the first UNMIK SRSG, the most important lesson to be gleaned from the Kosovo experience is that "peacekeeping missions need to arrive with a law-and-order kit made up of trained police, judges, and prosecutors and a set of draconian security laws. This is the only way to stop criminal behavior from flourishing in a postwar vacuum of authority."[85] Even though the obstacles associated with mobilizing CIVPOL personnel had been recognized before Kosovo, the only significant adaptation that had been made was by NATO.[86] There existed no ready pool of international judges or prosecutors to draw on. As a result, it was not possible to ensure solid expertise with serious criminal justice cases, and the caliber of judges ranged from extraordinary to embarrassing. With regard to the penal system, there was no international organization or NGO to turn to for professional expertise because this had never been attempted before. Eventually, a core group of advanced democracies took on the burden.[87]

Recruitment remained a chronic and debilitating barrier years later, even after the United Nations had established a routine hiring process. Delays left this vital area woefully understaffed. The UN personnel system was grudging even about providing basic information to the head of the Department of Justice regarding existing and impending openings and when the process of filling them could begin. Efforts to hire capable and hardworking candidates were regarded with unmasked suspicion, as if there was an ulterior motive involved. Thus, one of the greatest obstacles to establishing the rule of law came from the UN system itself, owing to its incapacity to provide sufficient qualified personnel in a timely manner.

Financing

The sharp distinction between the UNMIK mission budget and the consolidated budget for the Kosovo government hampered a smooth transition of responsibilities to local authorities. All equipment, computers, vehicles, protection gear, and so on provided by the United Nations for use by UNMIK Police could not, by definition, be handed over to the locals. The result was a duplication of assets, which retarded the transition process because local authorities either had to find bilateral donors to assist with major acquisitions or seek funding through Kosovo's poorly financed consolidated budget.

CONCLUSION

As suggested in chapter 1, peace becomes viable when violence-prone power structures have receded and a balance of power has been constituted in favor of legitimate institutions of government. A strategy for institutionalizing the rule of law contributes to this outcome by creating a supportive context that is able to sustain the rule of law by reducing the impunity of obstructionists while simultaneously nurturing the capacity of the domestic legal system. As portrayed in figure 7.1 (see p. 167), viable peace is the decisive turning point in the transformation from lawless rule to a point where political and criminal elites no longer enjoy impunity and the legal system is capable of preserving order, protecting basic rights—especially for minority groups—and applying the law equitably.

Capacity of the Legal System to Uphold the Rule of Law

One prominent lesson to learn from Kosovo is that it is vital to make a proper determination at the onset of the mission of the extent to which international personnel will be needed to perform essential legal functions. In the Kosovo case, it would have been more effective to assume control of all institutions required for the rule of law at the beginning of the mission. It was unrealistic and counterproductive to expect members of the Kosovo Albanian judicial community to begin administering equal justice to members of ethnic communities they identified as former oppressors. The relationship between international personnel and members of the local legal community and police force should have begun with international custodianship, subsequently evolving into a partnership, and eventually transitioning to local ownership as performance warranted. This would have greatly reduced the prolonged gap in administration of justice that permitted war-hardened power structures to cement their dominance over the political economy. When the local judiciary proved incapable of dealing with the threat posed by these criminalized power structures, or of dispensing equal justice to Kosovo Serbs, international judges and prosecutors had to be inserted into the system of justice. Because this was not done at the inception of the mission, it created the impression of usurping authority from the local judiciary and was not conducive to establishing an effective partnership.

By the end of 2003, UNMIK had made significant progress in developing Kosovo's police, judiciary, and corrections system into capable institutions. With a force that had reached six thousand personnel, the KPS had begun to assume responsibility for running police stations across Kosovo, with thirteen of thirty-nine operating under its control. The judicial system consisted of 420 judges and prosecutors, who handled 97 percent of all cases. The most politically sensitive and dangerous cases, however, involving interethnic violence, politically motivated murders, and organized crime, continued to be handled by international judges and prosecutors. The KCS had 1,416 personnel and a capacity for 1,358 prisoners, although this was still not adequate for Kosovo's needs.

By certain measures, the performance of the legal system was commendable. The police and corrections services were genuinely multiethnic institutions. Serb and Albanian police went on patrols together in mixed communities, and they served side by side in the prisons. Crime clearance rates were better than those of police forces in some major European countries. The rioting that took place in March 2004, reportedly involving some fifty thousand people across Kosovo, could not have been quelled without the contribution of KPS members, many of whom stood shoulder to shoulder with their UNMIK Police colleagues. Members of non-Albanian communities, however, did not have equal access to justice, and that is the quintessential measure of a legal system's capacity in a society struggling to emerge from internal conflict.

Shaping the Environment by Depriving Obstructionists of Impunity

Perhaps the most salient lesson emerging from Kosovo is the need to recognize and effectively address the threat to the rule of law in the local environment. Stabilizing a lawless environment requires a coordinated civil and military approach to dislodge the most serious sources of political violence and organized criminality. Cooperation must extend from those who gather intelligence to those who have the means to disrupt and deter the activity of spoilers, as well as to investigations leading to arrest, prosecution, and incarceration. Delay in fielding these resources merely compounds the difficulty of confronting obstructionists because they will continue to deepen their penetration of political and economic structures over time. Had the mechanisms to confront these threats been available from the outset of the mission, the process of reshaping the environment would have been considerably enhanced.

During 2002 the components of the intelligence-to-incarceration continuum were sufficiently well established for UNMIK to begin making high-profile arrests. Daut Haradinaj and members of his command were convicted of the 1999 torture and assassination of Ibrahim Rugova's bodyguards. Another senior ex-KLA commander, Rustrem "Remi" Mustafa, was found guilty of multiple assassinations. The culprit in the murder of prominent ex-KLA commander Ekrem Rexha, better known as Drini, who had been notably supportive of UNMIK's early efforts, also was convicted. Some seventy former KLA members were arrested and tried for major crimes. Fatmir Limaj and several other lesser former KLA figures were incarcerated in The Hague. The record with Serb spoilers is not as extensive, in part because of their ability to flee to Serbia to avoid arrest; however, the leader of a violent assault on UNMIK Police in April 2002 was ultimately convicted of a minor offense. All war crimes cases have been tried by international judges, resulting in seven convictions.

The impact has been twofold. First, the aura of impunity began to be stripped from violent underworld elements that ultimately expected to wield power in Kosovo. Second, a few members of the general population began to come forward and provide testimony in politically sensitive cases. Likewise, as prominent criminals were jailed, local judges, prosecutors, and police began to develop confidence that it was possible to prosecute such cases successfully. Selected members of the KPS were incorporated into various investigative units such as the KOCB and the central CIU and were performing valuable service.

Development of Safeguards to Institutionalize the Rule of Law

To institutionalize the rule of law, a collaborative partnership between the international community and Kosovo's criminal justice system is essential. Local institutions responsible for the rule of law continue to depend heavily on the resources and support of internationally run mechanisms, even as international personnel are transferring their overall responsibility to local actors. Institutional safeguards, primarily the oversight mechanisms for the KPS, the KCS, and the local judiciary, are still needed to provide a continuing source of assessment of the progress of local institutions at all stages of the transfer of responsibilities, and simultaneously to provide an assurance against backsliding.

The Unfinished Quest for the Rule of Law

For viable peace to result, there must be a capacity to provide equal access to justice for individuals on all sides of the internal conflict, and no one should be immune from prosecution. The "Standards for Kosovo" document, approved by the Security Council in late 2003, specified that before Kosovo's final political status could be negotiated and responsibility for maintaining the rule of law transferred to local institutions, there would have to be progress toward meeting the following conditions:

> Police, judicial and penal systems act impartially and fully respect human rights. There is equal access to justice and no one is above the law: there is no impunity for violators. There are strong measures in place to fight ethnically motivated crime, as well as economic and financial crime.[88]

As of 2004, successful prosecution in cases involving interethnic and extremist violence was possible only with international judges and prosecutors in full control of the process. International resources remained essential to breaking the impunity of political-criminal power structures on both sides of the ethnic divide, and their involvement as a safeguard on performance will likely continue to be required even after Kosovo's political status has been determined.

NOTES

The authors wish to acknowledge the generous assistance of colleagues who have provided comments, corrections, and feedback on previous versions of this chapter. Although defects that may remain are solely attributable to the authors, this work has been substantially enhanced by the assistance of Colette Rausch, Michael Hartmann,

Victoria Holt, William Irvine, Agnieszka Klonowiecka-Milart, Fredrick Lorenz, Elizabeth Press, Elizabeth Rolando, and Kevin Rousseau. Paul Mecklenburg provided extensive assistance. His perspective, which spans the entire period from UNMIK's inception to the publication of this book, was invaluable in lending continuity and coherence to the authors' work.

The views expressed by Clint Williamson in this chapter are his and do not necessarily reflect the position of the National Security Council or the Executive Office of the President.

1. Dukagjin refers to a medieval Albanian ruling family that also gave its name to the western part of Kosovo—known to many as Metohija—as well as to a large portion of northern Albania. It is not certain whether the name Leke is the name of an actual member of the noble family (it is an abbreviation of the Albanian form of "Alexander") that codified the law. Regardless, many scholars believe the Kanun cemented many customary practices already in place at the time. See Noel Malcolm, *Kosovo: A Short History* (New York: Harper Perennial, 1999), 17.

2. The Military Technical Agreement called for complete withdrawal in eleven days. See NATO, "Military Technical Agreement between the International Security Force and the Governments of the Federal Republic of Yugoslavia and the Republic of Serbia," Article II, Paragraph 2(d), http://www.nato.int.

3. For a description of the clan structure and social ties of Kosovo, see the chapter "Orientation: Places, Names and Peoples," in Malcolm, *Kosovo*, 1–21.

4. Although there is no concrete number for Serb refugees and internally displaced persons (IDPs), the UN High Commissioner for Refugees (UNHCR) has assessed the situation of ethnic minorities in general. Those relocating to Serbia proper and Montenegro, a large contingent of whom are Serbs, number about 231,000. The number of displaced within Kosovo was estimated at 22,500. See International Crisis Group, "Return to Uncertainty: Kosovo's Internally Displaced and the Return Process," Balkans Report no. 139 (Pristina and Brussels: International Crisis Group, December 13, 2002), 1. See also UNHCR/OSCE, "Preliminary Assessment of the Situation of Ethnic Minorities in Kosovo," July 10, 1999, Paragraphs 9–29.

5. See International Crisis Group, "UNMIK's Kosovo Albatross: Tackling Division in Mitrovica," Balkans Report no. 131 (Orsitina and Brussels: International Crisis Group, June 3, 2002), 3–5.

The "bridge watchers"—a group of some 150 to 200 young men—received this name because they sat in a café near the main bridge connecting (or dividing) the predominantly Serb area of Mitrovica north of the Ibar River with the Albanian-dominated sector to the south. They watched the bridge and alerted the Serb community if an incursion appeared imminent. The name was subsequently applied more generally to refer to enforcers for Serb obstructionists. In the Serbian media, the group is referred to, much more laudably, as the "Guardians of the Bridge." See International

Crisis Group, *UNMIK's Kosovo Albatross: Tackling Division in Mitrovica,* Balkans Report no. 131 (Washington, D.C.: International Crisis Group, June 3, 2002), 3.

6. UN CIVPOL in Haiti and Eastern Slavonia did execute some police functions but it was not explicitly responsible for public security.

7. UNMIK named these Special Police Units (SPUs). Subsequently, the United Nations adopted "formed police units" as a generic term for this capability.

8. William G. O'Neill, "The Kosovo Judiciary and Legal Reform," in *Kosovo: An Unfinished Peace,* IPA Occasional Series (Boulder, Colo.: Lynne Rienner, 2002), 75.

9. UN Security Council, Resolution 1244 (1999) S/RES/1244, June 10, 1999, 9(f).

10. Ibid.

11. Ibid., 11(i).

12. UN, *Report of the Secretary-General on the United Nations Interim Administration in Kosovo,* S/1999/779 (July 12, 1999), 12.

13. UN Security Council, Resolution 1244, 11(j).

14. Ibid., 11(b).

15. UN, *Report of the Secretary-General on the United Nations Interim Administration in Kosovo,* 14, 24.

16. Michael Steiner, SRSG, "Address to the Security Council," April 24, 2002, UNMIK/PR719, 1, http://unmikonline.org/press/2002/press/pr719.htm (accessed January 27, 2003).

17. Ibid. See "Section III. Benchmarks," 2.

18. Thus, "rule of law" as used here entails the maintenance of public safety and the peaceful resolution of disputes through the use of institutions of government established for that purpose in a manner that is respectful of human rights and equally applicable to all.

19. UNMIK, "Standards for Kosovo," UNMIK/PR/1078, December 10, 2003, 3.

20. Robert B. Oakley, Michael J. Dziedzic, and Eliot M. Goldberg, eds., *Policing the New World Disorder: Peace Operations and Public Security* (Washington, D.C.: National Defense University Press, 1998), 511–512.

21. UN, *Report of the Secretary-General on the United Nations Interim Administration in Kosovo,* 9.

22. UN Security Council, Resolution 1244, 9(f). Nevertheless, this was not a fully integrated structure. UNMIK Police and the Department of Judicial Affairs were later combined to form one of UNMIK's four pillars, called the Department of Justice.

23. Oakley, Dziedzic, and Goldberg, *Policing the New World Disorder,* 520.

24. UN, *Report of the Secretary-General on the United Nations Interim Administration in Kosovo, 2.*

25. Ibid., 17.

26. Michael Steiner, SRSG, "Three Times for Kosovo" (speech presented at Humbolt University, Berlin, November, 12, 2002).

27. In spite of the considerable difficulty associated with mobilizing a capable international police force, there were even more serious defects in the options considered at the time. One alternative would have been to use SPUs to perform the executive policing function, along with a temporary contingent of local police. This proposal was quickly abandoned and, in retrospect, for sound reasons. Because the United Nations had never attempted to field such a force, there were no units on call for deployment, and the first SPUs did not begin arriving for almost a year. Thus, this option would have left UNMIK with no policing capability during the most crucial stage of the mission, when the campaign of violence against the Serb population was the most intense and a vicious internal power struggle was raging within the Kosovan Albanian community. In July 1999 consideration was also given to recruiting local "community liaison officers" to provide unarmed law-and-order assistance on a temporary basis (e.g., monitoring and reporting on the security situation and focal point for complaints). Relying on minimally trained recruits to fill the policing void was also deemed unacceptable because UNMIK would have risked exposing these personnel to conflict with the KLA's ad hoc police force.

28. The original nomenclature was confusing, using "police primacy" for the more limited sphere of criminal investigative activity and "tactical primacy" for the full spectrum of patrolling activities, deterrent presence, and so on.

29. NATO, "Undertaking of Demilitarisation and Transformation by the UCK," signed June 20, 1999, Paragraph 25(a), http://www.nato.int.

30. Colette Rausch, head of the OSCE Rule of Law Division (October 2000–June 2001) and acting director of the OSCE Department of Human Rights and Rule of Law (June 2001–October 2001), interview by Michael Dziedzic at the United States Institute of Peace, Washington, D.C., November 2001.

31. Sandra Mitchell, drafter of the OSCE plan for the Kosovar Judiciary, interview by Michael Dziedzic, August 9, 2002. See OSCE, Mission in Kosovo, Department of Human Rights and Rule of Law, *Observations and Recommendations of the OSCE Legal System Monitoring Section: Report No. 2—The Development of the Kosovo Judicial System (10 June through 15 December 1999)* (Pristina: OSCE Mission in Kosovo, November 1999), http://www.osce.org/kosovo/documents/reports/justice/report2.htm.

32. It was superseded through Emergency Decree 1999/3.

33. UNMIK's Legal Department drafted Regulation 26/1999, which extended the length of preindictment detention to a maximum of one year. See O'Neill, *Kosovo*, 78.

34. The AJC was created through Regulation 1999/7 on Appointment and Removal from Office of Judges and Prosecutors.

35. These shortcomings were largely rectified during 2000 through bilateral funding for infrastructure repair and "quick-start" judicial packages.

36. Colette Rausch, "Kosovo: Justice and Police Reforms" (unpublished manuscript, April 2002), 26.

37. Ibid., 25–26.

38. Ibid., 25.

39. Ibid., 26–27.

40. OSCE Mission in Kosovo, Office of Press and Public Information, "OSCE Trains 700 Kosovar Jurists," Monitor Final Edition, Pristina Media Highlights, from *Koha Ditore,* May 9, 2003.

41. O'Neill, *Kosovo,* 90.

42. This included serving as acting director of the Department of Human Rights and Rule of Law from June to October 2001.

43. Rausch, "Kosovo," 19.

44. CPT Alton L. Gwaltney III, "Law and Order in Kosovo: A Look at Criminal Justice during the First Year of Operation Joint Guardian," in *Lessons from Kosovo: The KFOR Experience,* ed. Larry Wentz (Vienna, Va.: Command and Control Research Program, July 2002), 259, http://www.dodccrp.org

45. William Irvine, director of the Penal Management Division for UNMIK, interview by Michael Dziedzic in Pristina, November 2002.

46. Simon Chesterman, *Justice under International Administration: Kosovo, East Timor and Afghanistan* (New York: International Peace Academy, September 2002), 5.

47. UNMIK, "On the Authority of the Interim Administration in Kosovo," UNMIK/REG/1999/1, July 25, 1999, http://www.unmikonline.org/regulations/1999/reg01-99.htm.

48. O'Neill, *Kosovo,* 80.

49. Ibid., 80.

50. UN, *Report of the Panel on United Nations Peace Operations (The Brahimi Panel Report on Peacekeeping),* A/55/305-S/2000/809 (August 21, 2000), 14, http://www.un.org/peace/reports/peace_operations.

51. "Strategy for Defeating Inter-ethnic Violence," drafted by Michael Dziedzic, UNMIK strategic planner, Spring 2000, 3.

52. Lawyers Committee for Human Rights, *A Fragile Peace: Laying the Foundations for Justice in Kosovo* (New York: Lawyers Committee for Human Rights, October 1999).

53. O'Neill, *Kosovo,* 84.

54. For example, UNMIK Regulation 2001/12, "On the Prohibition of Terrorism and Related Offenses," defines terrorism and makes it a criminal offense, effective June 14, 2001.

55. UNMIK Regulation 2001/20 deals with witness protection, and Regulation 2002/06 addresses use of covert measures.

56. Robert Perito, "'Odd Jobs': The Role of Special Police Units in Kosovo" (unpublished manuscript, July 25, 2002), 24.

57. O'Neill, *Kosovo*, 89.

58. In December 1999 UNMIK began to develop a concept called the Kosovo War and Ethnic Crimes Court (KWECC). The KWECC would have been staffed by both local and international jurists with authority to deal with war crimes, genocide, crimes against humanity, and serious interethnic crimes committed after January 1, 1998. UNMIK administrators conceived of the KWECC as a local version of the International Criminal Tribunal of Yugoslavia (ICTY) focused on past war crimes and current ethnic violence. It was not conceived of as an instrument for dealing with barriers to the rule of law stemming from the nexus between ethnic violence and organized crime. The focus on prosecuting war crimes also gave the KWECC a price tag that ultimately doomed the concept.

59. UNMIK/REG/2000/6.

60. UNMIK/REG/2000/34.

61. The arrest of former KLA fighter Afrim Zequiri for murdering three Serbs, including a four-year-old, with an assault rifle provoked concern that he would be summarily released by the local judiciary. An international judge was quickly reassigned from Mitrovica to serve as the investigating judge.

62. As stated in a briefing on Regulation 2000/64 provided to SRSG Michael Steiner, the "sixty-four panels," as they were called in reference to the regulation creating them, were established "to minimize the probability for certain miscarriages of justice." SRSG Briefing on Regulation 2000/64, 1. This also indicates how limited a guarantee of fair treatment the involvement of Serb judges would have been, even if they had been willing to remain in numbers proportional to their percentage of Kosovar society (roughly 10 percent).

63. SRSG Briefing on Regulation 2000/64, December 2000, 1.

64. See Michael E. Hartmann, *International Judges and Prosecutors in Kosovo: A New Model for Post-conflict Peacekeeping*, United States Institute of Peace Special Report no. 112 (Washington, D.C.: United States Institute of Peace, October 2003), 10–12. Also, in its April 2002 report, the OSCE observed that without formal criteria for case selection, "cases of a similar nature and seriousness risk being treated differently. It also permits political and other irrelevant considerations in assigning panels to cases." OSCE, Department of Human Rights and Rule of Law, *Kosovo: A Review of the Criminal Justice System, September 2001–February 2002* (April 29, 2002), 30.

65. Steiner, "Address to the Security Council," 1.

66. Gwaltney "Law and Order in Kosovo," 247.

67. UN, *Report of the Secretary-General on the United Nations Interim Administration in Kosovo,* 13.

68. Ibid.

69. Ibid.

70. Rausch, "Kosovo," 28–32.

71. OSCE, Department of Human Rights and Rule of Law, *Kosovo: A Review of the Criminal Justice System, February 1, 2000–July 31, 2000* (August 10, 2000).

72. Subsequent reports reiterated many of the same themes and raised added concerns about the treatment of juveniles and the mentally ill and about cavalier attitudes by some members of the judiciary toward trafficking in women. OSCE, Department of Human Rights and Rule of Law, *Kosovo: A Review of the Criminal Justice System, September 1, 2000–February 28, 2001;* and OSCE, Department of Human Rights and Rule of Law, *Kosovo: A Review of the Criminal Justice System, September 2001–February 2002* (April 29, 2002).

73. Rausch, "Kosovo," 30.

74. Ibid., 27–28.

75. The team's assessment is summarized in United States Agency for International Development, United States Office Pristina, and OSCE, "Kosovo: Justice Sector Assessment, Second Assessment Mission (JAM II)," January 22, 2002, 1.

76. UNMIK/REG/2001/8.

77. Of the four locals, one was a Serb. The composition could be altered, however, at the SRSG's discretion. Pillar III took exception to the dominant role of the SRSG, who both approved the composition of the KJPC and was the ultimate authority for ordering removals, arguing that this limited KJPC autonomy.

78. The JIU had been in de facto operation for several months, although it was not formally created until May through Administrative Direction 2001/1 implementing UNMIK Regulation 2001/15 of May 22, 2001.

79. International Corrections and Prisons Association, *Practical Guidelines for the Establishment of Corrections Services within United Nations Peace Operations* (Ottawa: International Corrections and Prisons Association, February 15, 2002), 23.

80. Rausch, "Kosovo."

81. UN, *Report of the Secretary-General Pursuant to Paragraph 10 of the Security Council Resolution 1244 (1999),* S/1999/672 (June 12, 1999), 4.

82. United States Agency for International Development and OSCE, "Kosovo," 9. See also "The New Draft Criminal Law and the Law of Criminal Procedure: Another Step in Building a Democratic Kosovo," UNMIK/FR/0049/01, June 22, 2001, http://www.unmikonline.org/pub/features/fr049.html.

83. Parallel with the work of JAC/LM, international experts established working groups to write regulations on different issues; there were cases when regulations were promulgated without the JAC having even minimal involvement in the process.

84. Memorandum from the International Judges and Prosecutors in Kosovo to the UNMIK Office of Legal Affairs, "The Provissional Criminal Procedure Code of Kosovo: Cautioning Comments by International Judges and Prosecutors," December 2, 2002.

85. R. Jeffrey Smith, "Kosovo Still Seethes as UN Official Nears Exit," *Washington Post*, December 18, 2000, A20.

86. Efforts by the United Nations to establish a rapidly deployable mission headquarters had been abandoned before the Kosovo mission because of opposition from the United States.

87. The Brahimi Report has recommended measures to rectify many of these resource deficiencies, but the response from member-states has not been overwhelming.

88. "Standards for Kosovo," 3.

8

Forging a Viable Peace

Developing a Legitimate Political Economy

Stephanie A. Blair, Dana Eyre,
Bernard Salomé, and James Wasserstrom

Within months of the return of refugees in 1999, the streets of Pristina began to sport a surprising number of luxury cars. Their suspected origins prompted a facetious tourist slogan, "Come visit Kosovo—your car is already here." Upscale German sedans mixed with rusty, smoke-belching Zastavas and Yugos. They commandeered the sidewalks as parking lots, competing for space with raucous street vendors peddling smuggled cigarettes, pirated music CDs, and counterfeit DVDs.

THE CHALLENGE

Navigating the streets of Pristina in the early days of the international intervention, one could observe in microcosm the components of Kosovo's economy: the remnants of a socialist past rusting away, enterprises of marginal legality vigorously springing up, and surprising displays of wealth. Not as evident but equally profound were the political dynamics associated with these activities as Kosovo sought to emerge from a political economy of conflict.

Although the nexus between wealth and power may not always be easy to discern, peace will seldom prosper if the political-economic incentives for continued conflict are overlooked. Anthony Lake suggests that one of the primary reasons for the neglect of this elemental issue may be the difficulty associated with thinking across disciplinary boundaries:

> Mention the deleterious political effects of a sound economic policy at a meeting of economic planners, and watch their fingers drum impatiently

on a table. Talk about the economic details at a conference of diplomats working on a political settlement and watch their eyes glaze. Tell a politician about the importance of painful economic sacrifice now for the sake of economic health later and watch his or her eyes widen in alarm. But economists, diplomats, and political leaders [and soldiers] must think in each other's terms, or reconstruction will fail. Such thinking is necessary from the beginning of the reconstruction process—as the diplomats fashion the political arrangements that could end the fighting, and as the economists plan for the first stages of economic recovery.[1]

As painful as it may be for diplomats, politicians, economists, and soldiers steeped in the relative conceptual clarity of their own disciplines, the experience of the United Nations Interim Administration Mission in Kosovo (UNMIK) demonstrates the vital importance of integrated thinking about transforming the political economy of war-torn societies. The purpose of this chapter is to capture that experience and use it as a basic guide for the development of a holistic and integrated political-economic approach to building a viable peace.

Although the transformation of the Kosovo political economy has been spotty, perhaps the most salient lesson is that politics and economics are inextricably linked. Depending on the nature of that nexus, a postwar political economy can either fuel further violence or promote peace. Exploring these relationships is the core task of this chapter.

Because the concept of a political-economic strategy to transform conflict is new, this chapter has a slightly different blueprint than the three previous strategy chapters. In our treatment of the *context*, we first define the general characteristics of a political economy of conflict. Later, in the section dealing with the *strategy*, we describe UNMIK's *economic* strategy, which was narrowly focused on long-term macroeconomic development, as captured in the phrase "construction, not reconstruction." UNMIK's approach evolved later, as its understanding developed regarding Kosovo's thorny connections between politics and illicit wealth. In time, UNMIK's thinking tilted in the direction of a *political-economic* strategy. The mission did not pursue an organizationally conscious, integrated political-economic strategy, however. Consequently, we identify the lines of effort that a model political-economic strategy should follow to transform conflict in war-torn societies. We then review the actions taken by UNMIK in each of these lines of effort.

By 2003 the mission had identified all the components of such a strategy, but many of its efforts were late, poorly focused, or under-resourced. Delays hindered UNMIK's ability to forge a viable peace in a reasonable time frame, contributing to both the lack of support for UNMIK by Kosovo's Serb community and the slow erosion of support among the Albanian population.

The Context

A Political Economy of Conflict

The term "political economy" refers to the relationship between wealth and power in society. The Overseas Development Institute defines this field of study as "concerned with the interaction of political and economic processes in a society: the distribution of power and wealth between different groups and individuals, and the processes that create, sustain and transform these relationships over time."[2]

For this concept to have value in designing a strategy for forging a viable peace, we must distinguish between a "political economy of conflict" and one that is capable of sustaining peace.[3] In abstract terms, a political economy of conflict has the following characteristics.

- *Economic transactions take place predominantly in the illicit informal marketplace.* Civil war can pay enormous dividends for those who wield power in a political economy of conflict. War profiteering is a major incentive for continued fighting because trafficking in arms and other contraband is lucrative business. Arms smuggling in a war-torn society is symptomatic, however, of a fundamental failure of the formal economy. The bulk of economic activity takes place in the subterranean or informal economy.

  The informal economy has two dimensions. The first is the *gray economy*, which involves commodities that would normally be considered legitimate; however, many of these transactions are conducted in illegal ways, such as the avoidance of taxes, violation of regulations, smuggling, the evasion of economic embargoes, currency manipulation, and the illegitimate exploitation of raw material resources. The second dimension of an informal economy is the patently illegal *black market*. Common black-market activities include money laundering and the trafficking of weapons, drugs, and women.

  In contrast, in the political economy of a self-sustaining peace, the majority of transactions are in the open *formal economy* and take place in broad accordance with legal and regulatory frameworks.

- *The state is captured by a criminalized elite sustained by illicit sources of revenue.* In failing states torn by internal conflict, cash and material assets from state-owned enterprises are siphoned off for private gain and partisan political purposes. Customs services, exchange rates, and internal markets are also manipulated to extract resources and dispense patronage to important power brokers. Additional unaccountable revenue streams are derived from shadowy gray- and black-market activities. International sanctions simply drive up the profit margins for thriving mafia-style elites who control profitable smuggling networks. Illicit wealth acquired from trafficking, smuggling,

Figure 8.1. The Political Economy of Conflict

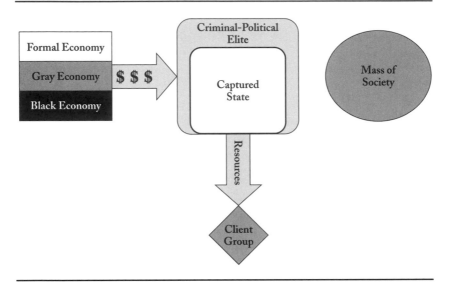

and extortion is used to reinforce the grip of this political-criminal class on power.

In addition to patronage and personal enrichment, these illicit funds provide the means to maintain a repressive apparatus that can be used for coercion, terror, intelligence activities, and paramilitary operations against dissent groups and rival ethnic communities. A criminalized political class can also exploit its control over basic commodities (e.g., food, fuel, shelter) to cow the population. This repression sets up a reinforcing cycle: capture of the state enables manipulation of markets and control over the population, which solidifies the grip of criminalized elites on power.

In contrast, within the political economy of a self-sustaining peace, the state is sustained by legitimate formal mechanisms, such as taxation and customs, and is largely independent of direct manipulation by any criminal elite.

- *Social conflict is manipulated to "legitimize" the regime.* Only a privileged "support group" that is identified with the political-criminal elite on ethnic, religious, tribal, or similar grounds benefits from the restricted distribution of wealth and power. To the extent that the state functions at all, it is exploited by a corrupt ruling elite to repress opposition and extract wealth from other social groups. Legitimacy is derived from the manipulation of societal cleav-

Figure 8.2. The Political Economy of Self-Sustaining Peace

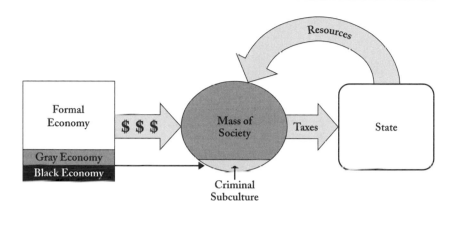

ages that reinforces the need for solidarity between ruling elites and their
support group. Other segments of the greater population are driven into
poverty and may be compelled either to seek employment in the diaspora or
to become refugees. (Refugee camps serve resistance movements not only
as a sanctuary but also as a rich source of new fighters.)

In contrast, within the political economy of a self-sustaining peace, the
state has a market-enabling role, facilitating engagement in open, legitimate
commerce by the population as a whole.

In a political economy of conflict, therefore, criminal, illicit, or informal
activities dominate all three realms: political, economic, and social, as shown in
figure 8.1. Those who control the shadow economy increase their power and
wealth while depriving the legitimate formal economy of growth and revenue. A
large segment of the general population pays the price in both cases.

Forging a viable peace in a war-torn society hinges on understanding fundamental differences between the structure of a political economy of conflict and
one that undergirds and sustains peace, as depicted in figure 8.2. In the latter case,
the bulk of economic activity is derived from legitimate formal transactions that
are conducted in accordance with the prevailing legal framework. Even though
shadowy informal markets continue to exist, political elites are no longer sustained primarily by these illegal economic activities. Consequently, illicit revenues
do not play a decisive role in defining who wields political power and controls

state functions. The integrity of the revenue stream that allows essential state services to be provided must also be maintained for the political economy to be sustainable. More equitable distribution of wealth and an expanding middle class are essential to nurture a genuine civil society and anchor the role of the state as a conflict mediator.

Kosovo's political economy in 1999 had been shaped by the ongoing disintegration of Yugoslavia and internal hostilities between Serbs and Albanians. The historical evolution of this political economy of conflict is highlighted here.

The Geocultural Heritage

Because Kosovo's general economic circumstances have never been particularly advantageous, the region has historically generated little wealth by producing marketable commodities. Kosovo's location and geography, however, have made smuggling a traditional mainstay of its economy. During the Ottoman period, local Balkan notables were appointed to protect roads and mountain passes from thieves. Often these appointments were exploited for local benefit by granting rights to certain thieves to plunder Ottoman caravans or other travelers in return for a share of the proceeds. These bandits enjoyed a legitimate status in Balkan society because they provided for their clans and villages and created a sense of brotherhood.

Kosovo's Economy (1950s–1980s)

Kosovo was the poorest part of the Socialist Federal Republic of Yugoslavia (SFRY—"Socialist" was dropped from the name in 1992, when the country became the Federal Republic of Yugoslavia, FRY). In the late 1950s the majority of Kosovo's population was sustained primarily by agriculture, with major industrial activity taking place only in mineral extraction, in particular the Trepca lead and zinc complex. Federal investments in the 1970s focused on developing Kosovo's lead, zinc, and lignite deposits, the latter being among the richest in Europe. Two coal-fired power plants were constructed adjacent to these coalfields with the intention of generating a surplus for export to Albania and Greece, although poor design prevented this goal from being realized. This period of investment also resulted in the opening of a ferronickel mine and plant in Glogovac, the expansion of Trepca, and the development of various secondary enterprises (e.g., an automobile factory, battery factories, a shock absorber plant, and a belt and rubber factory).

These industrial entities were collectively owned and managed by their workers and were known as socially owned enterprises (SOEs). Because plants were located in rural areas, most workers remained rooted in agrarian communities and farmsteads. Traditional family and clan ties to localities persisted. The result was the development of what has been called the "peasant worker" society.

The substantial federal investments of the 1970s and 1980s had only begun to transform Kosovo's agrarian economy when Yugoslavia went into steady economic decline. The federal development campaign was undercut by the collapsing Yugoslav economy. Kosovo faced the gravest consequences, with its unemployment rate rising to 54 percent by the late 1980s, three times the national average.[4]

Milosevic rose to power in May 1989 amid this context of economic turmoil. The basic political-economic characteristics of his oppressive regime were an extension of the logic of the Titoist system. Two elements were key. First, personal connections, or *veza*, were essential lubricants. Delivery of materials, availability of capital, and access to markets were all at least partly mediated by this closed system. Second, the boundary between institutional and personal wealth was blurred. It was accepted that those in positions of authority commonly diverted public resources for their own use. This was true whether the diversion enabled the construction of Tito's many palaces and retreats or provided perks to a factory director. When the Milosevic regime brought punishing international sanctions on the entire country, the result was a general collapse of legitimate economic activity, a return to dependence on still significant rural and family roots, and a burgeoning of informal gray and black markets.

The Evolution of a Political Economy of Conflict (1990s)

By the 1990s any formal and informal mechanisms of accountability present in the Tito era had atrophied. As Milosevic accumulated power, the exploitation of "public" wealth by select members of his regime expanded enormously. Official plundering included asserting state ownership over Kosovo's major public utilities. Thus, valuable socially owned enterprises became publicly owned enterprises (POEs). Kosovo's electric company was subsumed under a Serbian company run by Milosevic's cronies. They took over key business positions and systematically turned public or organizational capital into personal wealth, creating a "Sultanist" regime characterized by an absolute fusion of political power and personal wealth.[5]

This capture resulted in rapid decapitalization and stripping of assets from the Yugoslav industrial plant, a trend already under way owing to the reduction in investment capital. Higher oil prices, economic recession in Western Europe, and a reduction in Western loans to Yugoslavia compounded the adverse impact on Kosovo's fading formal economy. The inevitable result was "an economic collapse of extraordinary ferocity."[6]

In Kosovo this collapse was seen in "a growing dependence on agriculture, especially for self-consumption, a deterioration in agricultural practice, and a diminution in the physical stock in productive industry and infrastructure."[7] One report, looking at the region of Pec, noted, "Today, after five decades of socialist development, [Pec's] economy is back where it started . . . the transition from a pre-industrial agricultural economy to an urban manufacturing centre has failed."[8]

The effect of this collapse was magnified in Kosovo by Milosevic's politically inspired action in 1990 to deprive the province of its autonomous status. The Serb takeover resulted in the removal of ethnic Albanians from state-run enterprises, government ministries, and university faculties. Some Albanians turned to self-employment. Others relied on remittances from close relatives who went to Western Europe to find employment. The majority in Kosovo's growing diaspora toiled at honest pursuits. The combined effect of this experience was to instill a vibrant, enterprising spirit in much of the Albanian population. Linkages with organized crime across Europe, particularly the drug trade and prostitution, also flourished, however.[9]

Kosovo's exile Albanian population (approximately 180,000 in Switzerland and 150,000 in Germany)[10] contributed to the maintenance of a "parallel government" through an informal tax of 3 percent of income collected both inside Kosovo and from the diaspora. This revenue allowed Albanian clans to conduct a sustained period of passive resistance to the Milosevic regime in the early 1990s under the parallel government led by Ibrahim Rugova's Democratic League of Kosovo (LDK).

A parallel economy thus emerged in Kosovo along with Rugova's parallel government. International economic sanctions played a role in its emergence, further damaging Yugoslavia's struggling formal economy. Sanction busting became one of the major sources of wealth for the Milosevic regime. There is anecdotal evidence that Milosevic deliberately encouraged population flight from Kosovo because this resulted in the removal of unwanted Albanians and increased remittances of hard currency.

Kosovo's Albanians also took advantage of their unique position as middlemen. Yugoslavia needed hard currency and access to external sources of supply, both of which were available via the ethnic Albanian diaspora. Ethnic connections in the region facilitated transnational cooperation with the criminal underworld in neighboring Macedonia and Albania. A significant regional smuggling apparatus developed as a result. It is probably not mere coincidence that Albanians who continued to work for the Yugoslav customs service after the Serb takeover in 1990 are among the few Albanian officials who remained in government service but are not publicly denounced today as collaborators.

The Postwar Security Vacuum

The withdrawal of Milosevic's army and police forces from Kosovo in June 1999 produced a public security vacuum that Daan Everts, chief of the Organization for Security and Cooperation in Europe (OSCE) mission in Pristina, referred to as an "open invitation" to organized crime. As nearly eight hundred thousand Albanian refugees streamed back into Kosovo, Albanian criminal gangs rushed in along with them. A lack of border controls allowed almost anything to be smuggled in or out, including drugs, cigarettes, alcohol, cars, and petrol.

The Kosovo Liberation Army (KLA) quickly filled the vacuum as Belgrade's forces withdrew, establishing a "provisional government" as the de facto governing structure. Amid the chaos, local KLA groups set up "security companies" of doubtful provenance that enabled them to extort protection money from entrepreneurs, small businessmen, and farmers. Some former KLA members exploited criminal skills and connections they had developed during the conflict by engaging in trafficking in drugs, cars, weapons, and human beings. Others were widely believed to be involved in illegal trade in cigarettes, alcohol, and petroleum products, as well as other economic activities of problematic legality, such as the sale of counterfeit goods.

As former KLA members moved to assert control over Kosovo's levers of power and sources of wealth, they came into conflict with supporters of Rugova's LDK. Antipathy between the LDK and Hashim Thaci's Democratic Party of Kosovo (PDK) persisted, and violence believed to be associated with this struggle continued to plague Kosovo.

In the minority Serb community, Kosovo's political economy became radicalized through Belgrade's surreptitious funneling of support for Serb paramilitary "bridge watchers"[11] in Mitrovica in northern Kosovo, as well as support for similar militant elements in other Serb communities. At least until January 2002 the bridge watchers were funded out of the budget of Belgrade's Ministry of the Interior. Leading bridge watchers were reputed to be involved in organized crime, including cigarette smuggling, prostitution, extortion, and protection rackets.

Cultural practices also have had a heavy influence on Kosovo's political economy. Political leaders exercise significant control over a wide range of economic resources and wealth. The system of *veza* was not challenged in the political struggles of the 1980s and 1990s.[12] Patronage systems—which provide both power for elites and protection for their clients—continued after the demise of the Milosevic regime in 2000; merely the ethnic identity of those in control of the resources had changed. Thus, certain traditional practices continued, including patronage for clientele groups, the avoidance of taxation and regulatory requirements, nonpayment of utility bills through connections or abuse of public office, and off-the-books transactions between relatives and business partners. Some Albanian leaders in the 1990s sought to substitute their own autocratic control for the repression of Milosevic's regime. Their interests would be negatively affected by UNMIK's reform efforts to establish an honest civil administration, ranging from an impartial civil service to a transparent tax regime.

UNMIK faced a challenging transformation: a political economy in which illicit sources of wealth and de facto access to political power were intermingled. In the early stages of planning for Kosovo, attention was given to repairing war damage, yet this was probably the least problematic postwar requirement in terms of transforming Kosovo's political economy of conflict. The real strategic challenge was to disentangle the murky and often criminalized political-economic linkages that had sustained Albanians and KLA groups in their violent struggle against the Milosevic regime, and vice versa. Thus, UNMIK needed to ensure that the power of the gun, grounded substantially in illicit activities in the 1990s, did not translate into the power to dominate the postwar environment and consequentially the nascent political processes of Kosovo.

The Objective

The international community paid little attention to political-economic issues during the establishment of UNMIK. UN Security Council Resolution 1244 did not establish political-economic objectives; however, paragraphs 11 and 17 provide an indirect basis for doing so. They state:

> The Security Council . . .
>
> 11. Decides that the main responsibilities of the international civil presence will include:
>
> (g) Supporting the reconstruction of key infrastructure and other economic reconstruction;
>
> (h) Supporting, in coordination with international humanitarian organizations, humanitarian and disaster relief aid. . . .
>
> 17. Welcomes the work in hand in the European Union and other international organizations to develop a comprehensive approach to the economic development and stabilization of the region affected by the Kosovo crisis, including the implementation of a Stability Pact for South Eastern Europe with broad international participation in order to further the promotion of democracy, economic prosperity, stability and regional cooperation.

The connection drawn in paragraph 17 between a "comprehensive approach" and the creation of democracy, economic prosperity, and stability indicates recognition of the importance of political-economic linkages.

Beyond this general idea, however, there was relatively little indication of political-economic objectives to transform conflict, intended or implied, or of the means to achieve them. Economic development was seen to be important, and in some way linked to the long-term success of the peacebuilding effort. In contrast with democratic development and human rights promotion, however, which had reasonably well-established functional meanings (implying democratic elections, development of an independent media, civil society development, gender equality, and equal participation by all ethnic groups), there was a lack of common understanding about the functions implied by these paragraphs.

UNMIK thus entered Kosovo with only the vaguest of outlines for political-economic objectives and with relatively little international or local consensus about what Resolution 1244 implied. Key issues were not addressed. Was privatization to be a function of the interim administration? How about management of public utilities and other enterprises? Would UNMIK vigorously pursue private-sector development or would development be left to the initiative of the individual investors? Would Kosovo's market be rapidly opened to the outside competition or given a protective shading of tariffs until it established itself? Was the formal economy the exclusive realm of concern or would transformation of the informal economy also be required? How would this process relate to the transformation of war-hardened power structures?

If a political economic objective had been articulated, it would have addressed the transformation from a political economy of conflict to one that permits peace to prevail. For this to happen, peace must pay for those who participate in its building, and conflict must cost for those who oppose the peace effort. Making peace pay and obstructionism cost requires the development of autonomous public institutions that command adequate, relatively independent resources. These institutions must, over time, take over the international community's role in sustaining a winning coalition for peace, and the economic incentives and capacity for continued violent conflict must be curtailed so that illicit sources of wealth cannot determine who governs. Finally, the foundations of a broad and reasonably equitable distribution of wealth must be set, for this is the basis for long-term development of a prosperous economy and a self-sustaining peace.

THE STRATEGY

Lessons Applied from Previous Experiences

UNMIK's initial approach was shaped by the Western experience in supporting economic transitions in the former Soviet socialist bloc, the lessons from the recent postconflict efforts in Bosnia, and the established consensus among key donors and international financial institutions. This concurrence led not to a full political-economic strategy to transform conflict but to an economic development strategy with emphasis on macroeconomic fundamentals and a concern for generating revenues to fund the essential activities of the state. Activity in Kosovo's formal economy, as opposed to its insidious informal or underground markets, was regarded as the proper sphere of interest.

Focus on the Macroeconomic Fundamentals

One major area of consensus within the international community was the need to emphasize macroeconomic policy. Early in the planning process the World Bank, the G-8, the International Monetary Fund (IMF), and the European Union met in Brussels and agreed on the broad outlines of the approach to economic reconstruction and development. Kosovo was to have a market economy and fiscally responsible government and budget management. The province was also to be integrated economically within the region and with Europe.[13]

Accordingly, a stable currency and a functioning banking system subject to high standards of prudential regulation and supervision became foremost priorities initially. A strong regulatory framework was also required to create an attractive environment for foreign and domestic investment and to provide a disincentive for operating illegally. The essential elements were a business registration system, enterprise and contract laws, competition and investment laws, and mechanisms for solving disputes.

Nearly as important in shaping UNMIK's initial economic development strategy was the international community's view of Kosovo as a postsocialist economy in transition, albeit one suffering from the physical consequences of war. Thus, a November 1999 World Bank report noted that the twin challenges faced by Kosovo's economy were "recovery from the long decades of lack of basic productive investment . . . and the creation of incentives and institutions to make a rapid transition to a market economy."

This macroeconomic focus was reinforced by the international experience in Bosnia. By the spring and early summer of 1999 the international community had been involved in the implementation of the Dayton Peace Accords for more than three years. The international critique of efforts in Bosnia was captured in a report prepared for the May 1999 European Commission/World Bank donor conference. Institutional development and reform in Bosnia were regarded as "modest" and "slower than hoped."[14] Banking-sector reform was slow, pension reform had not yet begun, and the pace of establishment of critical Bosnian governmental institutions was called "much slower than hoped."[15] These lagging areas were regarded as "among the most complex of all of Bosnia and Hercegovina's post-war tasks."[16] As hot topics arising during the planning for Kosovo, these issues all received emphasis in the planning for UNMIK's economic strategy.

Capture Revenue to Fund the State

The urgent need for basic services, as well as the lessons of Bosnia, spurred early emphasis on public finance. UNMIK's dominant fiscal objectives were the formulation of a sustainable budget increasingly financed through domestic revenues with reduced reliance on external donor support,[17] the development of fiscal institutions ensuring the efficiency and probity of public spending, and the establishment of a liberal trade and customs regime that would permit Kosovo to realize its potential for growth and exports in the context of its geographical location in the south-central Balkans.

Focus on the Formal Economy

Economic reconstruction strategists viewed Kosovo's economy primarily through summaries of what it had been in the late 1980s. Thus, in a July 1999 World Bank paper, the economy of Kosovo was described as made up of "(i) a predominantly privately-owned agriculture that accounted for about one-third of GDP, and occupied more than half the active population; (ii) a number of state-owned industrial companies . . . another third of GDP; and (iii) a large variety of informal activities (mainly in the trade and services sector)."[18] Little note was made in any documents published in this period of the criminalization of Kosovo's political economy or its ties to organized-crime networks thriving in the region. To be sure, the effects of the last decade were noted, but these were conceived almost exclusively in terms of damage to infrastructure, a loss of human capital, and a lack of investment and consequent lack of maintenance or capital improvement. No mention was made in publicly available documents of the problem of overcoming the political-economic linkages of the thriving gray and black sectors of Kosovo's economy. This tended to be regarded as a social phenomenon that belonged to the police.

UNMIK's early macroeconomic approach to Kosovo's complex political-economic challenges was shaped by these basic ideas. The dominant model of the linkage between politics and the economy was a simplistic one, captured in the title of a November 1999 report by the World Bank, *Kosovo: Building Peace through Sustained Growth*.[19] Other areas, such as privatization and meso-economic development efforts[20] to enable specific economic sectors or industries, were marked by distinct differences of opinion. UNMIK's early approach reflected these differences.

The Economic Strategy: Construction, Not Reconstruction

Given that Kosovo's reconstruction effort would require substantial institutional resources, the UN secretary-general enlisted the expertise and capabilities of the European Union to lead UNMIK's Pillar IV, the mission's reconstruction endeavor. The European Union was charged with rebuilding the physical, economic, and social infrastructure and systems of Kosovo and supporting the reactivation of public services and utilities.[21]

The core idea behind UNMIK's initial economic strategy is captured in the phrase "construction, not reconstruction." The first head of Pillar IV, Joly Dixon, described the concept this way:

> A preliminary examination of the economic situation suggests that more emphasis should be put on economic governance and development than on reconstruction. A large part of the existing structures, both in terms of infrastructure and institutions, may well be incompatible with the goal of creating a sound economy. The goal is not to put humpty-dumpty together again. It is necessary to concentrate on economic and social development more than reconstruction. Furthermore, reconstruction is a static and backward looking concept. Development looks to the future. The objective is to build a strong and well-developed economy firmly based on market principles and the rule of law. Also globalisation implies that Kosovo's economy will have to be well integrated into regional and international structures.[22]

UNMIK sought to create the conditions for a free market to function. While not rigidly laissez-faire, this approach placed considerable faith in a positive response from market forces. In emphasizing the construction of an economic field on which the dreams of entrepreneurs would play, UNMIK was betting that "if you build it, they will come." The question was, Would they come quickly enough to demonstrate to Kosovo's massive unemployed population that peace would pay, an essential condition for advancing the peace process?

UNMIK also placed emphasis on the generation of local revenue to fund Kosovo's governmental functions. In the summer and fall of 1999, discussions with the G-8, the World Bank, and the IMF centered around the size of budget deficit that would be acceptable for 2000. Given the need to establish a tax and customs regime from scratch, significant revenue could not be anticipated before mid-2000. This created a contradiction between the political imperative for UNMIK to begin making peace pay by establishing effective governance and the economic dictates of the international financial community to avoid subsidizing the provision of basic services.

Revenue generation quickly became an urgent requirement. Finance ministers involved in deliberating this issue were reluctant to subsidize governmental functions. They were prepared only to fund a budget deficit of fifty million deutsche marks. This was not enough to pay for Kosovo's civil service and the anticipated deficit in utilities services, principally costs associated with operating the power station. This boisterous debate was resolved when the international community accepted a higher budget deficit and the European Union, as head of Pillar IV, proposed rapid implementation of a customs regime at the international border crossings between Kosovo, Federal Republic of Yugoslavia, and FYROM and Albania and a simplified business registration mechanism. The European Union's basic concept was to create a regime for collection of revenue that would make it more rational for businesspeople to pay taxes than to seek to avoid them.

The focus of Pillar IV's effort is clear in the initial report of its activities, published in September 1999.[23] It had three short-term priorities. The first was "keeping the economy going" and included essential services to get through the coming winter. The second was "building the macroeconomic framework." This priority is described in much more detail in the report and included developing the legal framework for a market economy and the institutional framework for economic governance and fiscal management (i.e., a tax system, a customs service, and a banking and payments authority). The third priority was "policy dialogue with the local population." Activities such as housing construction and infrastructure efforts were described as medium-term goals, along with development of the education and health sectors, the agriculture and food-processing industries, and business enterprises.

THE EVOLUTION OF A POLITICAL-ECONOMIC STRATEGY

UNMIK did not begin with a political-economic strategy. However, its initial strategy for economic development did evolve in response to events. As local political developments forced confrontation with issues not addressed in early planning, elements of a political-economic strategy began to emerge.

This evolution took place in two phases. The first, occurring between the fall of 1999 and the spring of 2000, can be characterized as "the problem of the missing middle" or the "relief-to-development *dis*continuum." At one end of the continuum, the international community recognized the need for immediate postwar humanitarian assistance. As a result there was no serious hunger or disease crisis in the postwar period. At the other end of the continuum, attention was given to the need for long-term economic reform (hence the development of the Customs Service, the Central Fiscal Authority, and the Banking and Payments Authority of Kosovo, among other institutions). The "missing middle" consisted of government salaries, utility reconstruction, and business revitalization that UNMIK was not adequately prepared to address. A gap developed, therefore, between short-run humanitarian assistance and the long-term process of economic development. The basic enablers of normal business activity had been relegated to the medium term, but they rapidly became central problems for UNMIK, particularly in the winter of 1999–2000 and the following spring.

The second phase can be characterized as "the (re)discovery of organized crime." As UNMIK's initial challenges were resolved and an interim political course was set, UNMIK turned to what had been considered longer-term challenges. Thus, recognition grew only over time that organized crime was intimately linked to political extremism and that it must be dealt with in order to deprive obstructionists of their financial underpinnings.

The aim here is to suggest what a generic political-economic strategy might consist of. The elements of this strategy serve as a framework for the ensuing discussion of the evolution of UNMIK's strategy for transforming Kosovo's political economy of conflict into one that is capable of sustaining peace. In a nutshell, this strategy requires simultaneous action on four lines of effort:

- *The economic foundations of obstructionist power must be undercut* (see #1 in figure 8.3). The economic incentives for continued conflict must be removed. For this to happen, the overpowering influence of criminally obtained wealth over the exercise of political power must be radically diminished. External funding for subversive activities (e.g., from neighboring states and organized-crime networks) must also be curtailed. These efforts must be sustained throughout the peace process.

- *Peace must pay so that the coalition for peace can prevail* (see #2 in figure 8.3). Peace is a political agenda, and as with any political agenda, local political leaders must be willing to carry it forward. Contending elites will have to take risks for peace, and if their backing is to be won and maintained they and their supporters must benefit from the peace process. Peace must pay for *all* the parties to the conflict, moreover, if they are to develop a stake in sustaining peace. The benefits of peace need to flow without regard to ethnic, religious, or political affiliation and regardless of collective attributions of blame. Peace must offer all parties the promise of tangible improvement in the quality of life. Expeditiously restoring power and basic public services very early in the mission, therefore, should be a top political and economic priority.

- *The state must be fiscally autonomous and sustainable* (see #3 in figure 8.3). Establishing the autonomy of the state from lawless forces that had held sway during the conflict is a primary concern. Essential to this end is the integrity of the revenue stream required to sustain essential state functions. If the political clout of warlords and similar obstructionists is to be contained, the state must have the ability to fund efforts to counter their subversive activities. If the coalition for peace is to be sustained, the state must also be

Figure 8.3. The Political Economy of Viable Peace

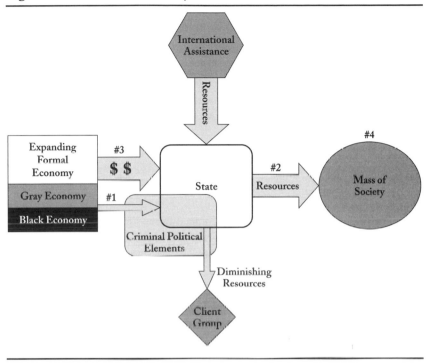

able to deliver benefits to society based on need, not exclusively on the basis of connection to patronage structures.

- *The macroeconomic foundation for expanding the formal economy and distributing the benefits of peace must be put in place* (see #4 in figure 8.3). Building the foundation for legitimate economic activity must start at the very beginning of the mission. This includes restoring the banking system and creating a legal and regulatory framework that promotes enterprise and protects the public sector from politicization and corruption. Alternatives to employment in the underground economy need to become sufficiently available so that there is a broad interest in maintaining transparent and accountable political and economic structures. This is the foundation for the political core of a self-sustaining peace—the long-term development of an economically stable middle class, which, through its demands for an increasingly open, accountable, and efficacious state, ultimately makes peace self-sustaining.

Although all four lines of effort of the strategy must be pursued more or less simultaneously, they have different gestation periods, and their impact on the peace process varies at different times. Undercutting the economic power of obstructionists and strengthening the coalition for peace are essential to reshape the balance of power in the early stages of the peace process. Ensuring the integrity of revenue required to sustain the state is a sine qua non for both the political and the economic transformations required to attain a viable peace. Laying the foundation for a legitimate formal economy that distributes wealth throughout society is critical if a self-sustaining peace is to emerge over the long term.

Difficult trade-offs must be made between long-term economic efficiency and mobilizing near-term political support for the peace process. When, for example, should public utility workforces, bloated by a history of state subsidy, be downsized? When should subsidies for public utilities or basic commodities be cut? Such actions may support long-term economic goals, but laid-off workers facing high levels of postwar unemployment may become ready recruits for subversive groups bent on obstructing the peace process. Disgruntled publics aroused by persistent privations may run out of patience before long-term economic projects yield results.

How UNMIK came to recognize and deal with such trade-offs is treated next.

Undercutting the Economic Foundations of Obstructionists

A natural symbiosis exists between the use of political violence and the revenues generated by criminal activity. Funding for obstructionists may come from various sources, including illicit or corrupt activities under their direct control or external funding by surreptitious patrons and conspirators operating outside the mission area. As described earlier, both of these sources were used by obstructionists operating in Kosovo. In the Balkans the roles performed by paramilitary organizations, unaccountable intelligence cells, and organized-crime networks have tended to overlap and reinforce one another.[24] They all share antipathy to the rule of law and have an overriding stake in preserving the nexus between political power and illicit wealth. The combination of income from crime and the propensity for political violence renders these elements intolerable obstacles to a viable peace. Their damaging influence on the political process must be neutralized and, to the extent possible, eliminated.

This entrenched threat was not collectively recognized as harmful to the peace process in Kosovo, though some individuals were aware of it. The tendency was to define the problem simply as organized crime and, therefore, a matter of secondary importance to be dealt with much later. UNMIK thus failed to distinguish between criminal activity that was instrumental to obstructing the peace process and that which was inherent in Kovoso's society. Indeed, the central challenge of conflict transformation was not even recognized until well into the mission.

While Bernard Kouchner was special representative of the secretary-general (SRSG) (July 1999–January 2001), UNMIK gradually began to acknowledge the existence of an organized-crime threat to the peace process. A statement prepared by UNMIK for the donors' conference held in Brussels in November 1999 recognized that

> the activities of organized criminal elements appear to include protection rackets, smuggling, extortion, gambling and the sale of narcotics. There are also indications of trafficking in persons, prostitution and trade in human organs. The presence of organized crime in Kosovo directly contributes to instability and the present weakness of the rule of law in Kosovo.[25]

Members of the Balkans Contact Group, particularly Italy and Germany, became concerned with the transnational aspects of Kosovo's organized-crime threat, leading to the creation of a Criminal Intelligence Unit (CIU) within UNMIK. There was reluctance initially, however, to link the CIU to any law enforcement response within Kosovo. The impetus for the CIU had more to do with major European nations' concerns about criminal activity on their own soil rather than with its adverse influence on Kosovo's peace process.

By the time of Michael Steiner's leadership of UNMIK (January 2002–July 2003), there was a general recognition that ending the impunity of those associated with criminalized power structures was a sine qua non for peace to prevail.[26] UNMIK's measures to develop reliable instruments to complete the entire rule-of-law continuum, from intelligence to incarceration, are described in chapter 7. The most challenging aspect was to develop the means to gather evidence against the sources of political-criminal violence. Among the entities that UNMIK created to fill this gap were the Kosovo Organized Crime Bureau, an investigative unit within UNMIK Police that possessed sophisticated technical means and experienced criminal investigators, and a Sensitive Information and Operations Unit within the Department of Justice for the prosecution of members of organized crime, terrorists, and transnational lawbreakers.

UNMIK took another vital step by establishing the legal framework to attack criminal networks associated with extremist violence. This entailed criminalizing terrorist activities and providing for witness protection. Also vital was the ability to target international capabilities on the most significant extremist threats by coordinating the efforts of KFOR and UNMIK. Most of these measures began to coalesce during 2002, leading to the arrest of dozens of former KLA fighters suspected of postwar murders of fellow Albanians. Those arrested included senior former KLA commander Rustrem "Remi" Mustafa and members of the intelligence apparatus he controlled.[27]

Although these efforts bolstered enforcement action against extremist networks on both sides of Kosovo's ethnic divide, UNMIK was slow to implement regulations to drain the revenue from Kosovo's underground economy that sustained their obstructionism. The mission began to confront this issue with the creation of an Economic Crime Unit in November 2001 and a Financial Investigation Unit (FIU) staffed by specialists from the Italian Guardia di Finanza in 2002.[28] The standards announced by Michael Steiner in April 2002, however, made no mention of illegal economic activity. In December 2003, when these standards were further refined as a basis for determining Kosovo's readiness for final-status negotiations, UNMIK officially specified economic and financial crime as a priority concern. Among the requirements established in the December 2003 "Standards for Kosovo" were the following:

- Effective legal, financial, and administrative mechanisms that conform to EU standards are in place to tackle economic crime in both the public and private sectors, including seizure of illegally acquired assets.

- Adequate investigative mechanisms have been created and are functioning effectively.

- Money-laundering legislation is effectively implemented and suspicious financial-transaction reporting is in place.[29]

Among the instruments that are most important for a political-economic strategy aimed at depriving obstructionists of illicit wealth, therefore, are criminalization of money laundering, the seizure of illegally acquired assets, and a competent criminal investigative body. It was not until UNMIK was four years into the mission, however, that these instruments began to be wielded. In implementing these anticorruption measures, UNMIK had to confront political interference, intimidation, and threats of physical harm that were indicative of the continuing nexus between ill-gotten wealth and structures of power opposed to peace.

UNMIK had to guard against empowering obstructionists through its own expenditures. Thus, its "mission economics" had to be carefully controlled. Although not all missions will command the magnitude of funding that was available to UNMIK, all spend substantial sums on routine operations in poor, war-torn societies. Humanitarian assistance, infrastructure repair contracts, supply procurement, utility bill payments, banking and insurance activities, and staff housing rent are but a few of the many economic transactions undertaken by a mission that are likely to contribute to a burgeoning gray market. The impact of these expenditures needed to be scrutinized and controlled by UNMIK so as to avoid inadvertently subsidizing the activities of obstructionists. If spoilers could demand that shopkeepers close for a day of protest, then UNMIK could surely insist that those who sold services to the mission adhere to a code of conduct that precluded such behavior. Because the United Nations did not pay taxes on imported fuel, this exemption had to be carefully controlled to preserve the integrity of Kosovo's new customs system. Audits of procurement, particularly of critical commodities such as fuel and large capital goods (e.g., construction equipment), were vital for controlling mission economics and undercutting funding streams to obstructionists.

Strengthening the Coalition for Peace by Ensuring That Peace Pays

Humanitarian assistance is key to demonstrating, at the outset of a mission, that peace pays. Humanitarian assistance has both political and economic consequences. Certainly, the overall level of popular support for any intervention will be influenced by the efficacy with which the international community delivers emergency relief. This external assistance may also begin to diminish the population's dependence on patronage provided by rival paramilitary leaders. Although relief efforts are not undertaken for these reasons, their implications should be taken into account by those responsible for implementing a strategy of conflict transformation.[30]

In Kosovo, the delivery of humanitarian aid to the ethnic Albanian community was generally successful, in both its humanitarian objectives and its political implications. Thousands of tents, 45,000 heating stoves, winter clothes for 250,000 children, more than 500,000 blankets and mattresses, and 160,000 tons of food were delivered to more than half the population of Kosovo.[31] Thanks to these efforts and the resourcefulness of the Albanians themselves, there was no humanitarian crisis in the winter of 1999–2000.[32] The immediate needs of the population were met, and there was no "crisis of confidence" over the international community's efforts in the initial stages.

The same was not true, however, for Serb and other minority populations. There was initially "little awareness of the plight of minority communities."[33] Although the UN High Commissioner for Refugees established an Ad Hoc Task Force on Minorities in July 1999, other agencies were slower to adapt to the unexpected challenge posed by violence against the Serb community in Kosovo. Although a more effective program of humanitarian assistance to the Serbs might have had only a limited impact on reducing the number of Serbs who eventually fled, the preservation of a multiethnic society was pivotal both for Kosovo's final status and for long-term regional stability. Thus, this highlights the unavoidable connection between humanitarian assistance and political outcomes, particularly in building a coalition that can sustain momentum toward a viable peace.

In contrast with the overall effectiveness of the early relief effort, the middle of the relief-to-development continuum was missing. UNMIK had much less success in reconstituting basic services that affected the daily lives and economic prospects of all residents. A host of factors severely limited the mission's responsiveness, among them the rapid return of refugees, the ensuing violence, and the difficulties associated with mobilizing, deploying, and funding the mission.

In addition, however, the conceptual approach taken by the international community to Kosovo's political economy was also responsible for the missing middle. Resources were focused on long-term construction of the private sector, to the detriment of immediate reconstruction of basic services that were provided by the POEs, such as Kosovo's power company.

Compounding this, the prevailing international economic orthodoxy opposed providing direct budgetary support to restore basic services, such as the recurrent costs of salaries of teachers, doctors, and government officials. Because these were local officials who were not UN staff, their salaries could not be paid by UN peacekeeping assessments. In the absence of any functioning mechanism to generate tax revenue locally, there was no way to fund government services in Kosovo. The only source of revenue to fill this short-term gap was the international donor community, but finance ministers who influenced these decisions initially refused to provide budgetary support, insisting that Kosovo be self-sufficient.

The desire of economists for immediate financial self-sufficiency clashed with the political imperative to make peace pay. The macroeconomic emphasis on long-term private-sector development did not address the immediate requirement to get the major publicly owned utilities operating. During the winter of 1999–2000, an acute gap in public utilities services emerged. The sporadic availability of electricity, water, sewage, and garbage collection[34] created a discontinuum between emergency relief and long-term development and severely undermined the credibility of and support for UNMIK.

The overall result was a pronounced gap between the point at which emergency relief activities concluded and the point at which long-term economic development, or construction, activities could be expected to kick in.

The most troubling condition leading to the missing middle was UNMIK's chronic inability to establish a reliable system of power generation. The ramifications were felt in both the economic and the political spheres. Recurring power outages had a ripple effect throughout the meager formal economy, driving up the costs of production and disrupting the water supply system, heating, and other productive activities. The political consequences were even more detrimental, however, because the lives of all the people of Kosovo were continually affected. Nothing did more to discredit UNMIK than this constant aggravation. The continual inability to rectify this problem created an adverse impression of UNMIK that became more pervasive over time. This loss of support played into the hands of obstructionists, who were eager to hasten UNMIK's departure before their influence could be undercut.

The challenges confronted by UNMIK in this area were monumental. Among them:

- Kosovo's two power plants were aging and poorly maintained, with one requiring major overhaul to be viable.

- Serb engineers and technicians who had been operating the system had fled.

- The power grid had been damaged during NATO's bombing campaign, hampering importation of electricity.

UNMIK initially took a laissez-faire approach. This allowed former KLA members to assume managerial control over Kosovo's electric company, Korporata Energjetike e Kosoves (KEK), and the associated coal mines. The result was a bloated, incompetent, and politicized workforce. The productive plant, already poorly maintained, suffered damage as a result. During the first winter, hard-liners inside KEK sought to use their control of the power grid as a tool to drive Serbs out by cutting off their power supply. KEK was also a source of largesse (e.g., jobs, patronage, and kickbacks) for those who were in a position to exercise de facto control. Only in 2002 was the power of this politicized workforce broken and competent management placed in charge.

The task of assessing and funding essential repairs was left to international donors, which led to an uncoordinated and incomplete response. The result was a chronically unreliable supply of electricity and the refusal of many consumers to pay their bills. When combined with the widespread practice of pirating power, even after four years of UNMIK administration, KEK was able to collect only enough revenue to cover 45 to 50 percent of its direct costs. This paltry revenue stream was barely adequate to pay workers' salaries and the cost of consumables such as fuel. This meant that expenses for repairs and for the import of electricity to cover shortages had to be subsidized out of government coffers or the repairs left undone.

In spite of major infusions of capital to keep the system afloat, the power supply remained sporadic. The core problem of management incompetence and cronyism remained unresolved. The largely self-appointed KEK workforce was inefficient, overstaffed, and unaffordable, and the political consequences continued to mount. Before May 2002, there were no standard employment contracts or job descriptions, so accountability was impossible to achieve. Only after professional standards were established and enforced was competent management put in place.

Because the top management position was in international hands, UNMIK became a convenient scapegoat for the power utility's inadequacies, exemplified by the conviction for embezzlement of an early KEK international manager. This was indicative of UNMIK's difficulties in creating a framework to regulate public enterprises and hold management accountable.[35]

The entire mission fell into disrepute as a result, and this continuing short-coming was a common theme in anti-UNMIK editorials. The inability to keep the power going, when the Serb-run system had continued to function even under persistent international duress, weakened UNMIK's ability to sustain support for Kosovo's essential political transformation.

To have averted, or at least minimized, these damaging consequences, UNMIK needed a strategy for improving the management of large and complex public utilities. It could have hired experienced international corporate manage-ment teams to assume control over the core functions of KEK and other vital POEs. The basic aspects of corporate governance, such as human resources, accounting, procurement, billing, and information management, should have come under international oversight at the beginning of the mission. This could have been achieved by recruiting a team of ten to fifteen managers to work under contract for the United Nations, supported by a contract with a major utility to provide technical expertise on a temporary as-needed basis. Regardless of the merits of the particular solution, it is clear that public utilities management should not be a peripheral issue for a mission such as UNMIK.[36] Immediate delivery of electrical power on a sustained basis was central to building a coalition for peace.

Perhaps the most vital lesson to be drawn from UNMIK's experience is that future international administrations should be prepared to fill the missing middle as rapidly as possible by asserting effective managerial oversight of vital public utilities. This would have to include the rapid introduction of corporate manage-ment teams, the resolution of indemnity issues, and the creation of a suitable regulatory framework for exercising due diligence and ensuring the long-term accountability of public-sector enterprises.

UNMIK needed to nurture a coalition for peace in the Serb community as well. Yet UNMIK had neither the means to curb the flow of funding that was used by the Milosevic regime to maintain parallel governing structures in Serb communities nor the capacity to substitute for the administrative services they provided.[37] Thus, Belgrade's funding ensured that the average Serb remained tied, directly or indirectly, to support from the obstructionist Milosevic regime. Belgrade continued to support social services such as education and health even after the demise of the Milosevic regime in October 2000.

Various political and economic factors constrained UNMIK from asser-tively seeking to stop Belgrade's harmful influence on the peace process. For example, when Hans Haekkerup was SRSG, UNMIK decided not to confront the issue because of the political imperative of obtaining Serb acquiescence for the Constitutional Framework and participation in parliamentary elections in 2002. Even if UNMIK had devised a way to staunch the flow of Belgrade's external support to the Serb community, it would have been unwise to do this without the capacity to provide a reliable replacement for the social services involved. For Serbs even to begin contemplating reliance on UNMIK, their lives would have to show demonstrable improvement under the mission's influence. The greatest opportunity to do this existed in multiethnic communities.

The reopening of the Brezovica ski resort in the predominantly Serb municipality of Strpce provides an illustration, albeit a rare one, of a major development effort specifically designed to give the Serb community a stake in the peace process.[38] This project was a combined effort by KFOR and UNMIK involving revitalization of facilities, repair of the access road, financing for the ski school and equipment rental, and use of the facilities by KFOR as a rest and recreation site for its troops. The resort's economic viability was reasonably assured owing to the patronage that could be expected from the international community alone. The political importance, however, was measured in terms of the use of the facility by ethnic Albanians and the advancement of a multiethnic society, in addition to its value in enhancing the sustainability of the Serb community in Strpce.[39]

While this venture contributed to a climate that fostered the return of ethnic Albanian residents to their homes in the municipality, it did not alone end Strpce's reliance on Belgrade or the continued presence of Serbia's Interior Ministry police in the enclave. Undercutting this experiment in peaceful coexistence was the refusal of the Serb resort management to pay for its consumption of electricity, compelling KEK to suspend service. Confrontation between the two ethnic communities continued, including demonstrations and a stone-throwing clash with U.S. troops over the return of Albanians to the area. Though modest in its specific contribution, the ski resort venture represents the sort of activity that was needed to nurture Serb support by demonstrating that peace pays.

Developing a Fiscally Autonomous and Sustainable State

The central issue is safeguarding the integrity of the revenue stream for the state. The tax base must be developed in tandem with institutional controls to prevent the diversion and capture of revenue, especially by actors who profited from the conflict and who continue to obstruct the peace process. The state must have the fiscal capacity to provide security and other essential services to sustain the base of support for peace.

One of UNMIK's significant successes in the effort to ensure an economically viable self-government was the Customs Service. UNMIK chose a strategy that emphasized state revenue generation at the international borders (and eventually at Kosovo's internal boundary with Serbia and Montenegro). Customs fees included a value-added tax (VAT) at the border rather than at point of sale. UNMIK's initial focus was on efficient revenue collection and not on the constriction of illegal revenue flows to obstructionists. The primary concern was ensuring that revenues would not be diverted by carelessness, incompetence, theft, or corruption. For that reason, proposals for various tax exemptions were rejected if the system lacked the administrative capacity to enforce them.

UNMIK was not very successful, however, in addressing the issue of fuel smuggling. This was due in part to the difficulty involved in establishing an audit trail for fuel importation, physical issues in the control of distribution, and the greater volume of fuel transportation.

One notable success, in both raising tax revenue and undercutting funding for potential obstructionists, was cigarette taxation. Cigarettes were among the most heavily smuggled legal commodities in the Balkans. UNMIK achieved notable success in combating smuggling with a simple strategy. Initially, it reduced the tax rate to only two euros per one thousand cigarettes, an almost economically negligible rate, to eliminate the incentive to smuggle. This allowed UNMIK to gather information on trade patterns, identify and license distributors (with significant penalties for noncompliance), build customs capacity, establish habits of compliance, and clamp down on counterfeit cigarette manufacturing inside Kosovo.

Because the tax rate in the former Yugoslavia was fifteen euros per one thousand, an unintended consequence was the use of Kosovo as a conduit to smuggle cigarettes into the country. UNMIK was not unconcerned about regional smuggling; however, it was necessary to lay this foundation for revenue control first in order to proceed with the introduction of more sophisticated controls later—for example, through the use of banderols. Once these were in place, rates were then increased to six euros per one thousand. This combination enhanced Kosovo's revenue collection and reduced incentives for regional smuggling. Compliance stayed at previous levels. At least one major political figure is rumored to have told relatives involved in the cigarette importing business to ensure that all activities were legal so that his political standing would not be tainted. Thus, the generation of tax revenue was moving in a positive direction in sustaining Kosovo's state apparatus, and this was having a beneficial impact on the accountability of those seeking political power.

Establishing the Macroeconomic Foundations for Expanding the Formal Economy and Distributing the Benefits of Peace

Economic well-being for all ethnic communities in Kosovo is the bedrock of long-term political stability. This requires putting in place the foundations for a functioning formal economy and a distribution of the benefits of peace that promotes legitimate enterprise and creates jobs while diminishing the prominence of economic and financial crime and black-market activity. The eventual goal is the rise of a middle-class market economy in which state revenues are grounded broadly in society. This is a long-term transformation initiative associated with a self-sustaining peace, but the foundation must be put in place for peace to become viable.

The macroeconomic components of a strategy to accomplish this transformation include a sound legal and institutional base that is conducive to business. This was the economic objective most clearly recognized by UNMIK at the start of the mission. This objective also requires a regulatory apparatus and corporate governance structure that is capable of holding public officials (both international and local) and the private sector accountable for criminal misconduct. It should be noted that UN officials serving in Kosovo, including those who hold public office, are subject to the secretary-general's right and duty to waive immunity in the discharge of their official function. This requirement was not addressed at the onset of the mission, and the delay in putting these mechanisms in place had detrimental political and economic implications.

The need to establish a strong legal and institutional framework to attract foreign and domestic investment was clearly recognized by international planners. Bilateral donors, the IMF, and the World Bank all shared the immediate priorities identified by UNMIK of creating an environment conducive to private-sector activities. These priorities included "resolution of basic property rights, regulation of banking and finance, clarifying conditions for foreign trade and setting up simple procedures for company registration."[40] By the end of 1999 UNMIK had issued regulations addressing most of these issues.[41] Especially notable was its success at establishing a functioning banking system with a stable currency.

In partnership with the IMF, UNMIK's Banking and Payments Authority of Kosovo served as both a payment bureau and a banking and insurance regulator. This allowed for the growth of a substantial banking sector. By mid-2003, seven banks, with more than one hundred branches, had begun operation. Two had controlling international partners, and five were locally owned. The challenge that accompanied this success was that capital began to accumulate in the banks before quality loan demand developed. Nonetheless, this success was one of the best examples of the early strategy to focus on developing the framework for an expanding formal market economy.

UNMIK's early efforts to invigorate the *private* sector were necessary and appropriate. Largely neglected, however, was the need to take assertive action to ensure responsible corporate governance over the *public* sector. This allowed Kosovo's POEs to come under the influence of actors with political or criminal motivations. Because the POEs accounted for the preponderance of Kosovo's formal economic activity, the damaging result was a serious "graying" of the white economy.

Even though UNMIK was successful at creating a legal and institutional context capable of attracting investment, Kosovo had few enterprises available to invest in. When UNMIK attempted to privatize Kosovo's SOEs and thereby stimulate growth in the formal economy, it faced enormous obstacles.

The SOEs had socialist governing structures and management councils. They had no boards of directors. In some cases internationals were superficially in charge, but they were unfamiliar with the way SOEs functioned. The legal status of SOEs was unclear even under Yugoslav law. They did have a legal character, but they did not have by-laws or corporate attributes. This created legal uncertainty.

Another constraint was the limited value of the assets involved. Only a few dozen of some 350 SOEs were worth salvaging, so privatization was not going to be a panacea for Kosovo's economic plight. On the other hand, even unprofitable ventures often sat on valuable real estate, and privatization was clearly essential to allow the limited potential that did exist to be exploited.[42]

The promulgation of an UNMIK regulation that would authorize a privatization process was blocked until the spring of 2002 because of philosophical differences within the Security Council (with Britain and the United States in favor and China, France, and Russia opposed). Another reason for delay was that the privatization process required an appropriate legal framework that protected the United Nations from possible liabilities as well as the need for the European Union (which is the lead organization over the pillar responsible for this process) to assume responsibility. Another year passed before the Kosovo Trust Agency was established to begin implementing the process. In the interim, a process of "commercialization" was used to place certain of the more remunerative enterprises in operation without affecting the status of their ownership. This was successful at generating jobs and investment and was far less contentious than privatization.[43] Subsequent demands for swift privatization by Albanian leaders exacerbated tensions between international and national actors, resulting in demands for the removal of the KTA head.

Regulating the public sector was another major concern. If measures taken to capture revenue lost to smuggling can be described as "whitening the gray," then actions aimed at preserving the integrity of transactions in the formal marketplace might be described as preventing the "graying of the white." In Kosovo the bulk of formal economic activity was accounted for by fifty-five POEs that collectively controlled assets estimated at $1 billion.[44] Basic services such as electricity, telecommunications, heat generation, water supply and waste treatment, and operation of the railroad and airport were provided by public utilities. UNMIK's economic strategy concentrated on creating a legal and institutional framework for liberating the nascent private sector, while public enterprises were left essentially unregulated, even though these monopolies were the dominant sources of legitimate revenue in Kosovo's economy.

Especially in a cash-based economy, there is a crucial need to audit large revenue-generating enterprises to prevent their diversion into patronage networks, partisan political activities, or private bank accounts. The vacuum of oversight and accountability provided abundant opportunities for fraud. KEK, for example, delivered twelve million euros' worth of electricity per month but collected only about five to six million euros in payments. UNMIK's understanding of KEK's actual cash flow was limited by its inability to conduct basic investigations of KEK's cash flow potential (e.g., through the conduct of technical audits monitoring power consumption in a given region, identifying and disconnecting illegal connections, and auditing individual consumer bills).

Even entities of Kosovo's provisional institutions of self-government have failed to pay their utility bills, yet local authorities have consistently followed a policy of trying to take over the utilities, particularly telecommunications and KEK. If only 10 percent of the uncollected revenue went into illicit pockets, then that would have amounted to a half million euros per month potentially diverted into obstructionist activities that would undermine progress toward a viable peace. Thus, UNMIK compounded its early failure to insert international management teams into the POEs, which was needed to get them efficiently back into operation, by failing to establish a regulatory regime that would ensure that they would be run in a manner consistent with the public trust and its own objectives.[45]

When responsibility for the POEs was transferred in July 2002 from the interim civil administration to the Kosovo Trust Agency, the head of Pillar IV requested an audit. Completed a year later, that 2,250-page document revealed systemic irregularities, including a general lack of accounting procedures, vast procurement abnormalities, poor or nonexisting asset records, billing and collecting processes vulnerable to fraud, a lack of personnel policies for hiring and firing, and unclear company ownership. In late 2003 UNMIK took comprehensive steps to assert control over the POEs and their substantial cash flow. These measures included the following:

- Creating an Office for Co-ordination of Oversight of Publicly Owned Enterprises

- Forming an Investigative Task Force composed of investigators from the UN Office of Internal Oversight Services, the EU Anti-fraud Office, and UNMIK's Financial Investigation Unit with jurisdiction over the activities of UNMIK, Kosovo's institutions of self-government, and the POEs[46]

- Lifting the immunity of internationals suspected of involvement in financial misconduct (while not a new measure, it may not have been used earlier in UNMIK because of a lack of investigations and evidence providing a reasonable basis for such a request)

- Reforming the management structure of the POEs with an emphasis on responsible corporate governance, including legal incorporation, finance and accounting, billing and collection, merit-based hiring and firing, transparent procurement procedures, and modern systems for management of information

- Ensuring that international staff are formally notified and cognizant of their obligations to avoid conflicts of interest and beginning an information campaign on this topic for personnel of the provisional institutions of self-government and the POEs

- Initiating operation of the local Auditor General and other accountability agencies[47]

Although there were profound philosophical disagreements within UNMIK about the proper mixture of public and private enterprises, there was no political or economic merit in allowing monopolies with high volumes of cash flowing through them to operate in a regulatory vacuum. The most fundamental action required was to clarify their legal status by requiring the POEs to be incorporated, with by-laws and a board of directors capable of holding management accountable. Incorporation also makes it possible for the POEs to be taken to court for violations of their public obligations. Regular audits and annual financial statements were also needed to establish accountability.

Just like the private sector, the POEs required a legal framework that would allow them to operate profitably and attract needed investment. They were handicapped by a lack of policy on disconnection for chronic nonpayment,[48] on the role of the police in enforcing collection of overdue bills, and about how the rights of consumers could be protected. Basic issues such as whether competition was to be allowed, who would license it, how much to charge for service, whether the POEs should be privatized, whether they could borrow money, and what share of their assets or future earnings could be used as collateral remained unresolved for more than four years.

With all these uncertainties, coupled with the politicization of the workforce and other hidden liabilities, prospects for investment in Kosovo's public enterprises were far from maximized. These issues needed to be resolved in the early stages of the mission, not only to provide a basis for expanding Kosovo's formal market economy, but also to prevent it from slipping into the realm of illicit, gray-market transactions.

PROCESSES AND RESOURCES

Processes

Identify and Resolve Political and Economic Trade-offs

A political process that does not take into account the persistence of economic incentives and motivations for continued conflict will founder. Economic reforms that undermine political processes for resolution of the conflict will be futile. International missions that separate political affairs from economic matters can result in barriers to integrated efforts, unless mission leadership ensures close collaboration among these key functions, consistent with the mission's overall mandate.

Trade-offs and interaction between political and economic purposes need to be identified and resolved in a way that supports the mandate and promotes progress toward a viable peace. An integrated political-economic planning process is an essential mechanism for this purpose. There will be an inclination to divide the planning process into discrete categories that simply mimic the structure of the organization, however, and this will have to be avoided. The ability to think outside disciplinary straitjackets must be encouraged and rewarded. Ultimately, the head of the mission should make an informed determination about how the interaction and trade-offs between the two realms should be handled.

Take Culture into Account

A political-economic strategy to transform political-criminal sources of conflict must be developed on the basis of an understanding of the cultural influences and historical context of the relationship between wealth and power. Which elements of economic and financial crime have cultural roots and are, therefore, more resistant to change? Which elements are an artifact of the conflict and, thus, more amenable to transformation? How much is cultural and how much is situational? What is the role of the diaspora, in terms of both monetary flows and prospective support for the process of transformation? Basic concepts such as "investment," "company," and "accounting," among others, are taken for granted in Western economies. Local understanding of these foundational ideas may be significantly at variance with the meanings in the modern capitalist world.

Ensure Accountability for Internationals

Members of the international community serve in an environment where economic transactions are cash based, conditions are chaotic, and they are granted immunity. Some may be given authority over major public enterprises, and others will oversee the expenditure of vast sums of assistance monies. In the absence of effective systems of accountability, some are likely to succumb to the temptation for embezzlement, kickbacks, and other financial misconduct, perhaps in collusion with local actors who are obstructing needed transformation in the political economy. At a minimum, the international presence will be discredited by such misconduct and the fund of local consent will be squandered.

From the inception of a mission, audit and accounting processes must be in place, along with stringent internal monitoring and enforcement mechanisms for criminal activity. Scandalous misconduct cannot be allowed to result merely in repatriation. Immunity must be lifted, and punishment meted out, as warranted, not only as a deterrent to international officials, but also as an example to local civil servants that internationals are held, at a minimum, to the same standards that they are. Accordingly, the secretary-general has a right and a duty to waive the immunity of any official where, in his opinion, the immunity would impede the course of justice and would not prejudice the interests of the United Nations.

Adapt Public Information to Local Understandings

An understanding of the media culture and its relationship to criminalized power structures will be essential to the ability of the mission to get its message across. The depth of comprehension of market principles must also be gauged and properly addressed if policies that are heavily reliant on privatization are to prosper. If the population in general lacks an understanding of market forces, much will be wasted through ill-conceived investments. Missions must base their campaigns on the understandings of capitalist concepts that the population holds, not on the understandings held by international experts.

Resources

Funding Operations of Basic Public Services

The pace of the dispersal of funds from the European Union during the first year of the mission did not match the urgency of the task, especially in the face of the need to restore basic public services. Compounding this, no provisions had been made to fund the activities of local government. Lacking an operational budget until November 1999, UNMIK's municipal administrators were in no position to dismiss self-appointed former KLA "officials" without risking a collapse of services and possibly violent opposition. For the first six months, therefore, the KLA collected (illegal) fees and taxes, which did not foster UNMIK's standing in the eyes of the local population.

When a mission suffers months of delay in obtaining funding to restore basic services and government functions, the reservoir of goodwill that accompanies the arrival of internationals can soon be exhausted. This complicates the challenge of building a coalition for peace precisely when the political challenges are apt to be most severe and perhaps mission threatening. Although the United Nations has a capacity to convene donors' conferences and secure pledges of financial support, the dispersal of these funds is seldom timely, and when funds do arrive they may be tied to specific projects. This can leave the mission with very little flexibility to respond to the immediate imperatives of a political-economic strategy.

Competent Staff Managers and Technical Experts

Municipal administrators and municipal affairs officers were appointed in Kosovo's municipalities as early as August 1999; by October UNMIK had deployed international staff into the vast majority of Kosovo's municipalities. For at least the first year of operation, the U.S. government provided the bulk of the staffing for Pillar IV. The lack of international staff to oversee the restoration of the supply of electricity set in motion a troubled history of ineffectual involvement that continued to haunt the mission for years. Thus, the availability of a pool of civil administrators and utilities managers, in addition to political affairs specialists, police, and others involved in establishing the rule of law, is crucial to prospects for success. International staff also need to be adequately trained and prepared for the rigors of international service.

UNMIK lacked the staff to draft all the necessary economic regulations with efficiency, especially when overriding political questions had to be resolved (e.g., the Constitutional Framework). Philosophical differences also contributed to delay. Protracted review prolonged the process further. The resulting delay was detrimental for two reasons: it retarded the transition to a free market, and it kept the SOEs in a state of limbo that resulted in a great deal of blatant misconduct.

Information on Political-Criminal Networks and Activities

The core requirement is to understand the scope of gray- and black-market activities and the extent of their political relevance. By definition, these transactions are unrecorded, which means they are not captured in economic statistics. In Kosovo even the most basic statistics about the formal economy were lacking. Accurate economic statistics are required for trade, gross domestic product, inflation, and unemployment as a vital starting point, and these data must be supplemented by assessments of the flow of remittances and the underground economy.

CONCLUSION

UNMIK was only partly conscious of its political-economic objectives, though this awareness increased over time. Although it clearly recognized short- and medium-term economic objectives, the political payoff for these objectives—a market economy that would enable a self-sustaining peace (see the upper right-hand side of figure 8.4)—was mostly imagined in the long term.

The consequences of this framing were that short- and medium-term political-economic objectives were not recognized, resources critical to intermediate objectives were not made available, and the trade-offs and risk management activities central to clear strategic thinking were often neglected.

Capacity of State and Economy

Perhaps UNMIK's greatest success was in ensuring a fiscally autonomous and sustainable state. UNMIK's creation of a central fiscal authority and the efficient

Figure 8.4. Viable Peace: The Turning Point in Developing a Legitimate Political Economy

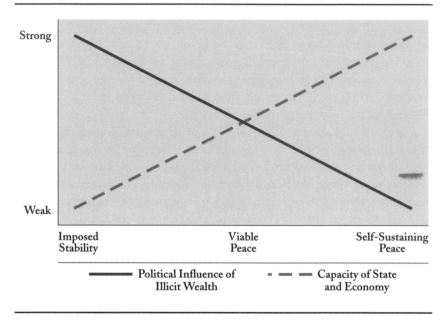

Strong			
Weak			
	Imposed Stability	Viable Peace	Self-Sustaining Peace

————— Political Influence of   ▪ — — Capacity of State
Illicit Wealth   and Economy

operations of the Customs Service together built a self-sustaining state, with a revenue stream that was auditable and whose integrity could be maintained. The budget of the provisional institutions of self-government was essentially self-funded within about three to four years after the start of the mission. Although this was in part due to the fact that the international community continued to bear many of the costs of the law enforcement system and of capital investments, it nonetheless remains a remarkable achievement.

UNMIK recognized the importance of a functional formal economy for the long term. It pursued efforts to transition from a socialist economy and for the most part succeeded in putting in place the economic foundations for the long-term evolution of a market economy. Compared with the international effort in Bosnia, UNMIK was successful in many of these foundational efforts. Achieving an economy that provides and distributes opportunities and benefits widely throughout society, however, may take a generation or more.

UNMIK had mixed success addressing short- and intermediate-term objectives of a political-economic strategy. In the short term, UNMIK succeeded in ensuring that "peace paid" in the immediate aftermath of the war through a robust humanitarian assistance program. Peace clearly paid in the medium term for the Albanian elite who succeeded in taking control of economically viable enterprises such as the Grand Hotel and the Peje Brewery; whether this contributed to the upsurge in mansion building by members of the elite in Pristina is a matter of speculation. The crisis of the missing middle, however, reflected the difficulties UNMIK had in providing services—water and power services, improved roadways and trash collection, and short-term business development assistance—for the majority population between the fall of 1999 and the spring of 2001. Complaints about KEK, for example, contributed to the slow erosion of UNMIK's credibility with the majority population.

UNMIK was even less successful in ensuring that peace paid for the Serb population. Because of the high degree of support they received from Belgrade, local Serbs were tightly tied to Belgrade. UNMIK's efforts, while always acknowledging the importance of the population, seldom robustly addressed their specific needs. Most notably, UNMIK's closure of the Trepca complex, compounded by a failure to move vigorously to restart economically viable elements of Trepca, meant that UNMIK was seen as substantially damaging to the economic well-being of Serbs. The combined effects of the absence of efforts to restrict funding from Belgrade, the closure of Trepca, and the lack of robust, minority-focused economic revitalization efforts meant that Kosovo's Serbian population remained tightly tied, economically and politically, to Belgrade.

Political Influence of Illicit Wealth

UNMIK had the least success undercutting the economic foundations of obstructionism. Both Serb and Albanian obstructionists, within Kosovo and throughout the region, seemed able to continue to operate without any clear economic impediment to their actions. Smuggling continued to be a common illegal activity, providing powerful incentives to ensure that state control remained weak. The link between such illicit wealth and the exercise of political power was only beginning to be effectively investigated by UNMIK and the international community in late 2003. Corruption and political-criminal wealth continued to hinder Kosovo's progression toward a viable peace.

NOTES

The authors are deeply indebted to David Kanin for his assistance in developing an understanding of the historical and cultural influences on the evolution of Kosovo's political economy. James Scaminaci and Oscar Vera have shaped our thinking on the critical influence of political-criminal power structures.

1. Anthony Lake, as cited in Geoff Harris, ed., *Recovery from Armed Conflict in Developing Countries: An Economic and Political Analysis* (London: Routledge, 1999), 63.

2. Sarah Collinson et al., *Power, Livelihoods, and Conflict,* Case Studies in Political Economy Analysis for Humanitarian Action, HPG Report 13 (London: Overseas Development Institute, 2003), 3; and Philippe Le Billion with Joanna Macrae, Nick Leader, and Roger East, *The Political Economy of War: What Relief Agencies Need to Know,* HOG Network Paper (London: Overseas Development Institute, July 2000), 1. See also Gilles Carbonnier, "The Challenges of Rebuilding War-Torn Economies," in *International Security Challenges in a Changing World,* ed. Kurt Spillman and Joachim Krause, vol. 3, no. 1 (Bern: Peter Lang, 1999), http://www.fsk .ethz.ch/documents/studies/volume_3/Carbonnier.htm.

3. See Mats Berdal and David Malone, eds., *Greed and Grievance: Economic Agendas in Civil Wars* (Boulder, Colo.: Lynne Rienner, 2000). Le Billion provides a basis for this distinction in his discussion of "social" and "asocial" political economies. The "social" political economy is typified by balance in the system. Its characteristics are the following: power is well distributed across society; all members of society contribute to the economy; the economic burdens of adjustment and war are evenly distributed; wealth is not finite and can expand through productive activities; economic activities contribute to the provision of public goods; and there is a low level of human rights abuses. The characteristics of an "asocial" political economy are the following: power is in the hands of a few illegitimate and unaccountable free agents; the economic project requires few members of society; people are viewed mostly as a hindrance or a prey to economic activity; the economic burdens of adjustment and war are unevenly distributed; wealth is finite and economic activities are extractive or speculative rather than productive; economic activities do not contribute to the provision of public goods; and human rights abuses are widespread. Le Billion et al., *The Political Economy of War.*

4. Susan Woodward, *Socialist Unemployment: The Political Economy of Yugoslavia, 1945–1990* (Princeton, N.J.: Princeton University Press, 1995), 203–208.

5. Robert Thomas, *Serbia under Milosevic: Politics in the 1990s* (London: Hurst, 1999).

6. For more detail, see Michael Palairet, "The Economic Consequences of Slobodan Milosevic," *Europe-Asia Studies* 53, no. 6 (September 2001): 903.

7. Ibid.

8. European Stability Initiative, *De-industrialization and Its Consequences: A Kosovo Story,* Lessons Learned and Analysis (LLA) Unit Report (March 2001), 1.

9. United States Institute of Peace, *Lawless Rule versus Rule of Law in the Balkans,* Special Report no. 97 (Washington, D.C.: United States Institute of Peace, December 2002).

10. Noel Malcolm, *Kosovo: A Short History* (New York: Harper Perennial, 1999).

11. For details of the "bridge watchers," see chapter 7, note 5.

12. Economic reform was not in the Kosovar Albanians' original conception of the political struggle. For instance, *What Kosovars Say and Demand,* published in Tirana in 1991, consists of almost five hundred pages and includes nearly one hundred protest essays, but it does not call for reform of the economy or discuss the linkage between a market economy and democracy.

13. European Commission and the Word Bank, *Towards Stability and Prosperity: A Program for Reconstruction and Recovery in Kosovo,* prepared in support of the United Nations Mission in Kosovo, November 13, 1999, http://www.seerecon.org/calendar/1999/events/sdc/ecwb-kosovo.pdf.

14. European Commission and the World Bank, *Bosnia and Herzegovina: 1996–1998; Lessons and Accomplishments: Review of the Priority Reconstruction and Recovery Program and Looking Ahead towards Sustainable Economic Development,* report prepared for the donor conference cohosted by the European Commission and the World Bank, May 1999, 17.

15. Ibid., 19.

16. Ibid., iv.

17. A World Bank report notes, "Donors welcomed efforts by UNMIK to reestablish tax and customs collection at border." Europe and Central Asia Vice Presidency of the World Bank, "Strategic Directions for the Economic Recovery of Kosovo," a report presented at the donor conference sponsored by the World Bank, July 26, 1999.

18. Ibid.

19. World Bank, *Kosovo: Building Peace through Sustained Growth,* http://www.seerecon.org/kosovo/documents/kosovo_building_peace_1999.pdf.

20. Meso-economic analysis is the consideration of conditions and structures that particularly affect the economics of subsections of the larger macroeconomy but that are larger than the economics of a particular firm or organization. These subsections may be either a region (e.g., Kosovo) or a specific industry or sector (e.g., the lead zinc industry). The conditions and structures considered may include issues such as transportation, the skill base of the local workforce, or a specific regulatory environment.

21. United Nations, *Report of the Secretary-General Pursuant to Paragraph 10 of Security Council Resolution 1244 (1999),* S/1999/672 (June 12, 1999), para. 14.

22. Joly Dixon, "Kosovo: Economic Reconstruction and Development," Brussels, July 12, 1999, copy in author's files.

23. Joly Dixon, *Report on Pillar IV's Activities,* Washington, D.C., September 28, 1999, www.seerecon.org/news/1999/unmik4/pdf.

24. United States Institute of Peace, *Lawless Rule versus Rule of Law in the Balkans.*

25. Dimitri G. Demekas, Johannes Herderschee, and Davina F. Jacobs, *Kosovo: Institutions and Policies for Reconstruction and Growth* (Washington, D.C.: International Monetary Fund, April 2002). This is the first major donor or international financial institution report to mention the consequences of crime for the peace process.

26. Michael Steiner, SRSG, "Address to the Security Council," April 24, 2002, UNMIK/PR719, http://unmikonline.org/press/2002/press/pr719.htm.

27. See United States Institute of Peace, *Lawless Rule versus Rule of Law in the Balkans,* 11.

28. *UNMIK Chronicle* no. 7, November 26, 2001, http://www.unmikonline.org/pub/chronicle/uc7.htm. See also "Guardia di Finanza Investigator to Join UNMIK," UNMIK/PR/781, July 23, 2002, http://www.unmikonline.org/press/2002/pressr/pr781.htm.

29. UNMIK, "Standards for Kosovo," UNMIK/PR/1078, December 10, 2003.

30. Indeed, many organizations that implement these efforts renounce such motivations because neutrality is vital to their ability to perform their critical activities in zones of conflict.

31. Fernando Del Mundo and Ray Wilkinson, "A Race against Time," *Refugees* 3, no. 116 (September 1999): 4–15.

32. Indeed, for Kosovo Albanians it was the opening round of a phenomenal construction boom.

33. Conflict Security and Development Group, *Kosovo Report,* part of the study *A Review of Peace Operations* (London: King's College, 2003), http://ipi.sspp.kcl.ac.uk/rep005/index.html.

34. The accumulation of refuse in urban areas led to a rat infestation and an outbreak of tularemia.

35. For more information about UNMIK's inattention to a needed framework, see http://www.setimes.com/html/English/030617-IVAN-004.htm.

36. British troops did take over the power station and mines in the early days of the mission, and a temporary contract was awarded to maintain the equipment pending a more permanent solution. Pillar IV elected to appoint a supervisory board and provide a monthly subsidy; however, this did not confront the political need to assert its writ over the power station and dismiss the unsavory element that was insinuating itself into its management structure.

37. See OSCE, Mission in Kosovo, Department of Human Rights and Rule of Law, *Parallel Structures in Kosovo,* October 2003.

38. According to the 1991 census, there were 4,300 Albanians and 8,138 ethnic Serbs in Strpce.

39. One teenager of Albanian-Serb parentage described skiing at Brezovica as "heaven." The scenic beauty, she said, was spectacular, but it was the fact that she heard Albanian and Serbian spoken together that made it "heaven."

40. See the "Conclusions" section of the July 28, 1999, donor conference, http://www. seerecon.org/calendar/1999/events/kdc/conclusions.htm.

41. UNMIK, "On the Currency Permitted to Be Used in Kosovo," UNMIK/REG/1999/4, September 2, 1999; "On the Establishment of the Central Fiscal

Authority of Kosovo and Other Related Matters," UNMIK/REG/1999/16, November 6, 1999; "On the Banking and Payments Authority of Kosovo," UNMIK/REG/1999/20, November 1999; "On Bank Licensing, Supervision and Regulation," UNMIK/REG/1999/21, November 15, 1999; and "On the Establishment of the Housing and Property Directorate and the Housing and Property Claims Commission," UNMIK/REG/1999/23, November 15, 1999.

42. The value of land in Kosovo was regarded as being high by EU standards.

43. For a discussion of privatization issues, see Dana Eyre and Andreas Wittkowsky, *The Political Economy of Consolidating Kosovo: Property Rights, Political Conflict, and Stability* (Bonn: Friedrich-Ebert-Stiftung, 2002).

44. KEK's assets alone were revalued in 2003 at 647 million euros.

45. This was largely due to a policy disagreement between the U.S. Agency for International Development and the EU-led Pillar IV.

46. UNMIK Executive Decision 2003/16 (October 21, 2003).

47. Although the office of the Auditor General had been created previously, it became operational only with the arrival of the first auditor general and deputy auditor general in November 2003.

48. Even after UNMIK established an administrative directive in 2002 governing disconnection for nonpayments, KEK did not choose to obey it, and UNMIK was not able to enforce compliance for several more years.

9

Linkages among the Transformation Strategies

Michael J. Dziedzic and Len Hawley

A CENTRAL PREMISE OF THIS BOOK is that internal conflict may persist and thrive for various interrelated reasons: war aims that remain unmet, militant extremism, lawless rule, and a criminalized political economy that fuels hostilities. This chapter focuses on the linkages among the strategies that seek to transform these sources of internal conflict.

The requirement for such linkages is not new. Seasoned practitioners have repeatedly identified the necessity to integrate interdependent lines of effort. There are numerous examples. Relief operations may need protection by security forces. The military depends on the diplomatic process to provide a peace to keep. Criminal-political power structures must be denied control of judicial processes. Demobilized soldiers need jobs to dissuade them from returning to armed violence. Interdependencies are the norm.

No international entity can accomplish even its own mission without the contributions of others. Achieving a viable peace calls for coherent action by all, civilians and military. Deconfliction is simply not good enough. Success in these difficult situations requires unified direction, genuine partnerships, joint civil-military planning, and coherent action.

This chapter's aim is to advance an understanding of this complex issue, using Kosovo as an illustration. We begin with a review of the many linkages that must be made among the four essential strategies of conflict transformation that address

- Moderating political conflict
- Defeating militant extremists

- Institutionalizing the rule of law

- Developing a legitimate political economy

The chapter then describes integrating mechanisms that international officials need to strengthen collaboration and minimize exploitation of these dependencies by obstructionists. It concludes by highlighting implications for the design of a process that seeks to bring about viable peace within a reasonable time frame of about three years.

THE STRATEGY FOR MODERATING POLITICAL CONFLICT

The strategy of the United Nations Interim Administration Mission in Kosovo (UNMIK) to moderate political conflict consisted of five parts:

1. Nurture favorable conditions for the mediation process.

2. Mediate conflict incrementally.

3. Build a working coalition to run a civil administration.

4. Contain obstructionism.

5. Channel the competition for power into nonviolent processes.

Linkages with Defeating Militant Extremists

Nurture favorable conditions for the mediation process. Armed hostilities must end if political mediation is to advance. In Kosovo this involved the withdrawal of Serb security forces in compliance with the Military Technical Agreement. The Kosovo Force (KFOR) also had to address the threat of a return to war by supervising the conversion of the Kosovo Liberation Army (KLA) into the Kosovo Protection Corps and continuing to sustain demilitarization and reform of that paramilitary group as the peace process unfolded.

Mediate conflict incrementally. Political compromise requires that risk takers have a reasonable expectation that they will survive. To advance their mediation campaign, UNMIK's political managers relied on KFOR and UNMIK Police to provide credible confidence-building measures, especially in the early stages of the peace process when security was a most prevalent concern. The police were essential to protect moderate political leaders who took risks to support the peace process, particularly those within the Serb community. Military and police capabilities of performing these two functions were limited initially, which contributed to the prolongation of the process of establishing an interim civil administration.

Build a working coalition to run a civil administration. Security is the essential precondition for building a working coalition among rival parties. With a hundred murders taking place each week in the early months of the mission, KFOR's role as a surrogate police force, even though imperfect, was irreplaceable for initiating a process of nonviolent political dialogue among key leaders within the Albanian community, leading to a working coalition to run Kosovo's civil administration. Eventually, military and international police forces established joint operations to curtail violent assaults and intimidation against the Serb population. Without a decline in ethnic and politically motivated violence, there would have been virtually no prospect for the continued existence of the Serb population, let alone for their participation in any civil administration for Kosovo.

Contain obstructionism. Obstructionists cannot be allowed to derail the peace process. The mission's political leadership relies on the military contingent to help stop obstructionist behavior when it emerges and to attack it at its source when that can be done effectively. The most decisive linkage that needs to be made is to exploit intelligence so that evidence can be generated that is admissible in court. By 2002 UNMIK had accumulated evidence against suspects in scores of politically motivated assassinations. KFOR played a crucial role in supporting arrests in the most dangerous of these cases.

Channel the competition for power into nonviolent processes. Election processes need to be defended against violent extremists. "Framework operations" conducted by international military forces are needed to provide the coercive means to respond to the use of violence aimed at subverting elections and other legitimate political processes. Before municipal elections in the fall of 2000, the combined action of KFOR and UNMIK Police halted an early wave of campaign violence, thereby allowing the election to take place without further disruption.

Another vital contribution that military contingents can provide is politically relevant intelligence about the motivations for political violence, the illicit sources of wealth and criminal associations that sustain fighting, and the likely threats to faction leaders if and when they enter into the mediation process. Reforming military, paramilitary, and intelligence forces of the former warring parties is another institution-building process that must progress if violence is to be taken out of the political equation.

Linkages with Institutionalizing the Rule of Law

Nurture favorable conditions for the mediation process. Political dialogue cannot flourish without basic public security. Initially, KFOR had to impose order. It took the better part of a year for UNMIK to deploy an international civilian police force to carry out its executive policing functions. The absence of a properly functioning legal system was a major barrier to gaining the confidence and participation of Serb representatives in the peace process. To deal with grievances about discriminatory treatment and the lack of access to justice within Kosovo's judicial system, international judges and prosecutors eventually had to be integrated into the system. It was vitally important for UNMIK to set conditions for this to happen by asserting authority over executive, legislative, and judicial systems at the outset with the issuance of Regulation No. 1 on July 25, 1999.

Mediate conflict incrementally. For a mediation process to flourish, leaders of rival groups will eventually have to take risks for peace. Those who do so may require physical protection against assassination. During the first year in Kosovo, it became clear that international police requirements for close protection of key political figures had been substantially underestimated.

Contain obstructionism. Installing legal processes to bring perpetrators of war crimes and politically motivated violence to justice is indispensable. To accomplish this, UNMIK and KFOR had to ensure that the entire continuum of essential rule-of-law functions from intelligence through incarceration could be executed reliably. If the international community, with all its resources, had been unwilling or unable to administer justice to the most notorious obstructionists, who often had strong ties with organized criminal activities, newly formed local institutions certainly could not have been expected to do so. Politics would have remained zero sum, with the capacity for political violence continuing to determine the outcome of disputes, making civil society untenable.

Channel the competition for power into nonviolent processes. Majority rule must be accompanied by guarantees of minority rights. The law enforcement and criminal justice system must provide mechanisms for resolving intergroup disputes peacefully and protecting the rights of political minorities. It will also be relied on to punish electoral manipulation. The capacity to remove corrupt or repressive public officials from office is also vital for the survival of nonviolent political processes. The rule of law became one of the most decisive and demanding standards that the international community identified as a requirement for the eventual determination of Kosovo's political status. This included equal access to justice for minorities and the capacity to deny impunity to violent extremists.

Linkages with Developing a Legitimate Political Economy

Nurture favorable conditions for the mediation process. Consent for and political cooperation with the international intervention are powerfully affected by the effectiveness of humanitarian assistance and the restoration of basic services. Both of these lines of action are vitally important to build a reservoir of popular support for the peace process. The most urgent concern is to alleviate the humanitarian emergency. By successfully preventing further loss of life during the winter of 1999, the international community gained a measure of goodwill and consent from the Albanians. A second area that influenced public perceptions, in this case negatively, was a delay in repairing Kosovo's basic infrastructure and restoring essential public services, such as power, water, and trash collection. Serbs, in particular, persisted in looking to Belgrade for basic needs, which greatly limited their willingness to enter into the peace process.

Mediate conflict incrementally. To persuade faction leaders to take the risks associated with compromising on their war aims, peace must pay in tangible ways. The presence of well-funded international programs may provide an artificial stimulus to the economy and a sense among a limited segment of the population that economic conditions are improving. To transform internal conflict, however, political leaders and their followers need to be provided alternatives in the formal economy. This can be pivotal in persuading influential members of the political class to redefine their personal interests to be more consistent with the peace process. Effective programs to promote sustainable business activity were slow to materialize in Kosovo, and unemployment remained discouragingly high.

Build a working coalition to run civil administration. The rise of a working coalition to run civil administration is closely tied to the strength of the coalition for peace. When the peace process provides tangible benefits to everyone, popular support is likely to emerge for the international mission's mediation efforts to get former adversaries to participate together in governance.

Contain obstructionism and channel the competition for power into nonviolent processes. To minimize the destructive influence of illegally obtained wealth over the political process, the incentives for continued conflict must diminish and the rewards of pursuing peace must grow. In a criminalized political economy, an insidious relationship exists between political violence and criminal interests. A successful political-economic effort will alter the incentive structure for gray-market or smuggling activity by making it more cost-effective for entrepreneurs to pay customs duties and other taxes than to evade them. Increasing the risk of arrest and making smuggling less lucrative should diminish the capacity of obstructionists and organized criminal groups to oppose the peace process. Kosovo's internationally run Central Fiscal Authority (CFA) established a tax regime relying on collection of customs fees that became increasingly effective as UNMIK asserted greater control over its borders and boundaries. The CFA also helped to establish a context for embracing fiscal transparency and accountability.

THE STRATEGY FOR DEFEATING MILITANT EXTREMISTS

KFOR's strategy to defeat militant extremists comprised four core elements:

1. Adopt an assertive posture with a maneuverist approach.

2. Seek reliable intelligence to guide operations.

3. Mount framework operations to find, fix, and strike against militant extremists.

4. Conduct joint military-police planning and action.

Linkages with Moderating Political Conflict

Adopt an assertive posture with a maneuverist approach. Taking assertive action against militant extremists will be tantamount to war, not peace implementation, in the absence of a credible peace process for the military to defend. The political effort offers the prospect of moving beyond the basic containment of security threats to the defeat of militant obstructionists.

A political formula for either demobilizing or demilitarizing armed paramilitary groups must be devised in order to deprive rival factions of the military option. The KLA emerged from the conflict believing that it had won the war. KFOR was not prepared to face down an armed KLA. Without KLA member participation in the peace process, the NATO intervention would have been in jeopardy. Formation of the Kosovo Protection Corps provided a mechanism for demilitarizing the KLA. Although this did not eliminate the capacity of former KLA members to disrupt the peace process, this obstacle was at least "strategically fixed," and open hostilities between KFOR and the KLA were avoided.

The military also relies on international civilian authorities to control radio broadcasting that incites violence and inflames hatreds. Efforts need to be made to undermine popular support for the use of violence and terrorism by obstructionists. After years of ethnic repression and murder in Kosovo, this was a very difficult undertaking. International oversight of the media may be required to restrict access by extremist leaders and groups who persist in propagating intercommunity hatred and antipathy for the peace process.[1]

Militant threats from neighboring states need to be suppressed. UNMIK's leadership also needed to shape support for KFOR's operations among Kosovo's neighbors. This involved a range of diplomatic initiatives to deny sanctuary for militant groups across Kosovo's borders and prevent the infiltration of support from patron states for militant extremists operating in Kosovo.

Mount framework operations to find, fix, and strike against militant extremists. Ultimately, political judgment must guide the use of force. This is essential for "vertical integration" that ensures the primacy of the peace process.[2] UNMIK's political managers carefully sought to keep the door open to participation by hard-bitten rival leaders who often operated on the edge of compliance with the peace process. Judicious political decisions about coercive military operations must be made, particularly when strike operations are contemplated against influential militant extremists. Thus, it is the custodian of the peace process who must make the policy determinations about who should be regarded as an obstructionist deserving of armed coercion and when it is advantageous for the military to strike.

In the end, enduring stability rests on an acceptable political solution. When the determination of Kosovo's political status remained stalemated for nearly five years, fears accumulated among Albanians that their aspirations for independence might be in jeopardy. This created an opening for violence-prone, extreme Albanian nationalist elements to use armed violence to seize the political initiative. This was the dominant factor that produced the upheaval of violence on March 17–18, 2004.

Linkages with Institutionalizing the Rule of Law

Adopt an assertive posture with a maneuverist approach. A military force may be able to impose stability, but it alone cannot establish an environment capable of producing a viable peace. KFOR was able to detain those suspected of terrorizing the Serb population or of engaging in cross-border subversion only for limited periods. Initially, senior national military officers assumed formal responsibility for detention procedures using the national law of the five nations leading KFOR's multinational brigades. This quickly became a source of enormous frustration when suspects were released within a few days. Progress in securing the environment depended, therefore, on a system of justice capable of incarcerating the most ruthless and violent troublemakers in Kosovo's turbulent society. KFOR could seek to disrupt the killing and intimidation temporarily, and it could deter assaults on Serb communities by its presence. This addressed merely the symptoms, however, not the sources of insecurity and disruption to the peace process.

Conduct joint military-police planning and action. Establishing a secure environment requires the integrated efforts of international military and police to complete the intelligence-to-incarceration continuum. Without effective integration, neither KFOR nor UNMIK Police could maximize its respective capabilities against major threats. They worked for years to develop mechanisms to pool intelligence about political extremists and their criminal enterprises. Whether disruption strategies or investigation and prosecution are the aim, the pooling of information and joint planning are vital for achieving progress in transforming the security environment.

Linkages with Developing a Legitimate Political Economy

Adopt an assertive posture with a maneuverist approach. Improved living conditions soften resistance to intrusive military action against militants. Increased employment signals to the general population that "peace pays" and deprives extremist and criminal groups of support.

Mount framework operations to find, fix, and strike against militant extremists. Armed extremists and terrorists need sources of funding to sustain an insurgency. Security operations are aided immensely by the political-economic strategy's efforts to reduce illegal financial support for militant extremists to buy weapons, reward supporters, and fund their violent activities. The security environment will be directly affected by the success of the political-economic strategy to reduce these illegal funding sources.

THE STRATEGY FOR INSTITUTIONALIZING THE RULE OF LAW

UNMIK's strategy to institutionalize the rule of law included the following efforts:

1. Develop institutional capacity.

2. Shape the context by dismantling criminalized power structures.

3. Provide safeguards on performance.

Linkages with Moderating Political Conflict

Develop institutional capacity. If underlying issues that motivated conflict remain unresolved, this will have a major bearing on decisions about the institution-building process. The most basic requirement is to determine what corpus of law and criminal procedure will be applied in a fractured, war-torn society. Because Kosovo's final status remained unresolved, this choice had unavoidable political and security ramifications. An early decision by the UN Secretariat to follow the existing Serb penal code had no legitimacy with Albanians, because it implied Serb sovereignty and was regarded as discriminatory. UNMIK later had to reverse this unhelpful political decision and begin enforcing the legal code used before Milosevic deprived Kosovo of its autonomy in 1989.

The terms of a peace settlement are likely to have a profound impact on the composition of the local police force and its prospects for operating in a politically neutral manner that is essential for stability. Although the KLA regarded policing to be one of the spoils of war, it was not allowed to usurp this function.

UNMIK's political managers balanced the need to integrate the KLA into the political process against the need for Kosovo's new police force to be impartial, accountable, and an integral component of the rule of law. All applicants to join the Kosovo Police Service were vetted to determine if they had an unsavory record, and the decision to accept or reject them was made on the basis of their individual qualifications, not because of their membership in a particular group. Former KLA members were among the first to be evaluated, however, and initially up to half the members of Kosovo's new police force were determined to have been affiliated with the KLA.

Shape the context by dismantling criminalized power structures. Peace cannot flourish when power structures on all sides of the conflict are penetrated by criminal enterprises. Political elites need to be persuaded to relinquish criminal associations that may have flourished during fighting. Crucial political judgments have to be made about the extent of international involvement required to shape a lawful environment. UNMIK initially relied primarily on local Albanian judges and prosecutors to administer justice. However, it soon became obvious that ethnic bias and fear of retribution were dominant influences in cases involving war criminals, political extremists, or organized-crime kingpins. International judges and prosecutors had to be brought in to address this critical deficiency.

Provide safeguards on performance. Creating effective investigative and disciplinary mechanisms to serve as safeguards on performance required enlightened international leadership. This proved to be a decisive factor in creating effective investigative and disciplinary mechanisms to serve as safeguards on performance. The political decision to establish the Kosovo Judicial and Prosecutorial Council, with majority international composition, was a crucial step in achieving accountability for the legal system. The previously established body had proved incapable of effective oversight because the few international representatives were marginalized.

Linkages with Defeating Militant Extremists

Develop institutional capacity. The inevitable "public security gap" must be confronted urgently by international military forces during the first weeks of an intervention. Indigenous law enforcement organizations are likely to be in disarray or to constitute a predominant source of intercommunal abuse. Because the recruitment process for international police is inherently time-consuming, the military force will likely have to fill this institutional void by default. Military contingents need to come prepared to deal with dangerous suspects who pose a credible threat to a safe and secure environment. Violent troublemakers must be apprehended, securely held, and provided some form of due process if they are to remain in custody.

Shape the context by dismantling criminalized power structures. Intelligence sharing on threats to public security is a key military support activity to the rule-of-law campaign. Clandestine criminalized power structures may seek to suffocate the rule of law, and thus, both the military and the police will have to join forces to dismantle or neutralize them. In Kosovo the five countries with brigade sectors (France, Germany, Italy, the United Kingdom, and the United States) agreed to create a Criminal Intelligence Unit within UNMIK Police headquarters to pool relevant KFOR intelligence, particularly on the organized-crime threat. This helped develop a common picture between the military and the police on criminal threats to the peace process along with procedures for prioritizing and allocating their investigative resources in response.

UNMIK Police also relied on KFOR for assistance in high-risk arrest operations. Riots and civil disturbances are another threat to public security that can be met effectively only through coordinated action. Both KFOR and UNMIK possessed formed police units with a crowd-control capability, but the failure to develop integrated command-and-control procedures or conduct joint training resulted in an uncoordinated and inadequate response when Kosovo-wide riots erupted in March 2004.

Linkages with Developing a Legitimate Political Economy

Develop institutional capacity. Salaries of local law enforcement and court officials must be sufficient to sustain a workable and honest system of justice. Establishing a tax base and revenue stream for the new civil administration is thus vitally important. This requirement was a major impediment to building institutional capacities for the rule of law from the beginning because Kosovo lacked state capacity to generate revenue. Consequently, UNMIK sought financial contributions from the countries of the G-8 to fill initial funding shortfalls. UNMIK was confronted by the reluctance of finance ministers because of fears that these grants would create a dependency.

Shape the context by dismantling criminalized power structures. Obstructionists who benefit from conflict must be deprived of their financial base. When economic activity is heavily concentrated in informal transactions in illicit commodities, criminal networks reap profits that are apt to pervert both the political process and the legal system. This is a prescription for rampant impunity. Rationalizing the tax system by making it more cost-effective to pay taxes than to avoid them (i.e., "whitening the gray") is a major contribution to shaping the context so the rule of law can prevail.

THE STRATEGY FOR DEVELOPING A LEGITIMATE POLITICAL ECONOMY

Transforming a political economy of conflict into one that is capable of sustaining peace requires simultaneous action on multiple dimensions:

1. Undercut the economic foundations of obstructionist power.

2. Strengthen the coalition for peace by ensuring that peace pays.

3. Develop a fiscally autonomous and sustainable state.

4. Lay the macroeconomic foundation to expand the formal economy and distribute the benefits of peace.

Linkages with Moderating Political Conflict

Undercut the economic foundations of obstructionist power. To the extent that electoral processes begin to function, politicians who derive their power from criminal enterprises should be progressively forced to make a choice. If public awareness of their continued involvement in organized criminal activities could disqualify them from office, then some might opt to sever their criminal associations, while others may be forced out of office. The essence of the political strategy is that elites emerging from violent conflict begin to see that their interests are better served through nonviolent means. If peace is to endure, the political clout of those who obtain power through peaceful electoral processes must come to prevail over obstructionists who are sustained by shadowy underworld connections.

Strengthen the coalition for peace by ensuring that peace pays. Building a coalition for peace may require the custodian of the peace process to make economically "irrational" decisions. Investment in activities such as the Brezovica ski center situated in the Serb enclave of Strpce, for example, was done with the "willful ignorance" of potentially problematic ownership issues because this economic initiative would advance the peace process. In the case of the far more strategically significant Trepca industrial complex, however, the economic costs blinded the international community from recognizing the potential political gains of investment. Among the political goals that should influence the allocation of international assistance is the promotion of economic interdependence among the parties to the conflict.

Develop a fiscally autonomous and sustainable state. Establishing effective state fiscal institutions may entail complicated regional diplomacy. To collect customs revenue adequately, UNMIK had to be able to control not only the external borders with Albania and Macedonia but also the internal boundaries with Serbia and Montenegro. This required considerable international diplomacy. Efforts to facilitate trade also require a host of mundane activities such as insurance and customs agreements to allow transactions to flow. UNMIK initially underestimated the personnel resources needed to obtain such agreements but was later successful in negotiating these matters.

Lay the macroeconomic foundation to expand the formal economy and distribute the benefits of peace. Political stability is an essential precondition for economic recovery, foreign investment, and expansion of the formal economy. The more solid the political foundation for peace becomes, the more likely remittances from the diaspora will flow into productive enterprises. The same is true of traditional forms of foreign investment. Over the long term, political inclusiveness, minority rights, and democratic processes will also lead to political-economic decisions that will encourage a middle-class market economy to emerge that will support progress toward a self-sustaining peace.

Linkages with Defeating Militant Extremists

Undercut the economic foundations of obstructionist power. Legitimate economic activity must be protected against armed extortion and violence. A large degree of overlap is likely between criminal sources of revenue and the propensity to use armed violence and intimidation to obstruct the peace process. In a political economy of conflict, these potent forces coalesce into violence-prone, criminalized power structures that are a primary obstacle to a viable peace. The greatest challenge for military contingents is to recognize this threat. The natural inclination is to dismiss criminal activity as irrelevant and to scoff at efforts to confront it as "police work" and therefore outside the realm of the military's mission. The lack of continuity created by regular troop rotations also hinders comprehension that the threat to peace is subversive and criminal in nature.

Military intelligence can be invaluable for identifying criminal-political networks and their sources of revenue. This allows for the development of mechanisms to focus international resources precisely on disrupting those gray- and black-market activities that are associated with resistance to the peace process.

Strengthen the coalition for peace by ensuring that peace pays. A nascent coalition for peace is apt to be vulnerable to armed intimidation. One of the most effective ways to demonstrate that peace will pay in the future is to bring the most notorious war criminals, violent obstructionists, and outright terrorists to justice. This likely will require sophisticated military resources, including intelligence, surveillance, and support for operations to arrest high-profile figures. This may include military support for enforcement of such seemingly mundane issues as building permits when gangster elements seize control over prime real estate and assassinate local officials who uphold the law.

Develop a fiscally autonomous and sustainable state. Several critical revenue-generation activities require military protection and support. The most immediate source of state revenue is likely to be customs duties on imports, and a porous border diminishes this revenue stream. In this case, KFOR was needed to assert some measure of control over Kosovo's borders from the outset. In situations where the country has a rich natural resource or a prime commodity, military protection may be required to ensure that the state can generate needed revenues from these assets.

Lay the macroeconomic foundation to expand the formal economy and distribute the benefits of peace. The cessation of hostilities and the establishment of basic public security are essential conditions for the resumption of normal economic activity. The existence of a public security gap at the inception of a mission will allow lawless, war-hardened networks to cement their dominance over the economy. To transform this context, moreover, perpetrators of black-market crimes must be placed at risk for punishment. To transform gray-market activity into legitimate enterprise, there must be a credible capacity to enforce the collection of taxes and customs and to punish politically connected smugglers.

Linkages with Institutionalizing the Rule of Law

Undercut the economic foundations of obstructionist power. Curbing revenue flowing from the underground economy to obstructionists requires the effective operation of functions across the rule-of-law spectrum from intelligence to incarceration. This includes the specialized expertise required to investigate and prosecute financial crimes. A legal and regulatory framework needs to be created to accomplish the seizure of assets that have been obtained through illegal means and to take enforcement action against such crimes as money laundering and intimidation of witnesses. Ordinary regulatory activities, ranging from consumer protection to enterprise audits and cash flow control, also make a vital contribution.

Strengthen the coalition for peace by ensuring that peace pays. Grievances need to be redressed via the legal system for victims to have a sense that peace is preferable to vengeance seeking. For example, unresolved claims over real property that changed hands as a result of the conflict provide a principal incentive for renewed violence. Establishing a credible and just process for resolving property disputes and returning rightful owners to their homes reduces the potential for hard-liners to mobilize mass support against the peace process.

Develop a fiscally autonomous and sustainable state. The integrity of state institutions is of prime importance to conflict transformation, and bringing to justice officials who violate the public trust is essential. An autonomous state that is not riddled with entrenched corruption and criminalized power will have effective mechanisms to tackle economic and financial crime in both the public and the private sectors. This includes administrative procedures and sanctions that preserve transparency and accountability. A code of ethical conduct for public-sector employees is also essential, especially regarding conflicts of interest.

Lay the macroeconomic foundation to expand the formal economy and distribute the benefits of peace. A free market can flourish only if a legal framework protects the sanctity of contracts and provides reliable mechanisms for the resolution of disputes, including property disputes. A body of civil laws dealing with banking, property rights, business registration, contracts, bankruptcy, and the like must be in place along with the legal architecture to enforce them reliably, including a commercial court. Regulatory oversight and audits of so-called publicly owned enterprises must be established to control economic and financial crime and bring those involved to justice.

INTEGRATING MECHANISMS

These linkages require effective mechanisms to achieve the necessary integration. They will not emerge simply through goodwill. This discussion highlights the most essential of these integrating measures.

Consensus Top-Down Policy Guidance

Effective integration starts at the top. As discussed in chapter 3, a competent interagency advance planning effort is an essential precondition for gaining coherence among the four conflict transformation strategies. When advance planning is not undertaken, fragmentation will ensue from top to bottom, provoking a host of adverse consequences that obstructionists will seek to exploit to derail the peace process.

At the top, three overarching policy instruments are indispensable. The first is an integrated political-military (pol-mil) plan for the intervention that establishes the broad strategic purpose and essential conditions for a viable peace. A pol-mil plan also provides implementation guidance to all composite, civil-military lines of effort across the entire intervention.

The second instrument is the mandate. This is usually a UN Security Council resolution, which should designate a senior civilian official as the overall political authority for the mission. The resolution should prescribe that the civilian and military components work in genuine partnership toward the common aims of the mission. An empowering mandate is especially important. The preferred model for future interventions that aspire to transform internal conflict is a UN civilian mission in partnership with a combat-capable multinational national force (MNF). The mandate for Kosovo, UN Security Council Resolution 1244, embraced these principles, and it was accompanied by the secretary-general's report of June 12, 1999, which outlined the United Nations' concept for integrating all civilian aspects of the international mission.

The postwar settlement is the third instrument. Although a peace accord normally spells out obligations of the rival groups in the postwar period, it also prescribes the roles of the international mission and grants authorities to the custodian of the peace process to ensure the settlement is fully implemented. The settlement must establish mechanisms that empower the international mission to ensure the primacy of the peace process. This requirement is often overlooked by negotiators. Because Kosovo did not have a comprehensive settlement, many of these authorities had to be included in Resolution 1244.

Unified Direction and Genuine Civil-Military Partnerships

The ideal is to maximize implementation strategies to achieve the same overall political aim. To approximate this ideal, the highest international civilian official, normally the special representative of the secretary-general (SRSG), should be empowered to ensure that efforts of the international intervention are integrated. The SRSG should be the single political director guiding both the military and the civilian components.

The Kosovo experience initially involved close interaction between KFOR's military commander and the SRSG. General Michael Jackson publicly endorsed the primacy of the peace process and conveyed that principle by personal example throughout his military command. Overall political direction must come from the SRSG, who serves as custodian of the peace process, even though the force commander must respond to commands from higher military authority. Without impinging on national command prerogatives, unified political direction ensures proper application of Carl von Clausewitz's admonition that military actions (as well as parallel civilian efforts) should advance the political aim of the intervention.

A corollary to the principle of unified direction is a genuine civil-military partnership. The leaders of KFOR and UNMIK forged such a partnership from the very beginning. General Michael Jackson and SRSG Bernard Kouchner conveyed solidarity by their personal remarks and day-to-day actions. The public posture of both missions reflected this tight relationship. Both these leaders collaborated continually in their daily activities in managing the transformation process in Kosovo.

A genuine partnership means that one accommodates the needs of the other. On the civilian side, UNMIK's political directors recognized the need for military commanders to be given achievable missions and political guidance well in advance to permit them to carry out their deliberate planning process. At the same time, KFOR commanders conformed to critical aspects of UNMIK's political strategy, including the necessity to make incremental gains and cultivate ambiguity about desired ends. Genuine partners meet in the middle, not just to coordinate and deconflict, but to integrate their operations into coherent action on the ground.

True integration of the four conflict transformation strategies requires a common structure for joint planning. SRSG Kouchner and KFOR commander Jackson instituted a "joint planning structure" that proved to be critical for "weaving the strands of the rope" and melding civilian and military activities for the common purpose of advancing the peace process. UNMIK's political directors relied on KFOR's time-driven and sequenced operational strategy development process. Some of this joint planning served to cement better civil-military integration in planning for UNMIK's broader priorities. On specific security operations, the joint planning structure became completely fused. In these cases, UNMIK civilian planners worked side by side with KFOR military planners as part of the operational planning cycle.

Integrated Executive Leadership

Policy trade-offs will need to be made as a natural consequence of dealing with the linkages among the four conflict transformation strategies. This is where executive leadership in a mission is a key integrating mechanism. For a joint UN-MNF intervention, the preferred structure should include an executive committee that formulates policy and overall strategy for the intervention. Meeting regularly and chaired by the SRSG, the executive committee should serve as the overall integrating mechanism for each senior "cabinet official" within the mission to negotiate policy priorities among the transformation strategies. The executive committee steers the peace process through a strategic mission plan, sets near-term mission objectives, clarifies linkages among civil-military actions, and tracks progress in implementing each transformation strategy. In Kosovo the SRSG's Executive Committee consisted of the mission's senior civilian heads of each major line of effort as well as the representative of the KFOR military commander.

A Strategic Mission Plan

A strategic planning process should bring together planners from each of the main pillars of the mission, including the military. This joint planning group should produce a strategic mission plan that integrates crucial transformation activities across the mission and updates it periodically at the direction of the SRSG. As contemplated in the secretary-general's report of June 12, 1999, UNMIK was provided a joint planning group to prepare a strategic mission plan.

An Information Management System

Information enables civilian and military leaders to drive the peace process. They need timely and relevant information on day-to-day events, early warning of crises, assessments of developments within the social and political landscape, and critical information on key transformation benchmarks. One lesson from the Kosovo experience is that an international mission needs capacities, including an information management unit, a user-friendly internal communications system, relevant databases, standard field reporting, and collaborative tools that extend the reach of the mission through the Internet. These must be established in the first weeks of the mission.

Integration of Military and Police Operations

Effective security, the precondition for all other efforts, requires the integration of military and police operations. One barrier, as experienced in Kosovo, is the lack of philosophical convergence among contributing nations about how to relate military operations with civilian law enforcement agencies. Italy and France had a gendarme tradition. Because domestic law enforcement is the primary task of their gendarme units, they did not feel pressured to turn police primacy over to UNMIK Police. Germany and the United States, in contrast, believed that their military police should be confined to internal policing of military units and support of combat units. Because policing a civilian population was an alien concept to their military commanders, German and U.S. units wanted to get out of the civilian policing business as rapidly as possible. By comparison, British troops had extensive experience in an environment where police primacy shifts between military and civilian police, affording a level of operational flexibility that was well suited to Kosovo's fluid environment. Because KFOR's approach varied fundamentally across the five multinational brigades, with each military contingent responding to instructions from their capitals, UNMIK Police had to develop five unique solutions for collaboration with KFOR in the field.

To promote the integration of military and police activities, KFOR and UNMIK established the Joint Security Executive Committee (JSEC), which functioned as a regular joint policymaking forum. The JSEC was normally chaired by the principal deputy SRSG and KFOR chief of staff, or, when warranted, by the SRSG and KFOR commander.

Integrating mechanisms were also needed at lower levels. As UNMIK slowly expanded its deployment of police into the five KFOR brigade areas, the police commissioner assigned police liaison officers to each military brigade and battalion. To facilitate communications, police officers were matched by nationality with the military presence wherever possible. Security planning and coordination mechanisms at the brigade and battalion levels included commanders of both KFOR and UNMIK Police, and some also included representatives of other international agencies operating in the area of responsibility.

By May 2000 the JSEC had agreed on a series of core principles for joint military-police operations. Integrating mechanisms included the following:

- *Joint operations rooms.* To ensure effective use of military and police resources during both regular and crisis-response operations, joint operations rooms were established at both the brigade/region level and the battalion/municipality level. They were staffed on a twenty-four-hour basis by co-located command-and-control personnel from KFOR and UNMIK Police, who had access to communications systems and other resources of both organizations. The intent was to ensure that both were simultaneously aware of event information and of the tactical decisions made by their personnel on the scene.

- *Joint planning groups.* Organized at KFOR and UNMIK headquarters, as well as at regional levels, joint planning groups were expected to conduct regular situation assessments and plan responses for contingencies and major incidents.

- *Joint patrols.* Joint patrols by police and military had a more significant impact on promoting public order than either could accomplish alone. Frequent patrols by highly visible joint teams proved the strongest preventive measure inhibiting provocations and general disorder.

- *Intelligence sharing.* One of the most vital forms of coordination—the effective sharing of intelligence and deconfliction of intelligence operations—was slow to develop. This also presented a challenge within KFOR from the outset, given KFOR's multinational composition. Effective information links depended on the collective agreement of a handful of key actors from each structure and the establishment of secure mechanisms.

Despite JSEC's directive, the functionality of the military-police integrating mechanisms and the other core principles varied considerably among UNMIK's five regions. To the extent that such joint systems were made operational, however, the effect on public order was tangibly magnified, demonstrating the potency of the military and rule-of-law linkage. Over time, as primacy for policing was transferred completely to UNMIK Police, these collaborative mechanisms tended to atrophy in various MNBs. This led to a generally incoherent and uncoordinated response to the Kosovo-wide rioting that took place in March 2004. The exception was the U.S. sector, MNB East, where these coordination mechanisms had continued to function effectively.

Integration of Police and Other Rule-of-Law Activities

The rule-of-law strategy requires its own integrating mechanisms. Within UNMIK there was initially a three-way division of labor relating to the institutionalization of the rule of law. Law enforcement was assigned to UNMIK Police. The judicial and penal systems were managed as part of the interim civil administration. Capacity building for the local police, judiciary, and penal system and monitoring of their performance was yet another separate effort managed by the Organization for Security and Cooperation in Europe.

In May 2001 UNMIK Police were integrated with the new Department of Justice, consolidating all components of the rule of law (i.e., police, justice system, and penal management). The formation of this pillar had as its primary purpose the consolidation of functions that UNMIK would continue to perform for an indefinite period. It also encouraged greater functional policy coordination between the UNMIK Police and the Department of Justice.

Integration of Political and Economic Strategies

An important lesson emerging from the Kosovo experience was the lack of integrating mechanisms for identifying and resolving political and economic trade-offs. This was partly due to the fact that UNMIK did not have a political-economic strategy when the mission began.

Economic reforms that undermine political efforts to resolve the conflict will be futile. An international mission, however, tends to separate political affairs from economic matters in discrete pillars. When autonomous international organizations head these pillars, as was the case with UNMIK, with the UN Department of Peacekeeping Operations handling political matters and the European Union managing economic issues, "stovepipes" are created that become barriers to both the flow of information and the integration of effort. Trade-offs and interaction between political and economic purposes need to be identified and resolved in a way that supports the mandate and transforms conflict. Ultimately, the SRSG should make an informed determination about how the interaction and trade-offs should be handled (e.g., should subsidies and jobs programs be used to gain short-term political support or avoided because of the potential for long-term economic dependency?).

IMPLICATIONS FOR DESIGNING A PEACE PROCESS

The formula for a comprehensive peace process has traditionally embraced the following general sequence:

1. Get a cease-fire in place.

2. Provide urgent relief supplies and return refugees.

3. Help a provisional government get things running.

4. Hold a countrywide election.

5. Install the new government.

6. Start postconflict reconstruction.

A number of troubled peace implementation efforts demonstrate that this formula is prone to failure. When a brutal struggle for power plays out violently in the postwar period, an incapable international peacekeeping mission will be left to watch in paralysis. War-hardened power structures will continue to thrive and obstruct the peace process. This outcome is inevitable because the international mission cannot or does not come prepared to carry out strategies for transforming conflict.

The design of the peace process has important implications for cementing and exploiting the linkages among the four strategies. To transform internal conflict, the following design principles are likely to be relevant:

1. The primacy of the peace process should be the unifying imperative for implementing the four conflict transformation strategies and exploiting their linkages. Primacy of the peace process is the foundation for successful attainment of a viable peace in a troubled society emerging from internal conflict.

2. The military's role in imposing stability and creating a safe and secure environment is an absolute precondition for moving forward in the other three transformation strategies. This means that demobilization or demilitarization of armed groups is an essential task of the military. It also means that

military forces must impose public security for a considerable period until sufficient civilian police capabilities are operating effectively.

3. Transforming lawless rule and economic predation cannot be deferred. Both the rule-of-law strategy and the political-economic strategy should be pursued from the very inception of the mission. Neither requirement is well understood by the international community, however, and the United Nations and other multilateral bodies lack the necessary capabilities to implement them effectively today.

4. Galvanizing the linkages among strategies for conflict transformation requires a range of integrating mechanisms. Some of these, such as the linkages across the security, rule-of-law, and political strategies, are recognized and understood. Actions must be taken to weave them together day to day across the entire mission. In contrast, the interlocking linkages between the political-economic and other strategies are not widely understood. Exploiting these interdependencies requires integrating mechanisms that do not exist today.

5. Success in the political strategy depends on making substantial progress in the other three strategies. Initial political gains may be frustratingly slow until the desired consequences of the other three strategies become apparent. Obtaining a viable peace will likely require several years of hard work and substantial international participation from the outset.

In summary, the design of the peace process is critical to transforming internal conflict. Past designs have failed because entrenched war-hardened power structures that thrive on political tyranny, armed intimidation, lawless rule, and economic predation have remained in play, vitiating the peace process. In designing an effective peace process, the custodian must judiciously implement assertive strategies that transform intransigent power structures and the underlying conditions that fuel violence. The four strategies needed to do this must be solidly integrated if conflict is to be transformed and viable peace is to emerge.

NOTES

1. Jock Covey, interview by Len Hawley, San Francisco, November 6, 2002.

2. Major General R. A. Fry, interview by Ben Lovelock, Portsmouth, UK, July 16, 2001. Fry was commander of the Multinational Brigade (Centre) (MNB[C]) from August 2000 to March 2001.

10

Conclusion

Michael J. Dziedzic

THE QUEST FOR VIABLE PEACE in the wake of an international intervention is not unique to Kosovo. The distinguishing features of situations like Kosovo must be clearly understood, however, if the learning process that has taken place there is to be appropriately applied elsewhere. To move from the particular to the general, two questions must be addressed: What is this a case of?[1] and How will we recognize similar situations in the future? The preceding chapters answer the first question: the Kosovo operation belongs to a set of cases in which conflict transformation is required. The second question is addressed in this chapter, where the attributes of this demanding category of interventions are summarized.

For peace to become viable in situations like Kosovo, the motivations for and means of waging deadly zero-sum power struggles must be diminished, and at the same time resilient institutions for peacefully resolving disputes must begin to prevail. The Kosovo experience provided a rich learning laboratory for developing an understanding of what is required to achieve these goals. Four interdependent strategies aimed at moderating political conflict, defeating militant extremists, institutionalizing the rule of law, and building a legitimate political economy were necessary. The second order of business in this chapter, therefore, is to summarize these strategies and their central lines of effort.

Owing to the holistic nature of the strategies involved in conflict transformation, establishing mechanisms that link them effectively is imperative. The individual selected as the custodian of the peace process will also be a decisive catalyst, and the peace process will need to have primacy over other policy considerations. This chapter ends with an acknowledgment of these vital supporting factors and a summary of the advantages that a strategic focus on attaining viable peace brings to peace implementation.

WHEN IS CONFLICT TRANSFORMATION NECESSARY?

Before intervening, statesmen and policymakers must accurately assess the landscape of conflict. The distinction must be drawn between a situation that is truly postconflict and one that requires the transformation of continuing and violent internal hostilities. In the latter case, a fundamental change in entrenched, lawless structures of power is required to remove the sources of conflict. A response that emphasizes ad hoc measures and simplistic exit strategies will not lead to an enduring solution.

Following are the salient characteristics of interventions that require transformation of internal conflict:

- *"Peace" is but the continuation of conflict by other violent means.* When unrequited war aims persist in spite of a promising diplomatic settlement, "peace" is in reality a prolongation of violent conflict. This is likely to be the case when an intervention takes place to end a man-made humanitarian catastrophe. Moreover, if a despotic regime has either collapsed or been forced from power by external intervention, the ensuing power vacuum will be especially conducive to continued violent political (as opposed to conventional military) conflict.

- *Active security measures are required to defeat violent obstructionists.* When violent, obstructionist power structures involving a variable mixture of paramilitary formations, intelligence operatives, and the criminal underworld are seeking to subvert the peace, establishing a safe and secure environment requires more than a deployment of international troops operating in a passive, self-defense mode.

- *There is a void in the rule of law.* When the indigenous police and judiciary have been an integral part of the repression and dysfunction that precipitated the intervention, they are of dubious value in upholding the rule of law. Alternatively, these institutions may disintegrate entirely. In either case, no capacity exists to provide security while also respecting human rights, nor is it possible to bring perpetrators of politically motivated violence to justice.

- *Conflict is fueled by a criminalized political economy.* When the political economy has been criminalized, conflict pays and peace does not. In the most challenging cases, peace constitutes a direct threat to the economic interests of both a gangster state and the leaders of groups that have been in violent rebellion against it. These rival factions commonly exercise control over illicit economic activities such as smuggling, unregulated exploitation of raw material resources, drug trafficking, and money laundering. The repressive apparatus of the state seeks to extract resources from the powerless, thereby fueling conflict and increasing the likelihood that violence and its adverse consequences will spill over international boundaries.

STRATEGIES FOR CONFLICT TRANSFORMATION

To the extent that these dimensions of entrenched and persistent conflict are present, strategies must be designed that chart a course to transform them. The critical lines of effort in each of these strategies are summarized here.

Moderating Political Conflict

The political strategy that evolved in Kosovo recognized that various antagonistic factions were still at war. The rivals remained as committed to their war aims as they were during armed combat. The United Nations Interim Administration Mission in Kosovo (UNMIK) sought to channel the competition for power into local processes and mechanisms that could eventually be managed effectively at minimal levels of oversight by the international community. The thrust of the political strategy was to encourage rival leaders to redefine their zero-sum political motives and recognize that their interests could be better served in the future by pursuing less contentious aims through peaceful political processes.

As portrayed in figure 10.1, peace becomes viable when the powerful motivations for continuing violent conflict have been diminished to the point that they are within the capacity of domestic institutions to address and resolve peacefully.

The principal lines of effort of a political strategy that addresses cases like Kosovo should consist of the following:

- Nurture favorable conditions for political dialogue.

- Mediate conflict incrementally.

- Build a working coalition to run a civil administration.

- Contain obstructionism.

- Channel the competition for power into nonviolent processes.

Nurture Favorable Conditions for Political Dialogue

By meeting the humanitarian needs of returning refugees, the international community develops a reservoir of credibility that will enable it to confront the many challenges that will arise while the mission is at its weakest. If the peace process is to move forward, a suitable approach to demobilization or, as in Kosovo, demilitarization of former combatants is vital. As the political leadership of the former warring factions increasingly recognizes that it cannot rely exclusively on the

Figure 10.1. Viable Peace: The Turning Point in Moderating Political Conflict

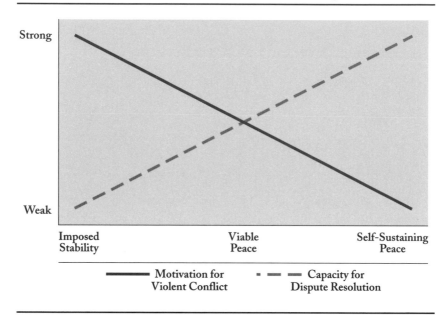

military option anymore, it will be compelled to pursue nonviolent methods of political influence that are consistent with the peace process.

Establishing favorable conditions also includes providing humanitarian relief, restoring basic services such as electrical power, addressing victims' grievances, maintaining public consent, and eliciting supportive public statements from influential leaders.

Mediate Conflict Incrementally

Especially at the outset of an operation, when the mission is weak and unlikely to win many head-on confrontations, it is important to open the door to participation by significant leaders on all sides. Hard-liners who feel excluded can easily derail the peace process through political violence. The decisive step in the mediation campaign is to persuade rival leaders to move beyond their war-hardened mentalities and to begin to envision themselves as political leaders in a lawful, nonviolent competition for power. The following five-step process, employed iteratively, is designed to accomplish this goal:

- *Establish contact.* The first step is to persuade political rivals to start talking, even if only about procedural matters. This opens the door for adversaries to make contact so that a useful exchange can follow.

- *Build confidence.* Deep hatreds and suspicions will persist long after the war ends; so, too, will internal pressures that constrain factional leaders from expanding contacts because of fear of reprisals from their own side. The leadership of an international mission must demonstrate in practical ways that it is impartial and capable of addressing a faction's basic needs, especially for security.

- *View interests in a different light.* The most decisive step is to persuade the leaders of rival factions that their personal interests and the interests of their followers can be better served by moderating their political aims and adopting peaceful means for achieving them. The mission should offer tangible inducements to all sides, the most basic being prospective roles in future political arrangements.

- *Take risks.* The flexibility available to faction leaders is often very limited because of the potentially fatal consequences of compromise. The mission must have the capability to coerce obstructionists who persist in using violent means to thwart the peace process. Both capabilities—to build consent and to use coercion—are needed to coax the parties to take the risk for peace.

- *Consolidate.* Each incremental step must be consolidated or formalized, and then the mediation process should repeat itself by taking on the next contentious issue among the disputants.

Build a Working Coalition to Run a Civil Administration

Establishing an interim administration is an integral part of the process of conflict transformation. It serves as a powerful inducement for participation in the peace process. To begin building local consent for accomplishing their objectives, international officials need to cultivate the support of prominent local figures who have influence with their constituencies. Hence, the central thrust of a public relations campaign to promote renunciation of violence should be to "speak through the leaders." UN missions that are responsible for establishing interim administrations and delivering essential services must deliver on pressing real-world problems. Local officials must be relied on to perform day-to-day functions of governance. Because the staffing of an administration has profound political implications, it must be done in a manner that sustains the overall peace process. Indeed, this is likely to be impossible unless the international mission first builds a working coalition among former warring factions. Even though contending factions may continue to distrust one another intensely, entering into an agreement to share the portfolios of government may be preferable to having no role in government at all.

Contain Obstructionism

Given limitations in capabilities early in a mission, the initial response to obstructionism may simply have to be to stop threatening behavior. Suasion and pressure are the basic tools. The goal is to bring troublemakers back into the peace process. Obstructionists or rogue actors who persist in opposing the peace process through violent means must be removed or deprived of the capacity for aggression. The custodian of the peace process will need to leverage the international military's capability to "find, fix, and strike" to defeat these extremists.

Channel Competition for Power into Nonviolent Processes

Conduct elections—but only when they serve to transform the means of competition from bullets to ballots. Elections should be conducted only when the political climate is favorable to locking in substantial progress and shifting the competition for power decisively toward nonviolence and accommodation. Hasty elections called before political violence has been adequately constrained can be an invitation for political extremists to obtain office, thereby legitimizing obstructionism. For elections to contribute to the transformation to nonviolent processes, minimum essential conditions of order, rule of law, and respect for minority rights must first be met. Unless the rights of minority populations can be reliably guaranteed, elections are likely to be perceived as a continuation of a life-and-death, zero-sum form of politics by at least one of the parties to the conflict.

Defeating Militant Extremists

The international military presence will need to support those who support the peace process and defeat those who violently oppose it. As portrayed in figure 10.2, for peace to become viable, the capacity for violent conflict must be diminished to the point at which the local security establishment is capable of dealing appropriately with it.

To accomplish this, a hybrid strategy should be crafted that combines principles from counterinsurgency operations with international practice for peace enforcement. This entails these generic lines of effort:

- Adopt an assertive posture with a maneuverist approach.

- Seek reliable local intelligence to guide operations and prevent harm to the peace process.

- Mount framework operations in support of civil authority to find, fix, and strike against militant extremists.

- Ensure joint military-police-civil planning and operations.

- Transform local security forces into contributors to peace.

Figure 10.2. Viable Peace: The Turning Point in Defeating Militant Extremists

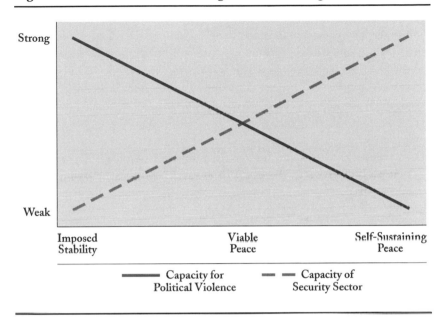

All these efforts must have the *primacy of the peace process* as their overriding guide. The definition of who should be regarded as spoilers or obstructionists and when it is suitable to confront them is a question for the mission's custodian. By adhering to this principle, the military can harness its assertive role in defeating militant extremists to set conditions for the transformation to viable peace.

Adopt an Assertive Posture with a Maneuverist Approach

To defeat subversive, militant organizations that are wont to exploit various forms of political violence to retain power, international forces cannot be merely deployed. They must be decisively employed. Instead of providing passive protection, military forces should adopt an assertive posture that will enable them to anticipate potential trouble and to disrupt the overall capacity and cohesion of violent extremists.

Seek Reliable Local Intelligence to Guide Operations and Prevent Harm to the Peace Process

By gathering intelligence among the people, military and law enforcement officials can locate potential perpetrators and use intelligence-led operations to strike at and eventually defeat them.

Mount Framework Operations in Support of Civil Authority to Find, Fix, and Strike against Militant Extremists

To take the initiative and place militant extremists at risk, military commanders must mount framework operations in close collaboration with civilian police forces. The three key components of framework operations, drawn from the counterinsurgency paradigm, are the following: *find*—that is, develop the local intelligence necessary to locate extremist threats by operating among the people, in coordination with the police; *fix*—that is, deny freedom of action to extremists while protecting groups and facilities that assist the peace process through the use of patrols, checkpoints, and other routine activities undertaken in conjunction with the police; and *strike*—that is, take coercive action against extremists, when directed by mission leadership, using intelligence-led operations with the aim of arresting them or disrupting their activities.

Ensure Joint Military-Police-Civil Planning and Operations

Militant extremists cannot be defeated unless they are separated from their support base. Popular support for the peace process is best achieved by integrated civil-military efforts to demonstrate that "peace pays" in tangible and material ways. When military commanders apply force, they should use only the minimum necessary to accomplish the mission. The purpose and nature of such activities also need to be explained to the local population through an information campaign.

Effective framework operations call for the joint participation of military, special police, and civilian police from beginning to end. The heart of the challenge is to exploit intelligence so that evidence can be generated that is admissible in court. Military operations cannot succeed without parallel progress in political and economic transformation and the development of functioning institutions of government, especially those that administer the rule of law.

Transform Local Security Forces into Contributors to Peace

The above lines of action are aimed at defeating militant extremists. For peace to become viable, the capacity of local security forces must also be addressed. To reduce the potential for organized paramilitary resistance by the former guerrilla army, individual members who meet qualifications and have acceptable backgrounds may be incorporated into the official security forces. This provides a mechanism for reintegrating former fighters. In the short run, it strategically "fixes" ex-combatants in a structure where they can be held accountable. Over time, as greater numbers of these individuals identify with their new profession, the capacity of local security forces to maintain the peace against obstructionist elements can increasingly expand.

Figure 10.3. Viable Peace: The Turning Point in Institutionalizing the
Rule of Law

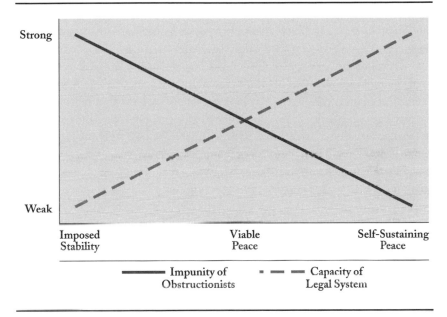

Institutionalizing the Rule of Law

Under circumstances such as those encountered in Kosovo, efforts to institutionalize the rule of law require a comprehensive strategy that combines capacity building with assertive international action to break the grip of informal
power structures rooted in illicit underground activities. As portrayed in figure
10.3, for peace to become viable, the impunity of those belonging to extremist
power structures must be diminished to the point where the local legal system is
capable of confronting parties on all sides of the conflict and dispensing justice
equally.

A strategy to foster the evolution from lawless rule to the rule of law should
combine three lines of effort:

- Develop institutional capacity.

- Shape the context by dismantling criminalized power structures.

- Establish safeguards on performance.

Develop Institutional Capacity

One of the fundamental lessons derived from peace operations dating back to El Salvador, Haiti, and Bosnia is that a holistic approach must be taken to the promotion of the rule of law.[2] It is necessary to develop local capacity not merely for policing but also in relation to the judiciary, penal system, and legal code.

If the institutions responsible for order, law, and justice have collapsed, however, the international mission will have to provide temporary substitutes. By default, the military contingent may have to establish public order, provide detention facilities, and facilitate a rudimentary judicial process during the emergency phase of the mission. It is unrealistic to expect members of a previously subjugated and brutalized community to begin administering equal justice to a population group that they identify with their former tormentors. In such circumstances, the relationship between international personnel and the local legal profession should begin with international custodianship over cases of an intergroup or politically charged nature. As local capacity is developed, the relationship should evolve into a partnership between internationals and locals.

Shape the Context by Dismantling Criminalized Power Structures

In a context characterized by considerable overlap between criminal and political power, transitioning directly to local ownership after training programs have been completed will not be sufficient to inculcate the rule of law. Lawless forces will simply assert ownership over these institutions.

The international mission, therefore, must adopt a strategy that seeks to transform the context by disrupting and dismantling extremist networks bent on subverting the peace process. The deployment of specialized crowd control units is necessary but not sufficient for this purpose, because they address only the symptoms of obstructionism, not its sources. The international mission must ensure that the full spectrum of capabilities—from intelligence to incarceration—can function efficaciously in order to dismantle rogue power structures. To prosecute high-profile and politically sensitive cases successfully, international judges and prosecutors may be required because they can be buffered from intimidation and coercion, unlike their local counterparts.

Establish Safeguards on Performance

The final component of the rule-of-law strategy is the introduction of safeguards to ensure that public security entities and judicial institutions do not again become instruments of ethnic persecution or captives of political-criminal networks. To accomplish this, it is necessary to develop the capacity to observe performance (transparency) and sanction misconduct (accountability). Part of the solution lies in creating structural safeguards within the state, such as open elections that permit power to change hands, an independent judiciary, and autonomous oversight bodies with effective disciplinary mechanisms for each institution involved. Safeguards within civil society, such as a free press, are also essential.

Domestic safeguards, however, will be effective only after the environment they operate in has been transformed. Thus, there is likely to be a gap between the completion of capacity building and the point at which local ownership of the new or reformed capacity will result in impartiality and the capacity to overcome impunity. International safeguards ranging from continued training, mentoring, monitoring, and operational assistance may be needed to fill this gap. As local safeguards mature and their effectiveness is proven, the international role can diminish.

The timing of the evolution to local ownership of institutions responsible for the rule of law should not be governed by arbitrary "end dates" or determined solely by the development of local skills. Performance matters. Nurturing an environment that sustains the rule of law is also a fundamental prerequisite, as is the effectiveness of domestic safeguards.

Establishing a Legitimate Political Economy

Although the nexus between wealth and power may not always be easy to discern, it can either fuel conflict or promote stability. Peace will not prosper if the political-economic incentives for continued conflict are overlooked. When illegal money flows provide the motivation for and means of maintaining informal power structures that obstruct the peace process, the political economy is the problem. It must be transformed from a situation in which illicit wealth creates unchecked political power to one in which the formal economy can outcompete the shadow economy and the autonomy of the state is preserved.

As portrayed in figure 10.4, for peace to become viable, the political influence of illicit wealth must be diminished to the point that the state is capable of maintaining the integrity of the revenue stream for its essential activities.

The development of an integrated political-economic approach is essential to building viable peace. This requires simultaneous action on multiple fronts:

- Undercut the economic foundations of obstructionist power.

- Strengthen the coalition for peace by ensuring that peace pays.

- Develop a fiscally autonomous and sustainable state.

- Lay the macroeconomic foundation to expand the formal economy and distribute the benefits of peace.

Figure 10.4. Viable Peace: The Turning Point in Developing a Legitimate Political Economy

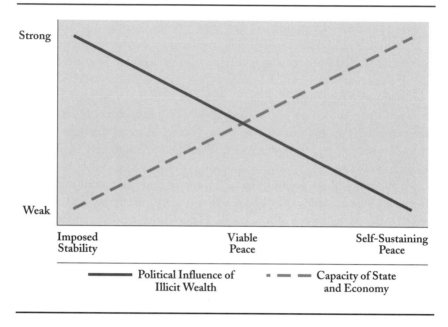

Undercut the Economic Foundations of Obstructionist Power

The economic incentives for continued conflict must be removed. For this to happen, the insidious influence of criminally obtained wealth over the exercise of political power must be addressed. External funding for subversive activities (e.g., from neighboring political entities) must also be curtailed.

Strengthen the Coalition for Peace by Ensuring That Peace Pays

Peace is a political agenda. As with any political agenda, local political leaders must be willing to carry it forward. Elites willing to take risks for peace, and their supporters, must benefit from the peace process if their backing is to be maintained. Ensuring tangible improvement in the quality of life by expeditiously restoring basic public services should be a top priority. Peace must pay for *all* the parties to the conflict, moreover, if they are to develop a stake in sustaining peace.

Develop a Fiscally Autonomous and Sustainable State

Establishing the autonomy of the state from lawless forces that held sway during the conflict is a primary concern. Achieving this goal demands that the integrity of the revenue stream required to sustain essential state functions be adequately protected. If the political clout of warlords and similar obstructionists is to be contained, the state must have the ability to fund efforts to counter their subversive activities. If the coalition for peace is to be sustained, the state must also be able to deliver benefits to society based on need, not exclusively on the basis of connection to patronage structures.

Lay the Macroeconomic Foundations to Expand the Formal Economy and Distribute the Benefits of Peace

The foundation for legitimate economic activity must be put in place. This includes restoring the banking system and creating a legal and regulatory framework that promotes private enterprise and protects the public sector from politicization and corruption. Alternatives to employment in the underground economy need to be made widely available, thereby creating a broad interest in maintaining transparent and accountable political and economic structures. With this foundation in place, prospects for the emergence over the long term of a middle-class market economy will be enhanced, thereby encouraging progress toward a self-sustaining peace.

THE OTHER VITAL INGREDIENTS

For peace to become viable, the four strategies for transforming war-hardened power structures that are sources of conflict must all be effectively integrated. As delineated in chapter 9, none of these strategies can succeed in isolation. Owing to their interdependencies, the linkages among them must be carefully and continually interwoven. Thus, mechanisms that effectively integrate the efforts of the multiple coalitions and actors involved (e.g., force and diplomacy, political and economic, military and police, relief and development, local and international) are essential ingredients for the attainment of viable peace.

Inevitably, trade-offs will be required among the many communities or disciplines participating in a peace mission. Each brings to the mission its own set of principles or body of doctrine that guides its routine efforts. None of these, however, is precisely tailored to chaotic settings where conflict must be transformed. Military officers often rail against becoming involved in what they regard as police work when it is necessary to dislodge criminal power structures that threaten the peace process. Economists may similarly resist funding the immediate requirements of government and instead stress their preferred long-term macroeconomic concerns. A fragmented or incoherent approach will only undermine the process of transformation and prolong the international presence. The primacy of the peace process should be the overarching guidance for all civilian and military peace implementation efforts.

The central actor in conflict transformation is the custodian of the peace process. Success will largely depend on how adroitly this appointed leader mobilizes international support and unifies the various components of the mission behind realistic strategies to promote the peace.

Implementation of these strategies cannot be accomplished effectively if the international response is ad hoc. Advance planning is of utmost importance. A clearheaded strategic assessment is just the first step. Once the strategic approach has been crafted and various building blocks have been specified, the agencies responsible for implementation must be authoritatively tasked and properly resourced. Viable peace is not a likely result when peace missions arrive too late, do too little, and seek to depart too quickly. That is, instead, a surefire formula for a hard and endless slog or a failed intervention.

VIABLE PEACE: A MORE REALISTIC AND ATTAINABLE GOAL

The attainment of viable peace requires strategies for transforming internal conflict. This is more realistic and attainable than the self-defeating pursuit of exit strategies. Prospects for peace can be fatally undermined when a major intervening power announces, even before peace implementation begins, that it intends to exit as rapidly as possible. Powerful local obstructionists, whose interests have been served by the conflict and who thus oppose the peace process, will have every incentive to delay and defy any real transformation. If the international community signals that it cannot be relied on to make a decisive difference in political realities before it prematurely exits, local voices of moderation are likely to conclude that taking risks for peace is foolhardy. Any who take such a risk can expect to be left behind to face dire consequences.

Viable peace also provides a basis for coherent political-military planning in the absence of clarity about the eventual end state. Since it is a decisive turning point, viable peace can serve as the desired near-term end state to guide peace implementation efforts after stability has been imposed externally. It offers an interim outcome as the focal point for planning the conditions that the intervention is seeking to bring about.

Another important advantage of focusing on achieving viable peace is that it is comprehensible and sustainable. The near-term intent is to transform internal conflict in a matter of a few years so that the international community can transition to a less costly, long-term presence that emphasizes civilian safeguards against a reversal of the peacebuilding process.

Securing the future, including achieving any sort of end state in the war on global terrorism, will depend on our ability to forge a viable peace in dangerous and dysfunctional neighborhoods around the world. We have repeatedly struggled to understand what we should do after we intervene in these war-ravaged places.

If we want to end the destructive dynamics that war-torn societies propagate internationally, we must adapt the instruments of international policy to the demands involved in transforming their internal conflicts. Civilian and military capabilities required to intervene effectively need to be prepared in advance. Organizational structures need to be created to field and employ these capabilities effectively. Collaborative mechanisms must be nurtured to allow a variety of international actors to work together smoothly and efficiently.

Neglect is not a strategy. It is, rather, a guarantee that the price of intervention will inevitably become exhaustive. The better alternative is to become proficient at transforming internal conflict. Viable peace will result only if this strategic challenge is properly understood and appropriately addressed.

NOTES

1. Charles C. Ragin and Howard S. Becker, eds., *What Is a Case?* (New York: Cambridge University Press, 1992).

2. Robert B. Oakley, Michael J. Dziedzic, and Eliot M. Goldberg, eds., *Policing the New World Disorder: Peace Operations and Public Security* (Washington, D.C.: National Defense University Press, 1998), 511–512.

Index

THE QUEST FOR VIABLE PEACE

This book is set in Adobe Caslon. The Creative Studio designed the book's cover; Mike Chase designed the interior. Helene Y. Redmond made up the pages. The text was copyedited by David Sweet and proofread by Karen Stough. The index was prepared by Sonsie Conroy. The book's editor was Nigel Quinney.